AQA Psychology A

Exclusively endorsed by AQA

A2

Revision Guide

Psychology

Julia Willerton
Dominic Helliwell
Sue Cave
Simon Green
Nick Lund
Janet Lord

 Nelson Thornes

Published in 2011 by:
Nelson Thornes Ltd
Delta Place
27 Bath Road
CHELTENHAM
GL53 7TH
United Kingdom

11 12 13 14 15 / 10 9 8 7 6 5 4 3 2 1

A catalogue record for this book is available from the British Library

ISBN 978 1 4085 0815 2

Cover photograph: Adam Korzekwa/iStockphoto

Page make-up by Pantek Arts Ltd, Maidstone

Printed and bound in Spain by GraphyCems

Contents

Introduction																			iv

Unit 3 Topics in Psychology

1 Biological rhythms and sleep													1

2 Perception																		14

3 Relationships																		29

4 Aggression																		43

5 Eating behaviour																	57

6 Gender																			75

7 Intelligence and learning														91

8 Cognition and development														107

Unit 4 Psychopathology, Psychology in Action and Research Methods

9 Psychopathology																	122

10 Media psychology																	144

11 The psychology of addictive behaviour										158

12 Anomalistic psychology															173

13 Psychological research and scientific method									188

Glossary																			205
Index																				208

Introduction

This revision guide will provide the essentials for your revision. These are:

- WHAT you need to know
- WHAT you will be asked to do in your exams.

What you need to know

For PSYA3, you will only need to revise the three topics you have studied. On PSYA4 you will study two optional topics and research methods, which is compulsory. On PSYA4, one topic will be from Psychopathology and one will be from Psychology in Action.

You can use the checklists below to ensure you are clear about which sections you need to revise. The date of the exams will be on the AQA website at http://web.aqa.org.uk (click on Administration and then Exam timetables).

PSYA3 Date of exam...

Topic	Topics covered (Tick at least 3)	Page numbers	Tick when revised
Biological rhythms and sleep			
Perception			
Relationships			
Aggression			
Eating behaviour (with focus on one eating disorder chosen from anorexia OR bulimia OR obesity)			
Gender			
Intelligence and learning			
Cognition and development			

PSYA4 Date of exam...

Topic	Option	Option covered	Page numbers	Tick when revised
Psychopathology	Schizophrenia			
	Depression			
	Phobic disorders			
	Obsessive compulsive disorder			
Psychology in action	Media psychology			
	Addictive behaviour			
	Anomalistic psychology			
Research methods	THIS SECTION IS COMPULSORY			

What you will be asked to do in the exams

The main difference between AS and A2 is that at A2 you are required to do *more extended writing*, with essay-style questions that are worth up to 24 marks.

PSYA3

You will be assessed on the three topics you have covered. You will have a total of one-and-a-half hours, which means that each topic should take you roughly half an hour.

A total of 24 marks will be available in each topic:

- 8 marks for showing your knowledge and understanding of the topic (AO1)
- 16 marks for analysis, evaluation and application (AO2/3).

The topics could be assessed by a single essay question or two or three shorter questions adding up to 24 marks in total. The three most important things to remember are:

1 There may be two or three questions on each of your topics. You must ensure that you answer *all* of the questions that are set on the topics you have covered. There is *no choice* of question *within* the topic and you must answer the questions that are set.

2 Almost twice as many marks are awarded for analysis, evaluation and application as compared to those awarded for knowledge and understanding.

3 When a question requires demonstration of knowledge and analysis and evaluation, two marks will be shown in brackets, the first is the number of AO1 and the second the number of AO2/3 marks for each question.

PSYA4

In section A (Psychopathology) you may be assessed by essays or a combination of 4-, 5- and 16-mark questions. Examples can be found at the end of every chapter.

In section B (Psychology in Action) you are likely to have three or four shorter questions. These are often based around a scenario and they are worth a total of 24 marks.

Section C (Research Methods) will involve mainly short-answer questions, and a total of 35 marks are available.

As you have two hours for the paper, you should allow about 35 minutes for sections A and B and 50 minutes for section C (which has more marks available).

A reminder about skills

Assessment objective	How is it assessed?
AO1: Knowledge and understanding	This is assessed through your ability to select and describe psychological theories, concepts, principles and research studies and your ability to select, organise and communicate relevant psychological information.
AO2: Application of your psychological knowledge and understanding	This is assessed through your ability to analyse and evaluate theories and studies. You will need to demonstrate that you can apply your knowledge to unfamiliar situations and can assess the validity, reliability and credibility of scientific information.
AO3: How science works in psychology	This is assessed through your understanding of how scientific knowledge is collected and how scientific understanding is developed in psychology. This will include your understanding of quantitative and qualitative scientific methods and ethical practices. Skills of designing investigations, analysing and interpreting data and how to report findings. It will also include your ability to analyse, interpret and evaluate the methodology of your own and others' psychological investigations.

Some common injunction words and what they mean

Term	What you need to do
Explain	Provide information about how or why something happens or is done.
Describe	State in detail the main points of the topic being examined. This could be a theory, approach (e.g. the behavioural approach) or research study.
Outline	An outline is basically a summary of the main features. Practise the skills of creating outlines of key theories, explanations or models using four or five bullet points.
	'Outline' tends to be used more often in the PSYA3 paper, given the shorter time limit for each question to be completed.
Evaluate	Evaluation requires you to put a value on something. This usually means weighing up the theory or study in terms of its pros and cons, advantages and limitations.
	You should be aware that evaluation does not simply mean 'criticise'. It is important to point out strengths and positive features as well as negative ones. Try to set out your evaluations in two sections: one positive and one negative. This will allow you to make a balanced judgement.
Discuss	This term means to describe and evaluate and can include commentary, consideration of implications and interesting points. The evaluation may involve a consideration of strengths and weaknesses or evidence for and against.
	When asked to discuss a topic, there is a large amount of potential material to choose from. You should think about including some detailed material and covering other issues in less detail so that there is some breadth to your essay.
Consider	This is a slight variation on 'evaluate', but the requirements are largely similar. Here, again, if you are asked to 'consider the effectiveness of …', then you are being asked to write about positive and negative aspects of the topic.
To what extent	This can loosely be translated as 'how far'. When you are asked 'to what extent', the examiner is requiring you to assess what part something plays within a larger picture.
	For example, 'To what extent can schizophrenia be explained by biological factors?' asks you to assess how much of a role biological factors play in schizophrenia and what factors other than biological ones may play a part in this disorder.

How to use this guide

Each topic includes the following features:

You need to know how to

A short checklist tells you exactly what you need to be able to do for each topic. You can use this list to tick off the different sections as you revise them.

Exam-style questions

Use these to practise writing answers, preferably allowing only the amount of time you will have in the exam.

Sample answers

These are examples – do not assume they are perfect! Think about how the candidate has used the material and what they could have done better.

Issues and debates

To achieve good marks in both exams, you will need to demonstrate that you have a strong grasp of the important approaches, issues and debates in relation to the specific topic. Do not try to go through every issue and debate in every essay. Select the most important and relevant issues and debates and use them in your answer to develop analysis and evaluation in your writing so that you demonstrate an understanding of some of the key issues confronting modern, scientific psychology.

Issues and debates are mentioned throughout the guide and in Unit 3 some important ones are shown at the end of each topic.

Biological rhythms and sleep

Biological rhythms

> **You need to know how to**
>
> ✔ describe the characteristics of circadian, infradian and ultradian biological rhythms
>
> ✔ explain the role of endogenous pacemakers and exogenous zeitgebers in the control of biological rhythms, including relevant research evidence
>
> ✔ explain what happens when biological rhythms are disrupted, and describe and evaluate relevant research evidence.

Introduction

Biological rhythms are regular variations in physiological and behavioural processes that can be found throughout the animal and plant kingdom. They are defined by the cycle length, the time between successive peaks of activity. The three fundamental types of biological rhythm are shown below.

Fundamental types of biological rhythm

	Cycle length	Examples
Circadian	24 hours	Human sleep–waking cycle Body temperature
Infradian	More than 24 hours	Human female menstrual cycle Hibernation Seasonal affective disorder
Ultradian	Less than 24 hours	Alternation between stages of NREM and REM sleep during the night

Biological rhythms are by definition very regular, but how are they controlled?

For the sleep–waking cycle, it seems clear that we sleep as darkness comes and wake up when it gets light in the morning.

Hibernation might well be triggered by the cold weather and the shorter days of winter.

However, there is no obvious environmental stimulus that might control the 28-day human menstrual cycle or the ultradian NREM/REM cycle.

Research studies show that squirrels kept in constant light and temperature conditions still prepare for hibernation at the appropriate time of year.

Research like this suggests that we have internal body clocks (or endogenous pacemakers) that can control biological rhythms.

> **Think about it**
>
> Why do biological rhythms exist? Often they seem to help coordinate the animal with the outside world. For instance, our circadian sleep–waking cycle means that humans sleep at night when activity is difficult and are awake and alert during the day. Hibernation helps bears and squirrels to survive the harsh conditions of winter.

> **Think about it**
>
> Is there one body clock, or are there many? Clearly, as there are many biological rhythms with different cycle lengths, there must be many body clocks. The Siffre (1975) study on page 2 provides evidence for at least two: sleep–waking and body temperature.

Endogenous pacemakers and exogenous zeitgebers

Biological rhythms seem to involve internal body clocks, the endogenous pacemakers, and in some cases environmental stimuli known as exogenous zeitgebers. The most studied biological rhythm is the sleep–waking cycle, and early studies clearly demonstrated the interaction between body clocks and the exogenous zeitgeber of light.

Key study

Siffre's (1975) cave study

Michel Siffre spent 179 days in a cave in Texas. There was no natural light, and in these conditions biological rhythms become free running. Siffre could ask for artificial lighting to be turned off and on. His sleep–waking pattern and various physiological functions were continually recorded. There were two key findings:

- Siffre's sleep–waking cycle increased from the normal 24 hours to between 25 and 32 hours (i.e. his days became longer) and when he came out, for him, it was only the 151st day, not the 179th.

- His body temperature cycle also extended, to about 25 hours, but overall it was more stable than the sleep–waking cycle.

Conclusion: In the absence of the natural light–dark cycle, the internal body clock can regulate circadian rhythms but not accurately. This is good evidence for the existence of body clocks, but it also suggests that they need light onset to trigger them at the right time.

Evaluation: This is a single case study of one man. There may be significant individual differences in how we react to the free-running conditions, and we would not base a whole theory on one case study. Studies on a range of participants would lead to specific hypotheses, which could be tested, and which would lead to reliable theories.

Later research has supported the findings of Siffre's study. Aschoff and Weber (quoted in Kleitman, 1965) found that the sleep–waking cycles of students kept in similar conditions to Siffre in an underground bunker also extended, to between 25 and 27 hours.

Siffre knew the nature of the study and gave informed consent. During the long period of isolation and afterwards, though, he suffered episodes of depression and suicidal thoughts. If the study was carried out now, he would be given counselling and psychological support during and after the study.

In free-running studies of the sleep–waking cycle, the endogenous pacemaker or body clock maintains the cycle in the absence of day/ night cues. A key structure is the suprachiasmatic nucleus (SCN) in the hypothalamus of the brain. Destruction of the SCN eliminates the circadian pattern of sleep–waking and locomotion in rats (Stephan and Zucker, 1972), showing its central role as a body clock.

Neural pathways connecting the SCN with the pineal gland allow it to control the release of the hormone melatonin from the pineal gland.

Think about it

When researchers suspected that sleep and waking might involve both internal body clocks and natural environmental stimuli such as light, they devised methods of testing the hypothesis. The simplest way was to eliminate one or the other and see what happened. This is the basis of the free-running studies such as the Siffre (1975) study, where natural changes in environmental conditions (light and dark) are eliminated by using unusual conditions such as deep caves.

AQA Examiner's tip

Some questions may ask you to evaluate evidence for the interaction of body clocks and zeitgebers using studies such as Siffre. Besides methodological evaluation, remember that findings and conclusions are the most important aspects of research studies, and focus on these.

Think about it

The SCN may function as a body clock, controlling the rhythmic activity of sleep–waking and other processes, but it can only work as part of a circuit of structures. For instance, for sleep and waking to be perfectly coordinated with light and dark, the SCN needs to be responsive to light in the outside world.

Melatonin has widespread effects on the brain and the body, especially in relation to sleep and arousal. Research has shown that:

- injections of melatonin can produce sleep in sparrows
- brain melatonin levels increase in darkness and decrease with the onset of light
- some studies have found that melatonin can be an effective treatment for circadian rhythms disrupted through jet lag.

Disrupting biological rhythms

Explanations

Our normal pattern works efficiently as we sleep when it is dark and wake when it becomes light. Body clocks and the onset of light are in synchrony. However, technological advances, especially electric lighting and jet travel, have radically altered our work and leisure habits. They have also led to situations where our body clocks become desynchronised from the main zeitgeber, light. This desynchronisation leads to the disruption of our normal pattern of biological rhythms. Research into disruption aids understanding of the role of exogenous zeitgebers. The effects of this are seen in two major areas.

Shift work and jet lag

- Shift work can lead to fatigue and depression, and it can affect judgement. The Chernobyl nuclear disaster has been linked to technicians working long hours at night time. People are making decisions when their body clock is trying to impose sleep.
- New York is about five hours behind London. The journey takes about six hours. Leaving London at noon means arriving in New York about 6pm London time, but it is 1pm local time. Our body clock thinks it is 6pm, and this difference with local time leads to the symptoms of jet lag.

Phase advance and phase delay

When we fly to New York our body clock ends up ahead of local time, and has to wait for local time to catch up. This is known as phase delay. When the body clock is behind local time, it is called phase advance. Research shows that phase delay is easier to adjust to than phase advance.

Disrupting biological rhythms reduces the effectiveness of the immune system, leading an increase in health problems.

Key study

Charles Czeisler and shift work (Czeisler et al., 1982)

Charles Czeisler was called in by a Utah Chemical plant that used a backwards shift rotation, with seven days working mornings, then seven working nights, then seven on evening shifts. Workers reported high levels of stress and health problems. Czeisler moved workers to a forwards shift rotation (this is equivalent to phase delay) and increased shift length to 21 days to allow the body clock to adjust. After nine months workers reported less stress and fewer health problems, and productivity increased.

Apply it

You need to understand how endogenous pacemakers and zeitgebers interact. Focus on the SCN and how it responds to outside light levels through the pathway to the retina. Then follow the pathway to the pineal gland and the release of melatonin. Think of Siffre in his cave – the sleep–waking cycle was maintained, but not very accurately. Explain this using your knowledge of the SCN and its connections.

Think about it

Research focuses on daylight as a zeitgeber. Is it the only one? How about Eskimos living through periods of continual light or continual dark? What zeitgebers might they use?

Think about it

If phase delay is easier to adjust to than phase advance, what would you predict about the severity of jet lag when flying east to west versus west to east?

Research evidence

Symptoms of jet lag are worse travelling east to west than west to east (Coren, 1996). This is linked to phase advance versus phase delay.

Recht *et al.* (1995) found that baseball teams won fewer games after travelling west to east than when travelling east to west, and linked the findings to the more severe effects of biological rhythm disruption by phase advance.

Coping with disruption of biological rhythms – jet lag

- Follow local zeitgebers by staying awake if it is daytime or sleeping if it is night-time.
- Expose yourself to morning daylight as soon as possible. Sunlight is the most effective way of synchronising the biological clock to local time.
- There is some evidence that melatonin pills taken before a flight can help reduce jet lag, but results are inconsistent.

> **AQA Examiner's tip**
>
> In questions about the disruption of biological rhythms, you will be expected not just to describe the effects. You will need to consider the implications and significance of these effects, how they can be explained and how they can be reduced.

Sleep

> **You need to know how to**
>
> ✔ describe the nature of sleep
>
> ✔ explain the different stages of sleep, the ultradian rhythm of sleep stages and lifespan changes in sleep
>
> ✔ describe lifespan changes in sleep and relevant research evidence, and consider some of their implications
>
> ✔ describe evolutionary and restoration theories of sleep and relevant research evidence
>
> ✔ evaluate evolutionary and restoration theories and the research evidence.

The nature of sleep

Sleep is found in all complex animals, and states looking like sleep are even seen in insects and reptiles. In mammals such as humans, sleep occurs in two distinct forms, first identified by Dement and Kleitman (1957) using the electroencephalogram (EEG):

- non-rapid eye movement sleep (NREM)
- rapid eye movement sleep (REM).

> **Think about it**
>
> Using electrodes attached to the skull, we can record the brain's electrical activity as the electroencephalogram. If the EEG has a clear wave form, it is called synchronised. If there is no wave form, it is called desynchronised. Waves of a synchronised EEG are defined by their frequency (waves per second, or hertz (Hz)), and amplitude (size). A fast desynchronised EEG is typical of the waking, aroused state.

Characteristics of NREM sleep

NREM sleep is characterised by four main stages.

	Description
Stage 1	EEG is characterised by theta waves, small amplitude, 4–7 Hz.
Stage 2	EEG is characterised by theta waves plus bursts of high-frequency spindles.
Stage 3	Delta waves appear, with higher amplitude and slower frequency than theta waves (1–4 Hz). Spindles disappear.
Stage 4	Dominated by large, slow delta waves. Deepest phase of NREM.

Characteristics of REM sleep

REM sleep has the following characteristics:

- In REM the EEG shows fast desynchronised activity although the person is deeply asleep.
- Body muscles lose their tone so the person is effectively paralysed.
- Rapid eye movements occur.
- Most (80 per cent) of dreams occur in REM sleep.

Sleep's ultradian rhythm

During sleep we move between the various stages and types of sleep. First we fall deeply asleep (NREM stage 4). Then sleep lightens and we move back to NREM stage 2. From there we move into a phase of REM sleep. After around 15 minutes in REM, we move back into stage 2 NREM and then down to stage 4. The cycle repeats itself about every 90 minutes, giving four or five complete cycles per night's sleep.

Lifespan changes in sleep

Newborn babies sleep for around 16 hours per day, of which 50 per cent is REM sleep. Over the first two years of life, this pattern gradually shifts to the adult pattern of about 6–8 hours sleep with about 20–25 per cent REM sleep. This is the most dramatic change in sleep patterns over the lifespan.

Major reviews of studies of sleep and ageing have identified other changes (Ohayon *et al.*, 2004):

- Total sleep time decreases from about 470 minutes at age 5 to 370 minutes at age 70.
- The percentage of Stages 3 and 4 NREM sleep (deep NREM) decreases from 24 per cent at age 5 to 9 per cent at age 70.
- The percentage of REM sleep falls steadily from about 25 per cent at age 5 to 19 per cent at age 70.
- Adolescents tend to sleep less during the week but more at weekends, but overall they sleep less than adults (Crowley *et al.*, 2007).

Functions of sleep

All animals sleep, so it is assumed that sleep must have essential functions. There are two broad categories of explanations – evolutionary and restoration.

Think about it

Why does a baby need so much REM sleep, and why does the need for NREM sleep reduce as we age? Use Horne's theory of the brain restoration function of 'core sleep' (i.e. REM and deep NREM sleep) to explain these two observations.

Think about it

Research material on sleep in dolphins. You will find that these water-dwelling mammals sleep with only one side of the brain at a time. What do you think this says about the essential nature of sleep?

Think about it

Sleep has two distinct forms (REM and NREM) and a complete explanation for sleep should cover both forms. But this can be a problem, especially for evolutionary explanations.

Evolutionary explanations

This explanation of sleep is sometimes referred to as the evolutionary/ecological approach. It focuses on patterns of sleep across different species. It tries to identify key factors that determine these patterns. These factors include:

- whether the animal is a predator or prey
- whether it has a safe place to sleep
- body size
- brain size
- metabolic rate (the rate at which the body burns up energy).

Key study

Studies analysing sleep across many species (Alison and Cicchetti, 1976; Zepelin and Rechstaffen, 1975; Lesku *et al.*, 2006)

A series of studies analysing sleep across many species has found some significant relationships between ecological factors and sleep:

- There is a negative correlation between body mass or size and sleep time – small animals sleep more than large animals.
- Brain mass is positively correlated with amount of REM sleep. More-advanced animals with larger brains have more REM sleep.
- Metabolic rate is positively correlated with sleep time.
- Animals sleeping in dangerous places have less sleep than those with safe sleep sites.
- Herbivores sleep less than carnivores. Note that herbivores (grass eaters) are often prey animals, and carnivores (meat eaters) are predators.

Evaluation: Correlations can only demonstrate an association, not cause and effect. For instance, small animals have a higher metabolic rate than large animals. So we do not know if they sleep longer because they are small or because they have a higher metabolic rate.

Many studies are also carried out in artificial environments such as zoos. We cannot be sure that sleep patterns in such environments accurately reflect sleep patterns in the wild.

The evolutionary approach takes into account the whole animal and its lifestyle. It is not reductionist. However, it cannot tell us which is the most important factor determining sleep patterns.

Apply it

The evolutionary approach relies heavily on observational studies of animals in their natural habitat or in zoos. Explain two advantages and two limitations of observational studies.

Think about it

The sloth was always thought to be a problem for the evolutionary approach. Early studies seemed to show that this large mammal slept for about 20 hours a day, far longer than predicted by its size and metabolic rate. But these studies were carried out in zoos. A recent study in the wild (Rattenborg *et al.*, 2008) suggested that the sloth actually sleeps for about six hours a day in its natural habitat. Why do you think this difference occurred?

Think about it

One consistent and striking observation is that the newborn baby has a very high proportion of REM sleep – about 8 hours a day, compared with about 1.5 hours in the adult. Does this finding support the restoration explanation of sleep? What is going on in the baby's brain that might explain the high proportion of REM sleep?

Evolutionary theories of sleep

Meddis (1975)	Webb (1982)
Proposed that sleep is simply to keep animals safe at times when active behaviour is impossible, e.g. at night, and is particularly important for prey animals. However, it would make more sense for an animal to be awake and alert rather than asleep, and this approach cannot explain why we have two types of sleep.	Used the model of hibernation to propose that sleep is a time to conserve energy, especially for small animals that burn up energy quickly due to their high metabolic rate. This is supported by the positive correlation between metabolic rate and sleep time. However, this does not explain why there are two types of sleep. In addition, REM sleep is a highly active state with energy consumption only a little less than waking. But overall we do burn less energy during a night's sleep, and this supports Webb's theory.

Restoration theories

These propose that sleep is a time for restoration of physiological systems, especially the brain, that are active during the day. Proteins, hormones and neurotransmitters are used during this time. Two slightly different theories are Oswald (1980) and Horne (1988).

Restoration theories of sleep

Oswald (1980)	Horne (1988)
REM sleep is for restoration of the brain. **Evidence**: Damage to the brain, e.g. through a drug overdose, increases the amount of REM sleep. NREM sleep is for restoration of the body. **Evidence**: Skin cells grow more quickly in NREM sleep. Marathon runners have more NREM sleep after a race (Shapiro *et al.*, 1981). *But*: Horne and Minardi (1985) found that after physical exercise we fall asleep faster but we do not sleep for longer. In addition, body repair during NREM would depend on nutrients from the evening meal. However, these are only available for about six hours after eating.	Both REM sleep and deep stages 3 and 4 of NREM sleep are for brain restoration. **Evidence**: Laboratory studies show that sleep deprivation affects cognitive processes in the brain, such as attention, perception and memory. There seem to be no effects on the body. When allowed to sleep, participants sleep more than usual, but they do not make up all the sleep they have lost. They recover far more REM sleep and deep NREM sleep than light NREM sleep. According to Horne, REM and deep NREM sleep make up 'core sleep'. The light stages of NREM are 'optional sleep'; their main function may be to keep the animal inconspicuous. Body restoration takes place during relaxed wakefulness.

Studies on sleep deprivation

Besides the scientific and controlled studies mentioned above, a variety of other investigations have looked at sleep deprivation:

- Several days of sleep deprivation in rats leads to death (Rechtschaffen *et al.*, 1983). Although this might support restoration ideas, rats were kept awake by very stressful procedures in the study that themselves might cause illness and death.

- Peter Tripp stayed awake for 201 hours, raising money for charity. He developed severe hallucinations and delusions, but slept for 24 hours after his epic and awoke fully recovered. This supports Horne's idea that sleep deprivation affects brain function rather than the body.

- Randy Gardner stayed awake for 264 hours. He developed visual problems and some paranoia. When allowed to sleep, he recovered about one-quarter of the sleep he had lost but this was concentrated in deep NREM and REM sleep, as Horne's theory would have predicted.

> **Think about it**
>
> The case studies of Tripp and Gardner are very memorable, but how scientific are they? Tripp, for instance, was in a glass booth doing radio broadcasts. This is not a very controlled environment. He also suffered quite severe effects of sleep deprivation, whereas Gardner seemed less affected. So individual differences are important. Horne's theory is based on putting together results of many controlled laboratory studies rather than relying on dramatic individual cases.

Sleep disorders

> **You need to know how to**
>
> describe explanations for sleep disorders, including insomnia, sleep walking and narcolepsy
>
> evaluate explanations for sleep disorders.

Insomnia involves problems with the quality and duration of sleep and it leads to daytime sleepiness. Symptoms include sleep onset latency (i.e. the time taken to fall asleep) of more than 30 minutes, sleep efficiency of less than 85 per cent, and increased night-time awakenings.

Explanations of primary insomnia

Primary insomnia is diagnosed when no obvious external cause is identifiable. So it is assumed that the cause must lie in the intricate brain systems controlling sleep.

Brain mechanisms and sleep

We have seen that one of the main endogenous body clocks involves the suprachiasmatic nucleus of the hypothalamus, pathways from the retina and pathways to the pineal gland that control the release of the hormone melatonin. There are also centres in the brain that control the ultradian rhythm of REM sleep and NREM sleep, using neurotransmitters such as noradrenaline, serotonin and acetylcholine. It would only take a slight malfunction in this complex system to affect sleep patterns and cause insomnia. It is likely that some forms of primary insomnia (idiopathic insomnia) reflect such a malfunction. There is evidence from family studies for a genetic component in primary insomnia (Reimann, 2010). It may be that a slight imbalance in sleep mechanisms is inherited, especially as we have already seen that endogenous pacemakers such as the suprachiasmatic nucleus clearly represent an inherited inbuilt biological clock.

Learned insomnia

People often have periods of insomnia at times of extreme stress and anxiety. When the stress disappears, sleep patterns should return to normal. However, in some people the insomnia persists even in the absence of stress and anxiety. It seems that they have tried techniques to deal with insomnia that are actually maladaptive, such as napping in the day or going to bed earlier and earlier. Even though the original stress has gone, they remain worried about sleeping, and this sleep-related anxiety leads to persistent learned primary insomnia. In support of this is the success of cognitive behavioural therapy in treating primary insomnia (Stepanski & Rybarczyk, 2006). CBT addresses the maladaptive learning and perceptions that underlie the disorder.

Sleep state misperception

This is an unusual form of primary insomnia where the person reports severe insomnia. However, careful recording in a sleep laboratory shows that in fact their sleep patterns are relatively normal. This is therefore a cognitive problem where the person misinterprets their sleep duration.

Explanations of secondary insomnia

Psychological disorders such as depression, anxiety and schizophrenia are associated with insomnia. This is known as secondary insomnia. Studies (Morin *et al.*, 1999) show that up to 40 per cent of patients seeking treatment for insomnia have an associated psychological disorder. Such as:

- medical conditions such as heart failure, chronic pain and asthma
- drugs such as alcohol, amphetamine and overuse of sleeping pills
- parasomnias – these are sleep disorders that can disrupt sleep but do not necessarily lead to daytime sleepiness. They include sleep apnoea and sleepwalking.

Evaluation

Secondary insomnia can have a range of causes so there is no single explanation. Accurate diagnosis of the insomnia and the underlying cause is essential. Once the cause is established, it is often possible to treat it and so relieve the secondary insomnia. But it is important to recognise that some personality characteristics, such as high levels of anxiety, can lead to sleeping problems including insomnia, and these can be very hard to treat. The impact of insomnia on the individual should not be underestimated. It can lead to problems with work and relationships, and so lead to anxiety and depression.

AQA Examiner's tip

It can be difficult to identify AO2/3 material such as research findings in relation to insomnia. Remember, however, that there are other sources of AO2/3 besides research findings. General commentary can include the implications of diagnoses, problems in diagnosing disorders, implications for treatment, impact of disorders on the individual, and so on.

Think about it

Treatments are not covered in the specification. However, the effectiveness of treatments may tell us something about causes. For example, relaxation techniques and cognitive behavioural therapy can be effective in cases where insomnia is associated with stress and anxiety. Avoiding stimulant drugs such as caffeine and alcohol is a simple technique if insomnia is drug related.

Personality and sleep

There are huge variations in individual sleep patterns. Apparently Napoleon slept for only four hours a night, while Albert Einstein needed 10 hours sleep each night. The average today is 7.5 hours (Empson, 1993).

People with anxious or neurotic personalities are more likely to suffer from insomnia (Vahtera *et al.*, 2007). This is predictable as anxiety and neurosis are associated with high levels of arousal, making sleep difficult.

Some people are aroused and alert in the morning ('larks') and some are aroused and alert in the evenings ('owls'). This is a stable aspect of personality based on circadian rhythms. The sleep–waking circadian rhythm in larks is about two hours ahead of that in owls (Kerkhof and Van Dongen, 1996). Your chronotype is therefore controlled by inherited brain mechanisms.

Narcolepsy

The symptoms of narcolepsy are:

- Extreme daytime sleepiness, including repeated short periods of sleep during the day.
- Cataplexy: this is a sudden loss of muscle tone while awake, leading to physical collapse. It can be brought on by excitement and over-arousal.
- Hypnagogic hallucinations: dreamlike experiences occurring during wakefulness, especially in the period between sleeping and waking.
- Sleep paralysis: inability to move, often when falling asleep or waking up.

Narcolepsy and genes

Early studies showed that cataplexy was highly heritable (genetic). Dogs in particular can be bred to be extremely vulnerable to cataplexy, collapsing while awake whenever excited. They also fall directly into REM sleep.

Research findings

- Cataplexy in dogs has been linked to a gene defect on chromosome 12 (Lin *et al.*, 1999).
- This gene is responsible for regulating the brain neurochemical orexin (orexin is sometimes referred to as 'hypocretin'). The defect means that orexin cannot perform its normal function.
- Orexin-producing cells in the brain are greatly reduced in people with narcolepsy (Thannickal *et al.*, 2000), and they have low levels of orexin (Sakurai, 2007).
- Animal studies show that injecting orexin into the brain increases the amount of REM, showing a close relationship between REM and orexin.

Evaluation

Findings from animals can only be extrapolated to humans with caution. However the genetic work in dogs has been supported by human studies. Some recent work has identifed a gene on chromosome 6 that is linked with narcolepsy in humans (Overeem et al., 2008). This gene helps regulate our immune system, and one current theory of narcolepsy is that orexin cells in the brain are destroyed when this system goes wrong. Narcolepsy is associated with one particular mutation in this gene. Not all people with narcolepsy have this mutation, while some people with the mutation do not have narcolepsy. The link between narcolepsy and orexin is well-established, but the detailed mechanism remains to be uncovered.

MZ twins do not have 100 per cent concordance for narcolepsy. Although genetically identical, it is not always true that if one has narcolepsy then the other twin is certain to have it. This implies that narcolepsy is not entirely determined by genetics. Environmental factors are also important.

Think about it

Think back to the characteristics of REM sleep. These include loss of muscle tone and dreaming. Loss of muscle tone can explain narcoleptic symptoms such as cataplexy and sleep paralysis, while dreaming is obviously related to hypnagogic hallucinations. So a popular explanation of narcolepsy is that it represents the invasion of REM sleep characteristics into waking life. This is supported by the observation that when people with narcolepsy fall asleep, they move directly into REM sleep rather than following the normal pattern of moving through the stages of NREM first.

AQA Examiner's tip

If you use MZ/DZ twin studies in an answer, make sure you explain the logic behind them. In particular, show your understanding of why the use of DZ twins controls for the fact that MZ twins share similar environments.

AQA Examiner's tip

Narcolepsy is an excellent area in which to review research findings from animals and humans, and this is the most effective source of AO2/3 marks. You can demonstrate your understanding by showing how findings are generally consistent.

Sleepwalking

Sleepwalking is a parasomnia, an event during sleep that does not result in daytime sleepiness. It tends to run in families, suggesting some genetic involvement and usually occurs in the deeper stages of NREM sleep early in the night. While sleepwalking, people carry out automatic tasks, although these can be quite complicated, such as making tea, driving a car or surfing the web. Sleepwalkers have no recollection of their actions when they wake up.

Explanations

- Genetic involvement: Twin studies show higher concordance for sleepwalking in MZ twins than in DZ twins (Bakwin, 1970). However, concordance for MZ twins is not 100 per cent, so other, environmental, factors must be involved.

- Psychodynamic theories: These include acting out conflicts repressed into the unconscious, and returning to a 'safe' place from childhood. The related idea that sleepwalkers are acting out dreams runs into the problem that dreams occur during REM sleep when the body muscles are effectively paralysed and movement is impossible. As with so many psychodynamic theories, there is no reliable scientific evidence that supports these theories of sleepwalking.

- Brain mechanisms: Normally the movement centres in the brain are inhibited during all phases of sleep. The greater frequency of sleepwalking in children suggests that these inhibitory circuits are undeveloped, allowing movement to occur. As the key circuits mature, so sleepwalking disappears.

Evaluation

There is evidence for some genetic involvement in sleepwalking, perhaps related to a delay in the development of brain mechanisms inhibiting movement during sleep.

Although the 'delay in brain development model' can explain sleepwalking in children, it fails to account for the 3 per cent of adults who sleepwalk.

Concordance rates from MZ/DZ twin studies show that environmental factors are also important.

The general diathesis–stress model can be applied to sleepwalking. A genetic vulnerability is triggered by particular environmental events or stresses.

> **Think about it**
>
> Sleepwalking can raise issues of free will. There have been dramatic cases where sleepwalkers have carried out violent acts including murder. The defence has relied on the fact that sleepwalkers have no free will but are operating on automatic pilot. Therefore, the sleepwalkers do not have responsibility for their actions and cannot be found guilty. This defence has actually been allowed in some cases, but only where the person has shown a clear history of sleepwalking.

Thinking about issues and debates

Studies using the scientific approach often use the sleep laboratory to measure sleep states. This is a highly controlled environment with high internal validity, but there may be problems of generalisability (or ecological validity). In contrast, case studies of sleep deprivation have low internal validity with uncontrolled variables, but they may have high ecological validity.

Explanations of biological rhythms and sleep disorders such as narcolepsy are often *biological* and on the nature side of the nature–nurture debate. However, the role of zeitgebers and the effect of environmental factors on sleep disorders is more of an *interactionist* approach.

Issues, debates and approaches in biological rhythms and sleep

Restoration explanations focus on physiology and so can be *reductionist*, ignoring higher-level influences such as ecological factors. Evolutionary approaches are not reductionist, but in turn they may ignore the physiological aspects of sleep. Make sure that you understand the correct meaning of reductionist.

Ethical issues, especially informed consent, are important in human studies of sleep deprivation. Use of animals can involve highly stressful methods. Can you also explain why *extrapolation* is an issue with animal studies?

The ecological approach often uses *correlations* between ecological factors and sleep time. Why are conclusions of correlational studies limited?

Exam-style questions

ere are some examples of the kind of exam-style questions that you could encounter
this topic and some sample student responses and associated examiner feedback.

ample 1

> **0 1** Outline lifespan changes in sleep. *(4 marks)*
>
> **0 2** Outline and evaluate the restoration theory of the functions of sleep.
> *(4 marks + 16 marks)*

ample 2

> **0 3** Outline the nature of sleep. *(4 marks)*
>
> **0 4** Discuss the disruption of biological rhythms. *(4 marks + 16 marks)*

ample 3

> **0 5** Outline and evaluate **one or more** explanations for the functions
> of sleep. *(8 marks + 16 marks)*

ample 4

> **0 6** Outline **one** example of a circadian rhythm. *(4 marks)*
>
> **0 7** Outline **one or more** explanations for narcolepsy. *(4 marks)*
>
> **0 8** Evaluate **one or more** explanations for sleep disorders. *(16 marks)*

Sample answers

Suggested content for the other example questions for this section can be found at
www.nelsonthornes.com/psychology_answers

Example 4

0 6   *An example of a circadian rhythm is the sleep–wake cycle, which has a cycle of 24 hours and determines when we sleep. The sleep–wake cycle is controlled by an endogenous pacemaker located in the suprachiasmatic nucleus of the hypothalamus. This endogenous pacemaker is influenced by exogenous zeitgebers especially light, which entrains the sleep–wake cycle to 24 hours. Moore (1973) found a pathway from the retina in the eye to the SCN, which allows light to influence the pacemaker.*

AQA   Examiner's comments

Excellent concise answer, accurate, covers basic characteristics of the sleep–waking cycle, and outlines the roles of endogenous pacemakers and exogenous zeitgebers. Reference to research is relevant and impressive. This answer would achieve a mark in the top band.

0 7   *The first explanation for narcolepsy is brain damage. Von Economo in 1916 found that patients with damage to their hypothalamus had similar symptoms to narcolepsy. It is thought that brain damage can affect cells that secrete the hormone hypocretin, which has been linked to narcolepsy.*

The second explanation for narcolepsy is the neurochemical hypocretin, as low levels have been found in the brains of people with narcolepsy. However, it has also been suggested that the receptors for hypocretin might be insensitive in narcolepsy, rather than low levels of the chemical itself.

The third explanation is genetics. It has been known since the 1970s that certain breeds of dog have an inherited form of narcolepsy. Selective breeding has identified some of the genes responsible.

AQA   Examiner's comments

Again, concise but comprehensive and accurate. Three explanations is possibly overdoing it, but each one is outlined and given some relevant elaboration. No time is wasted on extended evaluation. This answer would achieve a mark in the top band.

0 8

The link between narcolepsy and hypocretin is supported by a case study, where a 16-year-old girl developed narcolepsy after damage to her hypothalamus caused by removing a tumour. It was found she had low levels of hypocretin in her CSF compared to controls. Arii et al. (2001) suggested that removal of the tumour had damaged the cells in the hypothalamus that secreted hypocretin.

Studies in humans show that people with narcolepsy have an 80% reduction in hypocretin levels, suggesting that they have lost all or most of their hypocretin cells. This is supported by studies with dogs that show that dogs bred to be vulnerable to narcolepsy have a mutation that affects the hypocretin cells (Nishino). However, it is argued that findings with dogs cannot be extrapolated to humans. However, Thannickal (2009) found mutations in the HLA gene in people with narcolepsy. This gene controls part of our immune response and the mutation might mean that the abnormal immune response destroys the hypocretin cells in the hypothalamus. However, there is no direct evidence for this theory. In some studies people with narcolepsy were found to have normal levels of hypocretin, but it has been suggested that their hypocretin receptors might be insensitive to hypocretin.

The idea that narcolepsy is caused by genetic abnormalities with the hypocretin system is on the nature side of the nature–nurture argument. However, Mignot et al. found that concordance rates for narcolepsy in MZ twins were only about 25%. This shows that environmental factors must also be important in narcolepsy. A general explanation would be the diathesis–stress model, which says that a vulnerability to narcolepsy is inherited but it needs an environmental trigger to activate the condition.

Straight into relevant research evidence

Student could have commented on the problem of generalising for case studies

Sustained and effective evaluation (AO2/3)

IDA comment, rather brief and could be more detailed to demonstrate full understanding

Relevant evaluation of explanation

Good evaluative point. Again some slight lack of detail

A relevant debate followed by elaboration

Good point, could do with a little more elaboration to demonstrate understanding

Nice integrating conclusion

AQA   Examiner's comments

Excellent use of research evidence, usually the most effective source of evaluation (AO2/3) in questions like this. Detailed and accurate, sound understanding and interpretation. Some slight lack of organisation and one or two points could be more detailed, particularly in relation to approaches, issues and debates. For instance, the reference to the nature–nurture debate arises naturally out of the evaluation, but it could have earned more credit if the implications had been explored in more detail. This is an impressive and focused answer with an overall coherent and sustained line of argument that would get a mark in the top band.

2 Perception

Theories of perceptual organisation

You need to know how to

✔ summarise Gregory's top-down (indirect) theory of perception

✔ summarise Gibson's bottom-up (direct) theory of perception

✔ evaluate these two theories of perception in relation to evidence.

Gibson's bottom-up theory of perception

Also known as the direct theory of perception, this assumes that to understand what we are seeing, we only need the information from our senses. Light falls on our retinas and is converted to electrical impulses. These pass along the optic nerve to the visual cortex, which is located in the occipital lobe. Gibson's view of this process was that there is so much information in the light pattern that falls on our retinas that we do not need any higher brain functioning to interpret it. He believed in the innate abilities we have that allow us to perceive the world accurately without having to rely on learning.

The central elements of Gibson's theory are as follows:

The optic array:	there is enough rich detail for us to make judgements about objects in space. This detail comes from light being reflected differently off surfaces of different textures and angles
The optic flow:	Gibson realised that when we are moving, the point we are moving towards (called the pole) stays still, but everything else appears to move away from it. The further away from the pole an object is, the faster its apparent speed.
Movement:	as we stand, turn and walk, the position of our eyes changes in relation to objects around us. This information helps us understand better what we are looking at. Optic flow patterns only occur when we are moving.
Invariants:	certain aspects of our optic array remain the same in spite of our movement. These things, which do not vary, help us determine distance, depth and the orientation of objects around us.
Texture gradient:	one invariant is the texture of a surface. Close; we see a lot of the detail of its texture, as it slopes away the surface seems smoother. Think about standing in a grassy field – at our feet we see individual blades of grass; further away we see a smoother green surface.
Horizon ratio:	this is a second invariant, which relates to how much of an object appears to be above the horizon compared to how much is below it. Although an object seems bigger when closer, the horizon ratio stays constant.
Affordance:	Gibson thought we can understand what an object is because it is obvious; for example, a ladder looks as if it is for climbing up and down, a glass looks as if it is for drinking out of. He argued that we do not need higher cognitive processing for this.

Commentary

- Warren and Hannon (1988) presented sequences of moving dots to people to simulate optic flow patterns. They found that people could use them to judge which direction they were moving in, as Gibson's theory predicted.

- There is some biological evidence supporting the theory: *Graziano et al.* (1994) have identified neurons in the visual cortex that are involved in detecting optic flow patterns.

- The speed and accuracy of visual perception makes it seem likely that it operates as Gibson described, in a direct way.

- Bruce and Green (1990) suggested that affordances only explain aspects of perception relevant to lower order animals. Gibson's theory ignores the interpretations we put on things due to experience and understanding.

- It has been argued that the reason why illusions deceive us is because we use higher cognitive processes to interpret what we see. Gibson's response, that illusions are artificially created in laboratories, sidesteps the issue and ignores the fact that illusions can affect us in the natural world.

AQA Examiner's tip

If you are asked to describe and evaluate two theories of perception, there will be fewer AO1 marks to describe each one than if you were asked to describe only one. Practise being able to outline the key features in a reasonable amount of detail, but also more succinctly, in case you are asked about the direct and the indirect theories.

Gregory's top-down theory of perception

The top-down theory is also known as the indirect theory. Gregory realised that sometimes the information that our senses receive is incomplete or ambiguous, making it difficult to understand what we are seeing. Consequently we have to infer, or make our best guess about it. Our guesses are based on what we already know about the world, and so before we can make sense of what we are seeing, we have to apply higher cognitive functioning. It is as if we have been given a perceptual problem-solving task. This is why it is known as the top-down approach. Gregory's theory makes the following assumptions:

Perception is an active process. It involves more than just direct experience of input. Between receiving sensory input and understanding what we are experiencing, other processes are involved.

Perception is not directly driven by stimuli. It involves prior knowledge, expectations, emotion and motivational factors.

Because we make inferences, or guesses, about incomplete and ambiguous stimuli, we are prone to making mistakes. Gregory argued that the reason we are fooled by many optical illusions is because we interpret them as three-dimensional images.

Commentary

- Experiments using illusions provide evidence that people use their previous experience to make inferences about an image.

- Cross-cultural studies show that people with no previous experience of monocular depth cues cannot interpret what they see as westerners do so are not fooled by illusions.

- Ambiguous figures (e.g. Bruner and Minturn's letter B or number 13) have been used to demonstrate that we use clues like context to help us determine its meaning.

- The role of expectation has also been demonstrated in illusions such as the Ames room (Ittelson, 1951) and the hollow mask (Gregory, 1973).

AQA Examiner's tip

It is worth remembering that the evidence you use to support one of these models can also be used to challenge the other. Studies of the effects of illusions will support Gregory's indirect theory, but will also contradict Gibson's direct theory. This means that these studies can have two uses, and they are even more valuable as evaluative (AO2/3) material.

- The fact that higher cognitive processing takes place unconsciously is supported by the fact that we continue to experience the Müller-Lyer illusion even after we are aware that the two horizontal lines are the same length.
- Gibson argued that these experiments are not ecologically valid ways of testing perception. A lot of evidence for Gregory's theory is based on people's performance when viewing illusions.
- Daneman and Stainton (1993) found that errors are more common when proofreaders are analysing essays in their own handwriting than those written by someone else, because of expectations.

Gregory suggested that the information we receive on our retinas is quite poor. However, Gibson was able to show this to be an exaggeration. In fact, the information we receive is very detailed.

Development of perception

You need to know how to

✔ explain the development of perceptual abilities such as depth (distance) and constancy

✔ describe infant and cross-cultural studies of the development of perceptual abilities

✔ evaluate studies of perceptual development in relation to evidence.

Depth cues

Binocular depth cues

Binocular cues depend on our using both eyes to look at an object. Because no learning is involved, the use of this type of depth cue supports direct theory of perception:

> **Think about it**
>
> How do depth cues relate to perceptual development?

Ocular convergence: Our eye muscle movements tell us how far inwards our eyes are pointing, and this gives us information about how far away an object is from us.

Retinal disparity: Each eye receives a slightly different image. When an object is far away the two images are almost identical, but the closer an object is, the greater the difference between the images.

Sheedy *et al.* (1986) showed that hand–eye coordination tasks like threading a needle are performed 30 per cent faster when both eyes are used rather than just one eye. This supports the use of these two cues in judging depth.

Monocular depth cues

Monocular cues only require the use of one eye. These cues are used by artists to convey the impression of depth in a picture painted on a two-dimensional canvas. It is these cues that cause us to misinterpret optical illusions. They depend on learning and so support the indirect theory of perception. Some of them are:

- Relative size: an object that is drawn larger appears to be nearer to us in a picture.
- Relative height: an object that is lower down in the picture appears to be closer to us.
- Superimposition (overlap): if one object is partially obscured by another, it gives the impression that this is because it is in front of the other object.
- Shading: if a shadow is drawn next to an object, it appears to have three dimensions.
- Linear perspective: the convergence of lines that ought to be parallel (such as a railway track) gives the impression of distance.

Perceptual development

Studies of perceptual development have been conducted to determine whether the skills we have are present at birth or develop as we experience our environment. The explanations below focus on the role of nature–nurture. These studies fall into four categories:

- Neonate studies: studies have focused on the ability of very young children to perceive depth and understand perceptual constancies. Perceptual constancy is the perception that an object stays the same even though its appearance (size, shape, colour, etc.) may change. The problem with these studies is that the children cannot tell us exactly what they see.
- Cross-cultural studies: if perception is a learned ability, then different experiences will lead to differences in our perceptual skills. By studying people from different cultures (typically, non-Western, non-industrialised, and living in a non-carpentered environment), we can compare our skills and see how they vary, if at all. Perception of distance has been investigated, people's understanding of drawings, and whether they are fooled by optical illusions.
- Distorting the field of vision: if we can change the way an individual sees the world (maybe by using goggles that turn everything upside down), and they relearn how to cope with their new field of vision, this shows that learning is possible.
- Deprivation: if you could not see or interact with the world for the first year of your life, when you finally were able to, would you perceive things differently to an infant who had not had a restricted development?

Perceptual constancies

There are several aspects of an object's appearance that change, even though the object itself does not. These changes occur when the object moves, when the observer moves, or when there are changes in the conditions. When we understand these constancies, we will have fully developed perceptual skills. The constancies are:

- Size constancy: an object remains the same size, although it appears smaller as it moves away from the observer.
- Shape constancy: an object appears to be a different shape when we view it from different angles.

Apply it

Find some optical illusions, including the Müller-Lyer, the Necker cube and the rat-man figure. See whether you can determine which monocular depth cues have been used to create the illusion. Find the engravings of the Dutch artist, M.C. Escher, who deliberately misuses these cues to create unusual images of waterfalls and staircases. This will give you a better understanding of how monocular depth cues work.

AQA Examiner's tip

Only neonate and cross-cultural research appear in the specification. This means that examination questions will not be about studies using the deprivation of infants or distorting the field of vision. If, however, you are familiar with this wider range of studies, they will be useful in providing evaluative (AO2/3) material.

- Brightness constancy: an object will appear brighter or darker depending on the light source reflecting on it.
- Colour constancy: the hue of an object varies according to the time of day or the colour of the light that falls on it.
- Motion constancy: when we move we are aware of whether it is our own movement that we are detecting or the movement of the object.

Key study

The visual cliff (Gibson and Walk, 1960)

Gibson and Walk constructed an apparatus known as the visual cliff. This comprised a sheet of plexiglass over the top of a black-and-white chequerboard. On one side of the platform the chequerboard was just underneath the glass, on the other there was a 4-foot drop to the floor. The infants and young animals were coaxed to the shallow side, and then to the deep side.

All of the animals (humans as soon as they were old enough to crawl, one-day-old chicks, kids (i.e. young goats) as soon as they could walk, and rats as soon as they had opened their eyes) crossed to the shallow side, but only the rats crossed to the deep side. The rats crossed because they could feel the glass with their whiskers. When they had their whiskers cut off, they no longer crossed to the deep side.

The conclusion drawn was that these infants and young animals all had an innate ability to perceive depth. This was what stopped them from crossing to the deep side at such a young age.

Evaluation

- Human infants are usually around six months old before they can crawl. This means that they have had at least six months' experience of judging depth through things like being picked up by adults, carried upstairs and even shaken in the air. So what is being tested cannot be purely innate ability.
- In a variation of this experiment, the infants were held over the shallow side and the deep side. A measure of their heart rates was taken to signify whether they recognised that there was a drop or not. If their heart rate rose, it implied they felt fear from recognising the drop. The results confirmed the findings of the original study: the infants could perceive depth at two months old.
- It is not possible to generalise with any degree of accuracy from the performance of non-human to human infants. Human perceptual ability is learned to a greater extent than non-human perceptual ability. For example, by altering the field of vision with glasses that distort vision by 30°, Hess (1963) found that a human child could adapt, but hens could not.

Apply it

You could investigate any of these studies further to consider them in more detail

Size constancy in infants (Bower, 1966)

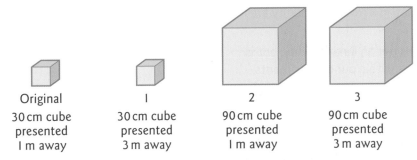

Original	I	2	3
30 cm cube presented I m away	30 cm cube presented 3 m away	90 cm cube presented I m away	90 cm cube presented 3 m away

Bower conditioned three–month-old infants to respond to the presentation of a 30 cm cube at a distance of 1 metre by turning their heads to the side. He then presented three further cubes to see whether they would respond in the same way.

The first alternative is the same size but looks smaller, the second alternative is bigger, and the third alternative is bigger but looks the same size because it is further away. Bower found that the infants reacted more to the 30 cm cube at 3 metres (same size as the original but smaller retinal image) than to the 90 cm cube at 3 metres. In other words, they could differentiate between the cube that was the same size as the original despite looking smaller and the one that merely appeared to be the same size as the original. This would suggest that they had developed size constancy.

Evaluation

- The conclusion overlooks the fact that they reacted just as much to the bigger 90 cm cube at 1 metre away. This was not the same actual size or apparent size of the original.
- They may have turned their heads whether they thought the cube was the same or not.
- Despite the conclusion that the three-month-old children had acquired size constancy, their performance was not as good as adults' performance. Therefore, it would be incorrect to say this is an entirely innate ability.

Cross-cultural study of depth perception (Turnbull, 1961)

Turnbull studied the BaMbuti tribe, who live in the dense jungle of the Congo. Because of the environment in which these pygmies live, they have never had the experience of seeing things at a distance. Turnbull took one of the BaMbuti pygmies out of the jungle onto a plain, and showed him a herd of buffalo in the distance.

The pygmy refused to believe the creatures in the distance were anything but insects because they looked so small. This was because he had never had the experience of things creating a smaller retinal image the further away they are. As Turnbull and the pygmy approached the buffalo, they appeared to grow bigger, and again, due to the lack of experience of this phenomenon, the pygmy was confused and accused Turnbull of using magic to fool him.

This study clearly shows that perception is not innate, it is determined by a person's life experiences.

Evaluation

- There is support for this cross-cultural study from other research that has found differences in how cultures perceive things. For example, Segall *et al.* (1963) found that Zulus living in a rural community are not fooled by the Müller-Lyer illusion.

- This supports the view that perception is not an innate ability, but is determined by the particular experiences within our environments.

- There are neonate studies that contradict the evidence from Turnbull's study, showing that perceptual abilities are already established from birth.

Key study

Cross-cultural study of monocular depth cues (Hudson, 1960)

In order to investigate the perceptual abilities of non-Western cultures, Hudson showed rural Africans pictures that used three-dimensional (monocular) depth cues. These cues included relative height, relative size and overlap. In one picture, a man is throwing a spear in the direction of two animals – an elephant and an antelope. The elephant is smaller than the man, and higher up in the picture, indicating that it is not directly in front of him like the antelope. People used to looking at this sort of picture will realise that it is the antelope that is standing in line with the man's spear, and that the elephant is in the background. However, the rural Africans tended to say it was the elephant the man is throwing his spear at. This indicates that the use of monocular depth cues is a learned ability.

Evaluation

- This study supports Gregory's indirect theory of perception. It also supports the nurture side of the nature–nurture debate, as it demonstrates that people with different cultural experiences perceive things in different ways.

- Deregowski *et al.* (1972) found that the Me'en people of Ethiopia could not recognise animals if drawn on paper, but they could recognise them if they were drawn on material. This indicates an imposed etic – a research tool that is developed by one culture may not be adequate for testing a different culture.

- There are ethical issues with this study, as there are with Turnbull's study. The implication is that in the Western industrialised parts of the world, we have superior perceptual skills, and by inference, other cultures are inferior. This is not dissimilar to the use of IQ tests used to make political points in the last century.

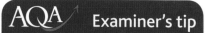

AQA Examiner's tip

Remember that referring to appropriate relevant issues and debates in your examination answers allows you access to higher marks. Finding cultural differences may be a result of cultural bias.

Evidence supporting 'nature' explanations

- Several studies of neonates show that perceptual abilities are present shortly after birth, including depth perception (Gibson and Walk, 1960), size constancy (Bower, 1966) and shape constancy (Slater, 1989). This shows that learning does not have to take place.

- The way that babies prefer gazing at some patterns compared to others (Fantz, 1961) suggests that humans are programmed to be able to make perceptual distinctions from birth.

- Hess (1963) attached goggles to hens. The goggles distorted their field of vision by 30°. Because the hens were not able to adjust to the distortion, Hess concluded that perception had to be innate. If it had been learned, they would have been able to relearn.

- Gibson's direct theory of perception supports the view that we are capable of understanding what we see without having the need for learning.

Evidence supporting the 'nurture' explanations

If perception were innate, then biology would dictate that all members of a species would have similar perceptual skills. However, any research that shows that cultures are different disproves this:

- Cross-cultural studies show that people from some cultures do not have depth perception skills (Turnbull, 1961).

- Cross-cultural research also shows how two-dimensional drawings are perceived differently due to lack of experience (Deregowski, 1972).

- People from a carpentered environment are more easily fooled by certain illusions than people who do not live in a world of straight lines and corners (Segall *et al.*, 1963; Annis and Frost, 1973).

- Perceptual deprivation studies performed on cats (Held and Hein, 1963) and cataract patients who have recovered their sight (Gregory and Wallace, 1963) show that perceptual development is retarded by lack of experience.

Face recognition and visual agnosias

> **You need to know how to**
>
> ✔ describe Bruce and Young's theory of face recognition, including case studies
>
> ✔ describe explanations of prosopagnosia
>
> ✔ evaluate research into face recognition and visual agnosias in relation to evidence.

Questions addressed by psychologists in trying to understand the processes involved in face recognition are:

- Are there different processes using different neural components for recognition of (a) faces and (b) other objects?

- Does the recognition of faces involve feature analysis, or is it a holistic process?

Shepherd, Davies and Ellis (1981) discovered evidence for the view that we process faces feature by feature. They asked participants to describe a set of unfamiliar faces and they found that they made reference to individual features – hair, eyes, nose, mouth, eyebrows, chin and forehead. They even tended to do it in the same order with each face. They did not describe the shape of the face or its expression – two things that would require an overall impression. This supports the feature analysis approach. However, when we are being asked to describe a face, we would of course refer to obvious characteristics. If we only need to recognise a face, the task is different and so the process might be different.

Contradictory evidence for the feature analysis theory comes from Yin (1969) and Bruce and Valentine (1986). Yin found that faces that are inverted are harder to recognise (known as the inversion effect). If faces were processed by feature analysis this would not happen. This suggests that we use a holistic process. Bruce and Valentine used pictures of famous faces whose features had been scrambled. People found the faces much harder to identify, which also shows that we do not recognise faces by processing individual features.

A further finding of Yin's research was that people are not confused by the inversion of objects in the same way that they are with faces. The implication of this is that objects and faces are not processed in the same way.

Key study

Theory of face recognition (Bruce and Young, 1986)

The theory of face recognition outlined by Bruce and Young proposed that it is a holistic process, that is, we look at a face as a whole rather than merely trying to pick out individual features. They identified eight separate components involved in the process, claiming that some worked in parallel (at the same time as each other) and some worked in sequence (one operated first, followed by another). The components were:

1 Structural encoding: this produces various descriptions (or representations) of faces.

2 Expression analysis: people's emotional state is inferred from the expression on their faces.

3 Facial speech analysis: facial movements are studied, especially around the mouth, to help understand speech.

4 Directed visual processing: specific facial features are processed selectively.

5 Face recognition units: information, or descriptions, about known faces is stored.

6 Person identity nodes: this is stored information about known individuals (e.g. their occupations).

7 Name generation: names are stored separately from other information.

8 Cognitive system: this stores additional information that might help the process of recognition (e.g. the fact that it is unlikely Cheryl Cole will be on the same bus you are on).

9 When processing familiar faces, we depend on structural encoding, face recognition units, person identity nodes and name generation. When processing unfamiliar faces, we depend on structural encoding, expression analysis, facial speech analysis and directed visual processing. This suggests two separate routes, one for familiar and one for unfamiliar faces.

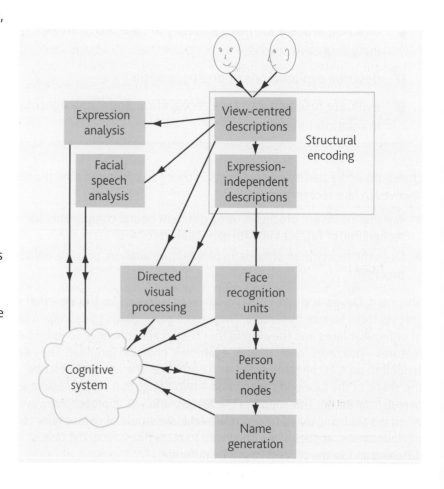

Evaluation

Attempts to investigate the Bruce and Young theory of face recognition have treated it in a similar way to models of memory. They search for evidence that the different components exist. Although much can be gleaned from healthy individuals, the majority of evidence comes from case studies of people who suffer from prosopagnosia (a condition in which sufferers cannot recognise familiar faces, even those of people they know well).

- Young *et al.* (1993) studied 34 brain-damaged men and found no grounds to confirm selectivity of processing. If these men had been better at processing familiar faces than unfamiliar faces, or vice versa, then this would have been evidence that there are separate processes.

- There is evidence that separate routes are involved in processing facial recognition and facial expressions. Humphreys *et al.* (2007) studied three sufferers of developmental prosopagnosia and found that they had an inability to recognise faces, but their ability to distinguish facial expressions was as good as healthy individuals. The findings have been corroborated by Young *et al.* (1993). Experiments with healthy individuals by Calder *et al.* (2000) also support these results. This confirms that there are separate routes involved.

- However, the majority of prosopagnosics suffer from an inability to recognise both faces and facial expressions. This indicates that the two processing routes might not be separate.

- The fewer steps the information needs to go through on the model, the quicker we would expect it to be accessed. Three elements which have been investigated are 'face recognition units', 'person identity nodes' and 'name generation'. Young *et al.* (1986) supported face recognition occurring faster than the other two. Kampf *et al.* (2002) showed personal identity happened quicker than name generation. Contrary to the model Brédart *et al.* (2005) found people could name colleagues quicker than retrieve their personal information, which suggests the model may need to be more flexible.

Explanations of prosopagnosia

Prosopagnosia is a condition in which sufferers cannot recognise familiar faces, although they can recognise familiar objects. Research has attempted to explain this in one of two ways:

- – face recognition is harder than object recognition, and so the condition is the result of some malfunction of the brain that means it cannot perform very well with more difficult visual tasks
- – face recognition is independent of other recognition tasks, and there is a specific part of the brain that has been damaged to cause this.

- Acquired prosopagnosia is caused by brain damage, and the patient will have had normal facial recognition abilities prior to the damage. Research has therefore tried to identify which parts of the brain specifically are the ones that cause prosopagnosia when damaged.

- Developmental prosopagnosia is not the result of brain damage. Research has therefore shown that prosopagnosia can also be caused without any apparent neurological abnormality. This makes conclusions about its causes difficult to draw. Each case study varies, and the evidence they provide is contradictory.

Case studies

Duchaine and Nakayama (2005) studied seven prosopagnosics, requiring them to recognise objects from several categories. As well as faces, the other categories were cars, guns, houses, tools, horses and natural landscapes. Duchaine and Nakayama found that some of the prosopagnosics had near normal abilities with all of the non-facial categories.

There have been several case studies of similar individuals, all of whom suffered from prosopagnosia but could still distinguish between other objects summarised in the table:

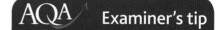

Examiner's tip

When using research evidence to evaluate a theory, make sure that you explain clearly why the evidence supports or challenges the theory. Highlight the implications of the evidence.

Case studies	Details
TA	Could not identify specific objects in a category, yet a galvanic skin response (GSR) test suggested he did unconsciously recognise familiar faces. (Jones, 2001)
RM	Could distinguish between individual cars in his model collection better than a control group of healthy participants. (Sergent and Signoret, 1992)
VA	Could tell his own handwriting and recognise coins from foreign currencies. (DeRenzi *et al.*, 1991)
Mr W	A farmer who could not distinguish human faces but could still differentiate between individual cows within the herd.
PS	Suffered brain damage and could distinguish between similar objects but Caldera *et al.* (2005) showed she relied on people's mouths when managing to discern faces.
EP	Was able to discriminate between objects in categories such as cars, flowers and buildings. (Nunn *et al.*, 2001)

The fusiform face area has been shown through EEG and fMRI to be more active when individuals are examining faces than when they are examining objects. Downing *et al.* (2006) presented people with images of faces and 18 other categories. They found the fusiform face area was more active with the faces than with any of the other stimuli. Other research has supported this, although sometimes the differences are only small.

It follows therefore that damage to the fusiform face area (located in the temporal lobe) might inhibit face recognition. This has been found to be the case. Prosopagnosics tend to have damage to this area of the brain (Farah *et al,*. 1995).

Think about validity

Prosopagnosia is a rare condition, so there is difficulty in acquiring evidence from controlled experiments with control groups for comparison. Consequently, much of the evidence comes from case studies, and much of it is anecdotal evidence. Think about the problems of using case studies as evidence. The visual abilities of each case vary, as do the origins of the brain damage. What is the impact of this on the validity of the conclusions drawn from this research?

Key research

The expertise theory (Gauthier and Tarr, 2002)

Gauthier and Tarr (2002) argued that we are good at recognising faces because we are experts at it. We have had a lot of practice and this is what makes the processing of faces different from the processing of other objects.

Participants were shown images of faces, birds and cars, and asked to perform recognition tasks. fMRI scans found the fusiform gyrus was active during the bird and car recognition tasks as well as the face recognition task. This indicates that the fusiform gyrus is not exclusively used for the recognition of faces. It is used for the recognition of any category of objects for which we have expertise.

This theory proposes that people who have expertise in a particular category of objects (e.g. cars) will not be able to perform a recognition task of objects in this category at the same time as a face recognition task because they will need to use efficiently the fusiform gyrus for both tasks simultaneously. Non-experts will be able to do this, because the fusiform gyrus will only be used to recognise faces. Gauthier and Tarr were able to demonstrate this supposition.

However, the case of RM contradicts this theory: he was able to recognise the makes, models and years of cars (a category in which he was an expert) but could not recognise faces (Sergent and Signoret, 1992). The theory of expertise would argue that if he could not recognise faces (one expert category), he should not have been able to recognise cars (another expert category).

Thinking about issues and debates

Cultural bias

Perception has less scope for cultural bias than some areas of research. Even cross-cultural research is used to explain a phenomenon that is relevant to the whole species rather than just to individual cultures.

NB: Cultural differences are not the same as cultural bias.

Reductionism

Trying to resolve the nature–nurture debate means concluding one thing or the other. Like all behaviour, perception is probably a combination of both innate and learned abilities. If we try to reduce it to an either/or question, we will miss contributing evidence from the opposing view. Consequently, we must conclude that we cannot satisfactorily reduce perception to either nature or nurture alone.

Issues and debates in perception research

Ethical issues

The use of infants in research is always going to be problematic. However, this and cross-cultural research is far more ethical than creating sensory deprivation in non-human animals. Holding a small child over a visual cliff is frightening for a while, but this is nothing when compared to having your eyelids sewn shut for six months, (Blakemore's study using kittens (1975)).

Psychology as a science

It is difficult to know how someone perceives an image. We have to rely on what they tell us or how they react. With infants, they cannot tell us, so interpretation of their behaviour is all we can use. This inevitably leads to problems of objectivity. Can we really know when an infant recognises an object?

A second difficulty lies in our inability to isolate innate skills from the effect of experience. One can never really be measured without the other.

Exam-style questions

Example 1

0 1 Describe and evaluate Gibson's bottom-up (direct theory) of
perception.   *(24 marks)*

Example 2

0 2 Describe Gregory's top-down (indirect theory) of perception.
                                                                     (8 marks)

0 3 Evaluate research that has been conducted to investigate
explanations of perceptual development.   *(16 marks)*

Example 3

0 4 Outline infant and cross-cultural studies of perceptual
development. Consider what these studies tell us about the
development of perception.   *(24 marks)*

Example 4

0 5 Outline explanations of prosopagnosia.   *(8 marks)*

0 6 Discuss Bruce and Young's theory of face recognition.   *(16 marks)*

Perception

Sample answer

Suggested content for the other example questions for this section can be found at
www.nelsonthornes.com/psychology_answers

Example 3

0 4

The two opposing theories of perceptual development are either that we are born with all the skills we need to understand our visual world, or that we acquire the skills we need through a process of experience, i.e. learning. The first theory suggests our innate abilities equip us from the moment we are born to be able to make sense of the things we see as well as an adult would. This has been investigated with the use of neonate studies. If it can be shown that newborn babies see the world like adults, we can conclude that experience is not needed.

One such study was conducted by Bower, who found that very young infants are able to distinguish between cubes placed at different distances. He concluded that by three months old, children already had a well-developed understanding of size constancy. This supports the view of innate abilities. However, although they did show some ability, they did not perform as well as an adult would. This means that at least some development had to occur. The accuracy of Bower's findings is also questionable; as the infants were too young to say what they saw, head movements were measured, although infants so young do not have full control of their heads.

Further support for innate abilities came from Gibson and Walk. They showed infants (humans as well as non-humans) seemed to have an innate ability to perceive depth, which they demonstrated with the visual cliff experiment. Although this evidence is not without its problems either. The use of non-humans is of limited value since it has been shown that some abilities are innate in non-humans, but learned in humans. This means it is very difficult to generalise between species. With the human infants that were used in this study, it must be remembered that they were at least six months old in the original study, and two months old in a variation. Consequently, what was being tested was not purely innate ability, as they had already had some experience.

The difficulty of drawing absolute conclusions from studies using neonates is that we can only interpret what they see from their behaviour. Non-human animals and very young infants do not have language, and so we are forced to assess their visual abilities, without their being able to tell us. Consequently, we might be misinterpreting their behaviour. This loses the degree of objectivity that psychological research strives for.

Introductory paragraph is not very effective. The candidate is referring to the nature-nurture debate but could be more explicit to gain more credit. They could also have referred to the development of perception clearly.

These paragraphs use evidence from studies well. The methods have also been criticised (AO2/3), which has an impact on the validity of the arguments they support.

An assessment of the accuracy of the previous studies, with reference to the issue of psychology being scientific provides good evaluative (AO2/3) material.

Cross-cultural studies have provided evidence for Gregory's theory that perception will be influenced by prior experience. Hudson found that rural Africans would misinterpret a picture that used monocular depth cues because they had not had any prior experience of the type of devices artists use to give the impression of depth in pictures. Because people from different cultures perceive things differently, we can conclude that perception is a learned ability that develops as we age. This is the nurture side of the debate. Furthermore, the way we are fooled by optical illusions, and tribes who do not live in a carpentered environment are not, also supports the theory that perception is a developmental process, affected by culture and experience.

Good evidence from research which is used well to make points.

The use of visual cues has been supportive of both the nature and the nurture side of the debate. The use of monocular depth cues is a matter of learning, since cross-cultural studies have shown, those who have not experienced them will interpret pictures differently from those who have. Binocular depth cues on the other hand rely on feedback from the eye muscles and retinal images. These are not affected by prior experience, and so suggest at least depth perception is to a great extent innate. It would be a mistake therefore to adopt a reductionist view that perception is entirely learned or entirely innate. Studies have supported both sides of the argument, and a complete conclusion would suggest development is caused by both factors.

Finally, the use of visual cues (gains AO1) is brought into the nature–nurture debate. A further reference to issues and debates adds to the evaluative marks (AO2/3) and shows that issues and debates can be used to build evaluation and pick up valuable marks.

AQA ⁄ Examiner's comments

The knowledge and understanding demonstrated (AO1) is reasonable but lacks the detail required for marks in the top band. The evaluative content (AO2/3) is reasonable in three of the paragraphs and is edging towards a mark in the top band.

3 Relationships

The formation, maintenance and breakdown of romantic relationships

You need to know how to

✔ describe theories that explain the formation, maintenance and breakdown of romantic relationships

✔ evaluate these theories and consider evidence that relates to them.

How relationships start

Two key theories have been put forward to explain how and why relationships get off the ground:

- The filter model (Kerckhoff and Davis, 1962) argues that relationships go through stages in which different things are important at different times.
- Reward/need satisfaction theory (Argyle, 1987) argues that people form relationships with partners who meet their needs and provide rewards.

Think about it

Both models put forward here are extremely Westernised. They are less relevant to relationships in other cultures where partners are chosen by way of arranged marriages. This links to the issue of cultural bias in relationship research.

Filter theory and reward/need satisfaction theory

Filter theory

Relationships develop in three stages. At each stage, different kinds of people are filtered out as unsuitable, leaving a smaller group of 'desirable' potential partners.

Social demographic filter. Most people meet others who are similar to them: they live nearby, go to the same school, college or work. These people tend to be similar in educational level, economic background and age. People from different social backgrounds are less likely to be encountered. Social sorting is an important and subtle filter.

Similarity of attitudes and beliefs. Once two people start getting know each other, similarity becomes important. People who share our attitudes, interests and beliefs are easier to talk to. Dissimilar people are filtered out as we do not have much in common with them.

Complementary needs. The third filter relates to how well the two people fit together and meet each other's needs. This becomes important after 18 months.

Reward/need satisfaction theory

Relationships are formed with people who meet our social needs and who provide rewards.

People come into relationships with their own unique set of needs, for example for self-esteem (to feel good about themselves) dependency (someone to rely on) and sexual needs. They seek relationships with partners who meet some or all of these needs.

Foa and Foa (1974) identified six kinds of rewards including practical and emotional rewards. Practical rewards are things like money, presents and help. Emotional rewards include status (being someone's girlfriend or boyfriend) and feeling loved. Relationships also provide rewards in the form of shared activities and time spent together.

If the rewards offered by one person meet the needs of the other, this is likely to motivate them to develop the relationship further.

Evidence and evaluation of filter theory and reward/need theory

Filter theory

- Sprecher (1998) found that couples who were similar in social/demographic background were more likely to develop a long-term relationship.
- Kerckhoff and Davis (1962) found that student couples who shared similar attitudes were likely to stay together for up to about 18 months, but after about 18 months similarity became less important and complementary needs became more important.

However:

- Gruber-Baldini *et al.* (1995) found that couples who were similar were more likely to still be together 20 years later, suggesting that similarity continues to be important.
- The filter model is a stage theory. Dividing relationships into stages is rather artificial: relationships change and develop but they do not fit neatly into stages.
- The social demographic filter may be less important today as we have greater mobility and the ability to make contact and stay in touch electronically with people who live further away. Social networking and texting allow us to get to know and stay in touch with people from more diverse social backgrounds.

Reward/need theory

- Long-term, happy relationships meet many of the needs of the two people involved. In contrast, unhappy relationships involve unmet needs (Smith and Mackie, 2002).
- This theory has close links to the behavioural approach with its emphasis on rewards and reinforcements.
- The idea of rewards also underpins other important theories of relationship maintenance such as social exchange theory and equity theory.
- This is a Westernised theory. In many parts of the world where arranged marriages are common, rewards may be less important in the formation of relationships.

Commentary

Both of these theories are dated. In the last 30 years or so, relationship researchers have become less concerned with presenting general 'catch all' theories, as these often ignore important differences/variations in relationships, for example between cultures or in same-sex couples. Theories of this nature were developed in the 1960s in the USA and they reflect the social values of that society and time.

Social exchange theory

Social exchange theory belongs to a group of explanations called economic theories. Economic theories assume that people run relationships in a similar way to bank accounts, keeping an eye on what they are putting in and getting out. Economic theories share the view that people are out to get the best relationship deal and may move on to another relationship if they think they will get more out of it. However, they differ in how self-centred they consider people to be.

AQA Examiner's tip

A good way to evaluate theories is to compare them. These two explanations each have a different focus. Reward theory focuses on why we have relationships and the motivations for engaging in them. It is closely associated with the behavioural approach. Filter theory focuses on how relationships develop over time. However, both agree that complementary needs are important in the survival of a relationship in the long term.

Think about it

This is a Westernised view of relationships, which assumes that people choose their partners and can move on and end relationships (voluntary). Arranged marriages do not share these assumptions. This links to the issue of cultural bias.

Key theory

Social exchange theory (Thibaut and Kelley, 1959; Homans, 1971)

SET argues that relationships involve the exchange of rewards and costs between two people. Both rewards and costs are defined differently by individuals. Examples of rewards could include affection and sharing activities, whereas costs might include arguments, loss of freedom and boredom. We maintain our relationships by aiming to maximise rewards and minimise costs (the minimax principle) and by bargaining over what we are prepared to give and what we want to receive. The balance of rewards and costs is referred to as the outcome of the relationship. If rewards outweigh costs, the relationship is in profit. If costs outweigh rewards, the relationship is in a state of loss.

Thibaut and Kelley argue that we compare an existing relationship with two bench marks to see how it is doing:

- The comparison level (CL) involves comparing the existing relationship with an expectation of how rewarding relationships are in general, gained from our past experiences. If the current relationship is better than previous ones, we should feel positive about it.

- The comparison level for alternatives (CL Alt) involves comparing our current relationship with other potential relationships that might be possible. If other possibilities compare favourably, we may be less pleased with our own relationship.

According to SET, a relationship is likely to break down when the costs involved outweigh the rewards. If the costs do not outweigh the rewards, it should be maintained. For example, if the relationship involved jealousy and arguments but few good times, it would be in a state of loss. As we evaluate relationships by comparing them with other possibilities, it may also break down if a better offer appears on the horizon. If the CL suggests that the relationship is less rewarding than it was in the past or than relationships in general, then the 'loser' may decide to end it. If the CL Alt suggests that a better alternative relationship has appeared on the scene, it may also be ended.

Apply it

Make a summary of SET using around six bullet points. Think of a mnemonic (memory aid) to trigger recall of your main points in the exam.

Evaluation

- SET has provided the basis for later economic theories (e.g. equity theory and investment theory) which have borrowed many of SET's ideas about rewards and costs.

- SET assumes that people continually keep an eye on the balance sheet of their relationships. Some theorists dispute this (e.g. Argyle, 1987 and Duck, 1994) suggesting that people only begin to count costs and rewards when the relationship has already run into difficulties.

- SET also assumes that relationships are run on the minimax principle in which we seek relationships with few costs attached. However, when relationships develop, there is often an increase in both the rewards and the costs attached to it.

- SET sees people as very selfish and likely to walk out of a relationship that has become unrewarding. However, many people stay in unrewarding relationships where there are many costs, for example, victims of violent or abusive partners. Rusbult and Van Lange (1996) argue that this is due to investments, which have been put into the relationship and cannot be retrieved, such as time and emotional support. Rhahgan and Axsom (2006) found that women living in a refuge for victims of violence had stayed in the relationship because of their investments. Jerstad (2006) found that the more time and effort put into a relationship, the more likely a person was to stay with an abusive partner. These studies contradict the predictions of SET as they show that people often stick with relationships that have become extremely unrewarding.

Equity theory (Walster, 1978)

Equity theory accepts SET's claim that people monitor their relationships and keep an eye on what they are putting in and getting out. However, it extends SET further by arguing that people do not simply think about themselves in relationships. They also focus on what their partner is getting out of the relationship. Equity theory suggests that couples maintain their relationships by aiming for fairness for both partners: what people get out should roughly equal what they put in.

■ If the relationship is unfair, with one person benefiting but putting very little in, the relationship is said to be 'inequitable'.

■ Inequity leads the person who is not getting much out of the relationship to feel dissatisfied. However, it also leads the person who is over-benefiting to feel guilty that their partner is unhappy. This is the main difference between equity theory and SET.

■ If the relationship is fairly new or not serious, the couple may simply break up. If the relationship is relatively serious and the couple have put lots into it, they may be motivated to try and repair the relationship.

■ Repair involves trying to restore equity to the relationship. This can be done by putting less (or more) effort into the relationship, or attempting to encourage one of the partners to put in more effort.

Evidence and evaluation

■ Equity theory provides an important explanation of why some relationships end. It is supported by studies of short-term (e.g. student) relationships and long-term (e.g. marital) relationships, which show that inequitable relationships are more likely to end.

■ Walster *et al.* (1977) tested equity theory using a sample of 500 male and female university students who were dating. Students were asked to comment on how much they and their partner were putting into the relationship and getting out of it. Fourteen weeks later, Walster returned to see which couples were still together. She found that those who had judged their relationships as being more equitable at the start were more likely to be still together than those who had judged their relationship as less equitable. Crucially, those who over-benefited were as likely to initiate a split as those who under-benefited.

■ Van Yperen and Buunk (1990) carried out a longitudinal study of 259 couples recruited through a newspaper advert. Participants filled in an anonymous questionnaire without their partner present. This was used to calculate an equity score between +3 and −3 for the relationship. One year later, Van Yperen and Buunk asked the couples about how happy they were together. They found that those with high equity scores were happier and more satisfied with the relationship, and this was especially true for women. The correlation between equity and satisfaction was 0.44 in women taking part in the study. Equity was less strongly related to satisfaction in men (correlation of 0.20).

AQA Examiner's tip

A useful way to evaluate a theory is to compare it with another theory that takes a different standpoint. When you do this, ensure that you do not simply describe the second theory (remember that no more than 8 marks can be given for describing in any essay). You should use it to make a sustained critical commentary. See the example essay on page 41.

Apply it

Make a list of the similarities and differences between SET and equity theory. Remember that comparing two approaches is a helpful way of developing evaluation skills.

Think about it

What are the differences in carrying out research on student couples compared with non-student couples? Why should we avoid generalising findings from one sample to another? (Clue: how are they different?)

- De Maris (2007) assessed the importance of equity in relation to splitting up. Using a sample of 1500 American couples, he found that a woman's sense of being under-benefited was the best predictor of the couple splitting up.

- However, equity does not appear to be equally important to all relationships. There is considerable evidence that it is more important to women than men. It appears to be most important in lesbian relationships (Dwyer, 2000). The idea of equity and fairness is more important in western relationships and less important in collectivist cultures.

Apply it

Compare SET and equity theory's explanations for relationship breakdown. Which do you think is better and why?

Evolutionary explanations of human reproductive behaviour

You need to know how to

✔ explain what is meant by sexual selection and how it has led to differences in reproductive strategies between men and women

✔ describe relevant research studies that show sex differences in behaviours and evaluate them

✔ describe explanations of sex differences in parental investment and evaluate evidence for them.

Sexual reproduction

Sexual reproduction occurs when a male gamete (sperm) and female gamete (ovum) unite. Human reproductive behaviours refer to the range of behaviours involved in sexual reproduction. Put simply, these include attracting and selecting mates (partners), having sexual intercourse, and care of the resulting offspring. The evolutionary approach argues that human reproductive behaviours have been shaped by sexual selection. Behaviours and bodily features that enabled our ancestors to produce more surviving offspring would be passed on to their children who would inherit the feature or behaviour.

There are two types of sexual selection:

- Intra-sexual selection occurs when members of one sex compete for mates from the other. For example, males who were large, aggressive and able to beat rivals in fights would get to mate more often with females and would leave behind more offspring than smaller males.

- Inter-sexual selection occurs when one sex (often females) choose which males to mate with. For example, females may prefer to mate with males who have a greater amount of resources.

How sexual selection has shaped male and female reproductive behaviours

According to the evolutionary approach, biology has programmed men and women to adopt different reproductive behaviours. The origins of different behaviours lie in the different biology of males and females – notably egg and sperm.

Apply it

Illustrate the concept of sexual selection with examples to show your understanding. In most cultures, males prefer females who are younger, and females prefer older males. Why?

Males who preferred younger females would produce more offspring (as they are more fertile) than those who preferred older females, who would be less fertile. Older males generally have more resources, which could aid survival of offspring, thus making them attractive to females.

As you read the following examples of sex differences, think about how the behaviours described may have evolved and how they link to reproductive success.

Think about it

Evolutionary psychologists are unable to travel back to hunter-gatherer times to observe behaviour directly. Therefore, they start from studies of modern human behaviour and work backwards to infer how and why behaviours developed. This process is sometimes known as 'reverse engineering'. This links to 'How Science Works'.

Comparison of sexual strategies for males and females

	Male	Female
Gamete	Sperm	Ovum
Description	Very small and mobile. Millions are produced in one ejaculation.	Largest cell in the body, usually one ovum is released each month, 400 are released over a lifetime.
Reproductive life	Sperm are produced from puberty until death although the number declines with old age. Longer reproductive life makes men capable of fathering thousands of offspring.	Ova are produced from puberty until menopause (around age 50). Shorter reproductive life makes women capable of mothering a smaller number of offspring.
How long does it take to make a baby?	As long as it takes to have sex.	Following conception, nine months of pregnancy followed by childbirth.
The best chance of reproductive success	Mate with as many fertile women as possible.	Ensure the survival of the few offspring produced.
Mate choice	Will seek young females as youth and fertility go together. Features associated with youth such as large eyes and an hourglass shape are attractive to men.	Will seek faithful, committed mates who are prepared to stay around and raise offspring. Powerful mates are also important as they can defend the family and provide valuable resources. Older males are more likely to do this.
Attitude to sex	Males should be promiscuous as any opportunity for mating increases reproductive success.	Females should be choosy and select the best available male. Promiscuity may lead to pregnancy with no support to raise offspring who may not survive.

Evidence from studies of human reproductive behaviour

	Male	Female
Mate preferences, qualities sought in partners (Buss, 1989 cross-cultural study)	Males are tuned in to physical attractiveness, which signals youth and fertility and leads to their reproductive success.	Women are tuned in to resources provided by potential mates as these will aid reproductive success by ensuring that offspring survive.
Promiscuity versus choosiness (Clark and Hatfield, 1989 and 1990)	Males are more promiscuous. Clark and Hatfield found that 75 per cent of male students who were approached by an attractive female stranger agreed to have sex with them.	Females are choosier. In Clark and Hatfield's study, none of the females agreed to have sex with an attractive male stranger.
Patterns of sexual jealousy (Buss, 1993)	Males showed greater stress when asked to imagine their partner having sex with someone else. Males are 'tuned in to' sexual jealousy as they could input resources into offspring that are not their own.	Females showed greater stress when asked to imagine their partner in love with someone else. Females are 'tuned in to' emotional jealousy as an emotional connection could lead their male to leave and remove valuable resources.

Commentary on approaches

The evolutionary approach takes the view that sex differences in reproductive behaviours exist because they have been sexually selected. However, the same behaviours (e.g. male promiscuity and female choosiness) can also be explained in other ways. In Western societies, social norms make it more difficult for females to behave promiscuously ('nice girls don't') whereas these behaviours are often encouraged in males.

Parental investment

According to the evolutionary approach, humans are programmed to maximise the number of their genes contributed to the gene pool in the form of surviving offspring. After an offspring has been conceived, parents must invest resources in order for it to survive to reach maturity and reproduce. Parental investment can be divided into mating effort (time and energy spent pursuing a sexual partner and having intercourse) and rearing effort (time and energy put into offspring after conception to ensure they reach sexual maturity).

Key theory

Parental investment theory (Trivers, 1972)

Trivers' theory claims that there are substantial sex differences in parental investment. These differences lead to differences in reproductive behaviour between men and women:

- Male investment in offspring is minimal. Males produce millions of sperm and they are not costly or time consuming to make. After the initial investment in mating, males do not have to invest in offspring or help with rearing them. Males therefore invest most in mating effort and least in rearing effort.

- Female investment in offspring is substantial. The gamete they supply (the ovum) is large and they have relatively few of them. As fertilisation is internal, females must continue to invest after conception, providing a safe prenatal environment and feeding the baby with nutrients from their own resources. They also give birth and continue to feed the baby until it is old enough to fend for itself. Females invest heavily in rearing effort. It does not matter how many males a female mates with in a single reproductive cycle, as she can only become pregnant with one of them. Mating effort is therefore less important for females.

According to Trivers, differences in investment lead to differences in reproductive behaviours. Females should be choosy as they gain nothing from mating with males who do not stay around and provide resources for offspring. In contrast, males with their minimal investment should be promiscuous as they gain greater reproductive success by mating with as many fertile females as possible.

Evaluation

Trivers' theory overlooks the fact that some women do have short-term relationships (one-night stands), and many men choose not to behave promiscuously. Sexual strategies theory (Buss and Schmitt, 1993) argues that both women and men pursue short- and long-term relationships, but seek different qualities in short- and long-term partners. Women seek generous mates in short-term relationships as they use affairs and flings to test whether a male would be a suitable long-term partner. Men look for very different things in one-night stands and long-term partners: a sexually willing partner is fine for a non-serious relationship, but for a long-term partner, faithfulness and good mothering skills are crucial.

Think about it

This theory is deterministic as it suggests that males and females are programmed to behave in certain ways. What are the implications of this?

AQA Examiner's tip

The studies on page 34 and on this page provide evidence for Trivers' claims. Each of these (Buss, Buss and Schmitt, Clark and Hatfield) demonstrates how sex differences in parental investment drive reproductive behaviour.

Apply it

See whether you can work out why faithfulness is so important for males in long-term partner selection. How might this link to Buss's study of sexual jealousy?

Effects of early experience and culture on adult relationships

> **You need to know how to**
>
> ✔ describe the main claims of attachment theory and research evidence for and against the continuity hypothesis
>
> ✔ describe how culture influences romantic relationships referring to research studies of relationships in different cultures and the difficulties with this research
>
> ✔ explain some of the difficulties with cross cultural research on relationships.

Early experience – attachment

Adult relationships are not just influenced by biological/inherited factors. Upbringing, socialisation and childhood also play an important part in later adult relationships. Attachment is the emotional tie between two people that is shown in their behaviours. Attachment theory, put forward by John Bowlby, argues that childhood relationships set the scene for later adult relationships. There is some evidence for this claim, but it is not wholly supported.

Key theory

Attachment theory (Bowlby, 1969)

Bowlby argued that attachment is an instinctive process that has evolved to ensure the safety, protection and survival of babies. In summary:

- Young babies possess instincts to elicit care-giving from their mother figure, and mothers have instincts to protect their babies.

- From the relationship with the mother figure, the young child develops an 'internal working model', which provides them with a view of how loveable they are, how trustworthy other people are, and of how relationships work in general. This model is thought to continue to affect adult relationships.

- The child develops a characteristic attachment style based on the responsiveness of the mother.

- There are three basic variations of attachment style: secure, insecure ambivalent and insecure avoidant.

Bowlby argued that the attachment style continues throughout childhood to adulthood, a claim known as the continuity hypothesis. The attachment style affects how adults run their relationships, how easily they trust other people and whether or not they behave possessively.

Think about it

Attachment theory is a deterministic approach as it suggests that childhood experiences determine later adult relationship experiences. Attachment theory also stresses the effect that upbringing and childhood attachments have on later adult relationships, emphasising the importance of nurture. There are strong links to both of these key debates.

Evidence for and against 'continuity'

Evidence *for* the continuity to adult relationships	Evidence *against* continuity to adult relationships
Hazan and Shaver's Love Quiz study showed a strong relationship between childhood attachment type and adult attachment type: ■ Secure babies often went on to become secure adults who found it easy to love and trust. ■ Avoidant babies became adults who doubted if love existed and feared involvement and commitment. ■ Ambivalent babies became jealous or possessive adults who were intense and worried about being abandoned.	Attachment style can change in adulthood in both directions: ■ When major life events occur – such as parental death or divorce – attachment patterns can change from secure to insecure (Zimmerman *et al.*, 2000). ■ When a disrupted early childhood is followed by later, strong relationships, an insecure attachment style can develop into earned security (Rutter, Quinton and Hill, 1999).

Commentary

Hazan and Shaver's Love Quiz study asked participants to write to a local paper, choosing one of three descriptions of their adult relationships and recalling their childhood relationship with their parents. It is likely that many participants would have had poor memories of their childhood and may also have produced socially desirable answers. Many researchers now use Adult Attachment Interviews rather than questionnaires to assess relationships.

AQA Examiner's tip

You can show your understanding of how science works by engaging in a methodological critique of research studies. Remember that you must focus your evaluation on attachment theory if this is what the question requires. You should make evaluation of this nature relevant by saying that problems with supporting evidence undermine the theory.

The influence of culture

Culture and relationships

Culture relates to the behaviours and beliefs of social groups that make them different to each other. But how does culture influence relationships?

There are a number of systems that attempt to classify cultures in different ways. One of the most widely recognised differences is between individualistic cultures and collectivist cultures (Hofstede, 1980):

■ Individualistic cultures: in Western Europe, Australia and North America, relationships are freely chosen by people on the basis of love and attraction. Common relationship patterns include cohabiting (living together). The number people choosing to get married is declining. Cohabiting and marital relationships can be ended if couples are unhappy.

■ Collectivist cultures: in Asian countries such as Pakistan, India and China, marriages have traditionally been arranged by relatives or well wishers. Criteria for choosing partners include wealth, profession and social status of the family. Relationships are viewed as permanent and divorce may be difficult or impossible.

Qureshi (1991) identifies three types of arranged marriage:

■ Planned/traditional: parents plan the process with very little discussion with their children, who cannot turn down the partner.

■ Delegation: children tell parents what kind of partner they want, and parents look for partners from 'appropriate' families who fit the criteria.

■ Joint venture: both parents and children are active in the selection.

Arranged marriages in collectivist cultures

Gupta and Singh (1982) compared 100 professional Indian couples. Fifty had married for love and 50 had taken part in arranged marriages.

Gupta and Singh used Rubin's Liking and Loving scales which showed high levels in love marriages but they declined rapidly over the first 10 years. In contrast, arranged marriages started with lower levels of liking and love but these increased and after 10 years, arranged marriage couples liked and loved their partners *more* than the couples who had chosen their partners.

Other studies have shown how Indian couples value the approval of the family for their partner however the marriage is organised. Umadevi, Venkataramaiah and Srinivasulu (1992) found that female Indian students were happy with the idea of arranged marriages as long as it involved the consent of the two people involved. They were also happy with the idea of a love marriage, but they stressed that the family would need to approve of their choice.

In the People's Republic of China, Xioahe and Whyte (1990) compared women who had chosen their own partners with arranged marriages. They found that those who chose their partners reported higher levels of happiness, suggesting that Western ideas of free choice are now becoming absorbed into collectivist cultures and altering attitudes and practices.

Commentary

Gupta and Singh's study shows that arranged marriages have traditionally been high in satisfaction and stability. Yelsma and Athappilly (1988) argue that the success of arranged marriages comes from the careful selection or matching of partners for education and social background. Similarity of many kinds is associated with happier and longer-lasting relationships. As separation and divorce are viewed negatively in collectivist cultures, there is much more emotional and practical help along with greater social support from families to help couples when things become difficult.

Over the last 20 years, many parts of the world including eastern Europe and East Asia have undergone dramatic economic and political changes, which have altered expectations about relationships. These changes are referred to as modernisation and Westernisation. Important changes include:

- developments in health and education
- reductions in family size
- increased educational opportunities for women
- the pursuit of Western ideals such as happiness and independence.

Xioahe and Whyte's study shows how these changes are beginning to alter traditional views about relationship formation in China. Other studies have indicated that divorce rates have begun to rise in collectivist cultures such as China and Japan, which have undergone rapid Westernisation (Whyte, 1990; Alexy, 2008).

> **Apply it**
>
> Researching further details of these studies will allow you to consider their implications.

> **Apply it**
>
> Consider how culture influences the processes of relationships to evaluate its effect.

Arranged marriages in individualistic cultures

There are differences in how marriages are arranged in different religious groups living in Westernised societies:

- Ghuman (1994) studied British and Canadian Sikhs, Hindus and Muslims and found that Sikh and Hindu families were more likely

to use delegation or joint-venture methods of arranging marriages, whereas Muslim families preferred traditional arranged marriages.

- Goodwin and Adatia (1997) studied 70 Indian couples who were brought up in Leicester and were Hindu in religion. Less than 10 per cent had fully arranged marriages with the remainder having a large element of choice over their partner.
- Zaida and Shuraydi (2002) studied a group of 20 second-generation Pakistani Muslim women who were brought up in Canada. They found that most of them disliked the idea of arranged marriages and would prefer to choose their own partner. They had internalised the views of Western culture – a process known as 'acculturation'. In contrast, their families who had been brought up in Pakistan were resistant to ideas of allowing them to choose partners and they experienced a clash between the values of the two cultures.

Commentary

The studies above demonstrate how new forms of relationships are being developed in second- and third-generation migrants who have moved from collectivist to individualistic cultures. In the above examples, traditional practices of wholly arranged marriages are being combined with Western ideas about choice, to present new cultural traditions for young British Asians. The move from traditional arranged marriages to joint-venture marriages is demonstrated in Goodwin and Adatia's study in Leicester.

Thinking about issues and debates

Cultural bias

Many of the models and theories presented here (e.g. SET, equity) have been developed from Western research studies and suffer from cultural bias. It is problematic when Western concepts (e.g. equity) and measuring tools are used in cross-cultural studies of relationships, such as Gupta and Singh's study of arranged marriages in India.

Psychology as a science

Relationships are difficult to study scientifically. They rely on self-report measures, and participants are also likely to present themselves in socially desirable ways. Find three studies of relationships that have used self-report measures where this criticism applies.

Evolutionary explanations cannot be tested in a scientific way as it is impossible to go back to hunter gatherer times. Instead, studies of modern human behaviour (e.g. sexual jealousy) are used to test hypotheses. Why is this a problem?

Issues and debates in relationship research

Socially sensitive research

Trivers' PIT also suggests that men are programmed to be unfaithful as this leads to reproductive success. Other evolutionary psychologists have argued that rape is a natural adaptation designed to increase reproductive success. What makes these claims socially sensitive?

Determinism

Attachment theory takes a deterministic view of early experience, suggesting that childhood attachment sets the scene for later relationships. Find two pieces of evidence which imply that attachment style *can* change and suggesting it is not determined.

Evolutionary approaches such as parental investment theory also take a deterministic view, suggesting that women and men have inbuilt preferences for certain types of partners.

What kinds of determinism are these?

Exam-style questions

Example 1

0 1 Outline **two** theories of the maintenance **and/or** breakdown of relationships. *(8 marks)*

0 2 Evaluate **one** of these theories in relation to research evidence/ other theories. *(16 marks)*

Example 2

0 3 Discuss the relationship between sexual selection and human reproductive behaviour. *(24 marks)*

Example 3

0 4 Discuss the influence of childhood experiences on adult relationships. *(24 marks)*

Example 4

0 5 Outline research into the influence of culture on romantic relationships. *(8 marks)*

0 6 Evaluate research into the influence of culture on romantic relationships. *(16 marks)*

Sample answers

Suggested content for the other example questions for this section can be found at
www.nelsonthornes.com/psychology_answers

Example 1

0 1 *Relationship maintenance involves the processes couples go to keep their relationship happy or together whereas relationship breakdown involves splitting up. Two theories attempt to explain both processes and are known as economic theories because they focus on the idea that people keep an eye on the 'balance sheet' of their relationship. This essay will focus on maintenance of relationships rather than breakdown.*

The first theory is social exchange theory (SET), which argues that we aim to maximise our rewards and minimise our costs in a relationship, known as the minimax principle. A relationship can be in a state of profit (when there are more rewards than costs) or loss (when the costs outweigh the rewards). SET argues that we compare the relationship with others in the past and we may split up if we perceive ourselves to be worse off (C.L.). We also compare it with other possible available relationships (C.L.Alt) and we may be motivated to end it if better rewards are available elsewhere.

In contrast, equity theory argues that we want to keep our relationships fair and, although we are motivated to gain rewards from them, we are also concerned that our partner is fairly rewarded. This theory takes an economic view of relationships arguing that we assess the costs and rewards when we are in the relationship and keep a mental balance sheet aware of who is putting in what and who is getting what out. If the relationship is relatively fair (equitable) we will stay together, but if it becomes unfair we are likely to try to restore the fairness – either by putting less in or making our partner put more in! If this does not work, the theory says that we will split up.

0 2 *SET has provided the basis for lots of later theories including equity theory and investment theory, which have borrowed many of its ideas about rewards and costs. However, lots of the ideas of SET have been challenged. For example, SET claims that people keep an eye on what they are putting in and getting out of their relationship. Some people dispute this claim (e.g. Argyle and Duck) suggesting that people only begin to count costs and rewards when their relationship has started to run into problems.*

This introduction does not pick up marks. It should be shorter

Two short summaries of theories. Accurate but less detailed. Just manages higher-band marks

Critical point about claims of theory

41

SET sees people as very selfish and likely to walk out of a relationship that has become unrewarding. However, many people stay in unrewarding relationships where there are many costs e.g. victims of violent or abusive partners. This means that there is evidence which contradicts SET and it cannot explain all relationships. Rusbult argues that people stay because of investments, which have been put into the relationship. These are things that can't be got back, like time and emotional support. Rhahgan and Axsom found that women living in a refuge for victims of violence had stayed in the relationship because of their investments and Jerstad (2006) found that the more time and effort put into a relationship, the more likely a person was to stay with an abusive partner. These studies contradict the predictions of SET as they show that people often stick with relationships that have become extremely unrewarding.

Presentation of contradictory evidence and alternative theory

Making this explicit provides a clear line of argument

SET is also challenged by equity theory, which suggests that fairness is more important than selfishness. There is evidence (Walster 1977) which shows that people who are over-benefiting feel guilty and are more likely to split up: SET says that they would just be glad to be in profit. Walter's study was carried out on students so it may not be representative of marriages.

More contradictory evidence

Another problem with SET is that it is an extremely Western theory. In many parts of the world (e.g. collectivist cultures) people cannot leave relationships just because they are unhappy. Hofstede argues that relationships are compulsory in some cultures. This makes SET culture biased as it does not apply well cross-culturally. The emphasis on selfishness is also very Western and in other cultures people do not pursue their own happiness in the same way.

An attempt at issues and debates. An appropriate debate but not very well developed

This last point needs to be elaborated. The candidate could have said that marriages are arranged and very hard to end via divorce when they become unrewarding. This demonstrates the limitations of SET as a cross-cultural model

AQA Examiner's comments

Reasonable evaluation. This question overall earns a mark in the basic/reasonable band.

4   Aggression

Social psychological approaches to explaining aggression

> **You need to know how to**
>
> ✔ describe at least two social psychological theories of aggression
>
> ✔ discuss at least two social psychological theories of aggression in relation to evidence
>
> ✔ describe and evaluate at least two explanations of institutional aggression.

Social learning theory (SLT)

One way to think of social learning theory is like a jukebox: once you have inserted a coin, you can make a selection based upon what music is in there. Everyone will observe lots of role models behaving in lots of different ways. So for each situation that we find ourselves in, we will select the most appropriate behaviour based upon what we have seen others use successfully in the past. Aggression is only one option. This is different from the psychodynamic approach, which states that aggression is unavoidable.

> **Apply it**
>
> Studies involving Bandura formed the basis of formation of SLT. Look up some specific studies in more detail.

SLT and various options for behaviour

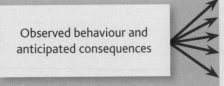

Observed behaviour and anticipated consequences →
- Aggression
- Constructive problem solving
- Withdrawal and resignation
- Dependency
- Self-anaesthetisation with drink or drugs

Evidence regarding SLT

- In 1961, Bandura, Ross and Ross showed that children will copy the aggressive behaviour of adult models. Children saw an adult role model performing aggressive acts towards a Bobo doll. During a 20-minute period of play afterwards, the number of aggressive acts they displayed was counted. The children were far more aggressive than a comparison group of children who had not witnessed an aggressive role model.

- In 1965, Bandura repeated the study with the variation of letting the children see the model being either punished or rewarded. He found that those who saw the model punished were less likely to imitate. However, when they were offered a reward themselves, they all copied what they had seen. This supports the motivation aspect of SLT: if a child thinks they will be punished, their motivation is low. But when they think a reward is available, the motivation to copy is high.

- It could be that young children do not behave in the same way as adults or even older children because they are more impressionable. This sample bias may restrict the ecological validity of the evidence.

> **Apply it**
>
> Can you understand why these studies are considered to be unethical? Think of who the participants were, and what they were being exposed to.

■ It could also be argued that conducting research in laboratories does not yield results that are applicable to normal, everyday situations. They lack mundane realism, and again the conclusions need to be drawn with care.

■ The studies only look at the immediate impact of watching a role model acting aggressively. In reality, exposure to role models might have different long-term effects.

■ Children on St Helena were observed before and after the introduction of television to see whether the exposure to images of people acting violently would increase their aggression (Charlton, 2000). No such effect was found. This demonstrates that exposure to aggressive role models does not necessarily lead to aggressive behaviour.

Deindividuation

Key theory

Deindividuation (Festinger *et al.*, 1952)

In 1952, Festinger *et al.* referred to deindividuation as the process by which people lose their sense of self-awareness and individuality. This happens when people feel their identities are hidden. As early as 1895, Le Bon argued that people in a crowd act quite differently from when they are on their own. This occurs because in large groups people can remain anonymous, which encourages the display of aggressive behaviour.

People are usually inhibited from acting aggressively because if they can be identified, there is the threat of punishment. Other situations that cause this phenomenon are the wearing of masks or disguises and the cover of darkness, both of which make it harder to identify a person's face.

When people are aware that someone is watching them, they become self-conscious. They monitor their own behaviour for fear of being judged by others, and they act according to a moral code that they have learned throughout their lives. When deindividuation happens, the individual loses this fear.

Evidence supporting deindividuation

■ In a variation of Milgram's electric shock experiment, Zimbardo (1969) used female undergraduates to investigate the role played by deindividuation in the delivery of punishment to a student learner. One group of participants wore their own clothes and had big name badges, the other wore laboratory coats with hoods, and were not identifiable. Zimbardo found that those whose identities were concealed delivered twice as many electric shocks as those who knew each other's names.

■ In a natural experiment, Mann (1981) analysed 21 reported suicides in the USA. In 10 cases, the crowd that had gathered to watch urged the potential suicide to jump. This happened at night, when the crowd was large and a long way from the jumper. In other words, they could not be identified.

■ In 1976, Diener observed 1300 American children going trick or treating. Those who were in large groups or who were wearing costumes that hid their faces were more likely to engage in antisocial behaviour, such as stealing.

AQA Examiner's tip

Remember that in the exam, if you are asked to describe *research*, the studies by Bandura *et al.* and Charlton may be used to gain AO1 marks. However, if the question only asks for *explanations*, you will gain no marks at all for describing studies. If explanations of aggression are required, you can only gain AO2/3 marks by referring to studies in two ways:

• by suggesting that their conclusions support or contradict an explanation

• by suggesting that the evidence they provide is methodologically flawed and therefore cannot validate the explanation.

Commentary

- Johnson and Downing (1979) criticised Zimbardo's research by saying that the outfits that his participants were required to wear resembled the outfits worn by the Ku Klux Klan. This might have led to an increase in the number of shocks given due to the expectations associated with aggressive stimuli rather than the concealing of the participants' identities. It is possible that deindividuation leads to an increase in any kind of behaviour that is usually restricted by social rules, not just aggression. Gergen *et al.* (1973) studied the interactions of 12 people in a dark room and found that many hugged each other and felt sexually aroused.

- It is not certain that becoming deindividuated by belonging to a large crowd will lead to aggressive behaviour. Diener (1980) found that deindividuation can create pro-social feelings at gatherings such as religious rallies.

- A meta-analysis of 60 studies by Postmes and Spears (1998) showed no consistent findings regarding the impact of deindividuation and the influence of groups on individual behaviour.

- Deindividuation also occurs with the victims of aggression. In the concentration camps of Nazi Germany, the inmates lost their identities by having to wear uniforms, or were dehumanised by having to live in demeaning conditions. It became much easier for the guards to perpetrate acts of violence towards the inmates when their victims were anonymous.

Institutional aggression

An example of aggression being institutional is when the village of My Lai in Vietnam was laid waste. The villagers were murdered by the US army because one man, who had legitimate authority, gave the order. It would have been virtually impossible for any of the soldiers under the command of Lt Calley to disobey his orders because of the rigid structure of command within the army.

Theories of aggression within institutions

Research in this field considers whether the cause of aggression is the situation that people find themselves in, or the personality of the people in the institution.

Deprivation model

The deprivation model refers to the lack of freedom, control, privacy, security and heterosexual relationships that prisoners experience. This of course is highly frustrating, and may lead to an aggressive reaction, as supported by the frustration–aggression theory (Dollard *et al.*, 1939). The prisoners are likely to express their frustration through violence directed towards the staff. The staff will be seen as the controllers of all privileges, and so it is they who cause the deprivation. This model rejects the argument that it is inmates' personalities that are the cause of violence, and that these have been 'imported' into the prison environment.

The Lucifer Effect

Also, the situation that people find themselves in may create what Zimbardo called The Lucifer Effect. This refers to the power of the situation to make ordinary people act in aggressive ways. The situation may cultivate an increase in aggression through a change in the power and status of those within the institution, feelings of helplessness in the victims of violence, and a sense of deindividuation on both sides of the aggressive behaviour.

Apply it

One way of evaluating a theory is to compare it with another. For example, watching violence on TV might be a bad thing (vicarious learning – SLT) or a good thing (catharsis – psychodynamic approach) depending on which theory you favour. It might even have no effect if aggression has a genetic cause.

Outline three similarities and/or differences between the social psychological explanations of aggression and other approaches.

AQA Examiner's tip

There are different types of institutions, from establishments like prisons and universities to organised bodies of people like the police, army or even terrorist groups. However, the best answers to an exam question on institutional aggression should focus mostly on prisons and the army because this is where the majority of recent research has been conducted. Also, with terrorist groups being uniquely different from other institutions, it would be hard to explain all aggression in the same way.

Importation model

The importation model refers to prison inmates bringing their existing antisocial or aggressive personalities into the institution, and continuing to behave in the same way. This suggests that ordinary people, if they had this kind of restrictive environment forced on them, would not be aggressive because they were not aggressive outside the institution. The people who are sent to prison are more likely to have an aggressive nature than those who are not. Gang members, for instance, would continue their gang culture inside prison. A high proportion of violent attacks by inmates on other inmates are gang related. An institution that people generally volunteer to join, such as the army, might attract people who are aggressive by nature. They may see the army as a reasonable outlet for their aggressive tendencies. So once again it is the expression of the personalities of those who join an institution that leads to aggression, rather than a temporary change due to the situation they find themselves in.

Commentary

- Jiang and Fisher-Giorlando (2002) studied 431 male prison records in the southern states of the USA and found that the deprivation model was the most likely to explain inmate violence towards staff. The prisons with the most restrictive regimes had the highest incidences of violence. However, the importation model was the most likely to explain inmate violence towards other inmates, as gang cultures persisted inside the prisons.

- DeLisi, Berg and Hochstetler (2004) supported the importation model when they studied the prison violence records of 831 inmates, and found that violent behaviour inside prisons was mostly caused by those prisoners who were violent outside prison.

- Zimbardo offered Abu Ghraib as proof of the power of the situation to create aggressive behaviour by the guards towards the Iraqi prisoners. The key elements of this particular situation were:
  - the provision of power to those who usually had none
  - the lack of supervision by a commanding officer
  - the dehumanising of the prisoners by removing their clothes
  - the opportunity to extract revenge on the out-group.

> **AQA Examiner's tip**
>
> It is very tempting when answering a question on causes of aggression in institutions to use material from Milgram's study. After all, his participants did commit potentially violent acts towards others. However, you must remember that this is the section on aggression, not obedience, so if you do choose to include Milgram's research, you must make it relevant to institutional aggression. Make reference to the existence of hierarchies in the army, for example, which create legitimate authorities and the agentic shift.

Biological explanations of aggression

> **You need to know how to**
>
> ✓ explain neural and hormonal mechanisms in aggression
>
> ✓ explain genetic factors in aggressive behaviour.

Neural and hormonal mechanisms in aggression

The structures of the brain that have been implicated in the initiation and control of aggressive behaviour are the limbic system and the prefrontal cortex. The limbic system, which comprises several structures, is responsible for instinctive behaviours such as eating, aggression and sexual activity. The parts that have attracted most interest are the hypothalamus and the amygdala. Through electrical stimulation, lesioning and more recently brain imaging techniques, it has been found that these two structures are responsible for making people act aggressively. The role of the prefrontal cortex is to control inappropriate displays of aggression. As we live in a structured society, there are rules governing the expression of aggression. It is the prefrontal cortex that allows us to learn these rules. Consequently, any damage to the prefrontal cortex will make it harder for us to control our aggressive instincts.

Evidence for the role of brain structures in aggressive behaviour

Delgado et al. (1954) stimulated the hypothalamus of monkeys with mild electric currents and found that they attacked other monkeys. This seems to show that the hypothalamus causes aggressive behaviour. Similar results have been discovered in cats.

Raine et al. (1997) compared positron emission tomography (PET) scans of the brains of 41 murderers with non-murderers and found the murderers had lower levels of activity in the prefrontal cortex and the amygdala. This might be the significant difference that leads them to kill. Raine also found a lack of activity in the prefrontal cortex of children suffering from ADHD, a disorder that makes it difficult for sufferers to control their instinctive urges.

Blair et al. (2001) studied institutionalised psychopaths, and suggested that their condition was caused by damage to the amygdala. The amygdala is responsible for recognising emotion in others, and if it is not functioning properly it increases the probability of harming others without remorse, as it leads to a lack of empathy.

A number of case studies have indicated that brain damage may be responsible for an increase in aggressive behaviour. One is Phineas Gage, whose personality became more aggressive after suffering a massive brain trauma in 1848 when an explosion sent an iron bar through his left frontal lobe. Another is Charles Whitman, who shot 12 people in 1966. A post-mortem revealed he had a tumour pressing on his limbic system.

Think about validity

Consider the methodological limitations of studies you use to evaluate this explanation. Firstly, it is not always possible to generalise research findings from non-human animals to humans. Secondly, it is not easy to make generalisations about behaviour based on case studies. This is because individual cases are unique, and different case studies may provide conflicting data.

Commentary

- Delgado's monkeys only attacked the other monkeys present when they were above the other monkeys in the hierarchy. When the other monkeys were superior, Delgado's monkeys cowered in a corner as if threatened, but dared not attack. This suggests that social learning is the overriding factor in determining aggressive behaviour, not brain structure.

- Although Raine et al. studied a good-sized sample, and he controlled variables such as age, sex, mental illness and drug-taking behaviour, there are still problems with drawing conclusions from his research. PET scans lack precision, and he did not control for different levels of violence in the murders (poisoning does not require the same level of aggression as strangling, for example). Furthermore, as his studies took place after the murders had been committed, the evidence was only correlational and cause and effect statements cannot be made with certainty.

- The damage to Gage's brain was so extensive, it would be difficult to pinpoint which part was responsible for making him more aggressive. We must also bear in mind that we have to rely on the accuracy of his doctor in recording his change in personality. Observations could be biased.

Think about it

Research using non-human animals must always be generalised to humans with care. However, Potegal, Ferris and Delville (1994) argue that differences are only qualitative (basically, humans and non-humans are more similar than dissimilar) and so we should be able to generalise with confidence.

Evidence showing that hormones cause aggression

An alternative biological explanation of aggression is biochemistry. This includes the role of hormones and neurotransmitters. There is much evidence to suggest that high levels of androgens (male hormones produced by the testes), especially testosterone, cause aggressive behaviour. It has also been shown that low levels of the neurotransmitter serotonin will have the same effect.

By most criteria, it seems that men are more aggressive than women. One obvious difference between men and women is the much higher levels of testosterone in men. It is concluded therefore that this hormone is responsible for this difference.

Researchers	What they found
Young *et al.*, (1959)	Injected pregnant monkeys with testosterone and found that if the offspring was female it would act like a male by play fighting as it grew up
Wagner, Beuving and Hutchinson (1979)	If a male mouse is castrated its levels of aggression drop. But when injected with testosterone, its aggression levels rise again
Kreuz and Rose (1972)	Higher rates of testosterone in criminals with a history of violent behaviour than in those without a history of violence
Floody (1968) (in a review of research)	In the week preceding menstruation women's androgens increase, correlating with increased hostility and the likelihood of committing crime
Haller and Kruk (2003)	A link between stress hormones (e.g. adrenaline and noradrenaline) and levels of aggression

Commentary

- There are societies that lead an existence free from aggression, and in which there are no differences between male and female levels of aggression (Deaux, Dane and Wrightsman, 1993). This suggests that aggression is learned and is not an unavoidable consequence of our biology.

- The levels of androgens in women cannot be measured at the exact time they commit crimes, so we cannot know for certain the strength of this correlation.

- It has been found that when watching a sporting contest (like a football match) there are increases in testosterone levels in the fans of the winning team. This means that our biology is influenced by our environment. So to look at our endocrine system without considering the impact that external factors have on it would provide an incomplete explanation of aggression.

Think about it

If we act more aggressively when we experience stress, and stress hormones increase at the same time, this is correlational evidence, and does not indicate cause and effect.

Evidence showing that neurotransmitters cause aggression

Davidson, Putnam and Larson (2000) found lower levels of serotonin in violent criminals than in non-violent ones. They suggested that the role of serotonin was therefore to inhibit aggressive impulses.

An investigation of 49 monkeys living on an island found that those with low levels of serotonin were more likely to be involved in dangerous activities, whereas those with higher levels spent more time grooming others and developing affectionate relationships (Lenard, 2008).

It has been found in Russia that silver foxes that have been bred as domestic pets over 30 years have higher levels of serotonin than the same species found in the wild. This equates to calmer, less aggressive behaviour in the tame animals.

It has been shown that increasing serotonin levels with drugs in both juvenile delinquents (Morand *et al.*, 1983) and in institutionalised patients (Greenwald, Marin and Silverman, 1986) reduces their aggressive tendencies.

Commentary

- Focusing on serotonin levels in the brain might be ignoring other physiological components that have led to aggressive behaviour. It might be that low serotonin levels are caused by an abnormality that also causes aggressive behaviour.

- Fluctuations in serotonin levels can also be explained by external factors. For example, light levels and disappointments like your favourite football team losing will both lower the level of serotonin.

- A lot of evidence comes from non-human animals, with the obvious difficulties of drawing conclusions across species.

- Despite these problems, analysing chemicals in the brain is an objective method using scientific measurements, which removes a lot of extraneous variables that may affect the results. Therefore, we can be fairly confident that the conclusions are accurate.

Evidence for a genetic explanation of aggression

The third biological approach to aggression suggests that the cause has a genetic basis.

Following the discovery of the 47 XYY karyotype by Sandberg (1961), Court-Brown found in a sample of 314 hospital patients that men with an XYY arrangement of the sex chromosomes were more aggressive than others.

Manuck *et al.* (2000) found that an abnormality in the MAOA gene was linked with aggressiveness in a study of 110 men. This genetic abnormality caused higher-than-normal levels of noradrenaline, which other research has linked to aggressive behaviour.

Nelson (2006) showed that selective breeding can lead to increased aggression in animals. This indicates that there is a genetic cause.

Commentary

Prior to his study, Court-Brown already had the idea that the XYY chromosome arrangement led to increased aggression. He made the mistake of letting this belief affect the interpretation of his results. It has since been accepted that the only consistent characteristic is increased height (Theilgaard, 1984), and not increased aggression.

- Caspi *et al.* (2002) only managed to find high levels of aggression in those with the deficient MAOA gene if they had also suffered from abuse as children. This suggests that a genetic explanation is incomplete. It is always difficult to separate genetic from environmental influences on behaviour. The research by Caspi *et al.* shows how the two provide an explanation only when both are considered together.

- Cairns' (1983) study of mice provided evidence for Nelson's view that animals can be bred to be aggressive.

- Biological elements are closely related, and difficult to separate when explaining aggressive behaviour. There could be a combination of genetic, biochemical and neurophysiological factors involved.

Think about it

All of these commentaries refer to the evidence on which the biological theories are based. An exam question could require an evaluation of *explanations* of aggression specifically rather than *evidence*. Consequently, the strengths and weaknesses of the evidence must only be used as commentary on the validity of the explanations themselves. So remember to make the point that a theory is only as good as the evidence that supports it.

AQA Examiner's tip

Remember to link these explanations to issues and debates in order to get top-band marks. There are two debates that you could write about quite easily with regard to the biological approach to aggression: determinism and reductionism.

When discussing the nature–nurture debate, remember that biological explanations fall on the side of nature.

Evolution and human aggression

You need to know how to

✔ understand evolutionary explanations of human aggression, including jealousy and infidelity

✔ describe evolutionary explanations of group display in humans.

Evolutionary explanations

The evolutionary approach suggests that any behaviour we display now must have had value in increasing our chances of surviving and passing on our genes in the past. An adaptive behaviour is one that gave our ancestors some advantage in their fight for survival.

The reason we might still be aggressive today is because of the genome lag. Mutating genes take hundreds of generations over thousands of years to change a complete society, so there will still be evidence today for adaptive behaviours of the past. To suggest that aggression has an evolutionary basis, we just need to be able to explain why it would have had survival value in the past.

Apply it

Have a look at the topics of gender and relationships. Read the evolutionary explanations of gender and relationships and try to understand how the approach relates to many other areas of behaviour.

Think about it

Remember, when studying the behaviour of humans from thousands of years ago (whether it is *Homo sapiens*, *Homo erectus* or even *Homo habilis*), that it is easier to compare this to the behaviour of other species of animal than it is to compare the behaviour of modern-day humans to other animals . Thousands (or even millions) of years ago, we had the same needs as other animal species. We had not removed ourselves from nature as we have done today.

Key theory

Lorenz (1966)

Lorenz distinguished between interspecific aggression (which is directed towards a member of a different species) and intraspecific aggression (which is directed towards a member of the same species). Lorenz argued that there are several reasons for intraspecific aggression:

- It helps to ensure that only the fittest and strongest survive. Females will select those for mating who win rutting contests. So those who are most aggressive have the best chance of passing on their genes.

- Offspring are better protected by parents who are aggressive.

- It helps to protect resources such as food supplies and mates. If resources are threatened by others, animals fight to protect what is theirs. This encourages other animals to find their own territory, and so the species spreads out.

Lorenz also made the point that most aggression is no more than a ritualised display. Animals appeasement gestures indicate to their opponents that they have had enough. These displays aid survival as they prevent death. This supports the argument that aggression is an adaptive response to the environment.

Commentary

- Morris (1990) supports Lorenz's view in that a lot of animal displays of aggression show restraint. The appeasement gestures of jackdaws (Gross, 1998) is a particular case.

- Tinbergen (1968), on the other hand, points out that, unlike other species, human aggression is not merely a ritualised display. It is born out of a deep desire to harm another person.
- Nelson (1974) argues that Lorenz fails to take into consideration psychological causes of aggression. In other words, the evolutionary approach is reductionist and fails to explain things like observational learning (Bandura), or situational factors like over crowding (Calhoun, 1962), or temperature rises (Baron, 1977).

Evolutionary explanations of human aggression

Jealousy

As jealousy is found in all human cultures, it is believed that it is a genetic rather than a learned behaviour. The purpose it serves is to ensure exclusivity in our mates. A man can never be certain of the paternity of his offspring. Although a woman can be certain that she is the parent, men do not know that their partners have been faithful to them. They may spend the rest of their lives raising another man's child and thus compromising the survival of their own genes. Jealousy serves to prevent this from happening. Displays of aggression will dissuade a man's partner from having sex with another man.

For a woman, especially in the environment of evolutionary adaptation (EEA), having children was very costly in terms of protection and finding adequate resources. Having a mate who would stay with her throughout her pregnancy and help her with the raising of her offspring was vital. If her partner left her to be with another woman, it would compromise her ability to obtain the resources she and her children needed to survive. Jealousy is a reaction to this possibility. It is an aggressive behaviour designed to prevent one's partner from committing his resources to another woman and/or her children.

Infidelity

Any behaviour that improves a man's chances of mating will be advantageous. The more partners a man has, the more children he will have and so the more of his genes will survive. It is worth his while then, from an evolutionary perspective, to be unfaithful to his regular partner.

Women, on the other hand, could have sex with a dozen men, but still only conceive once. So the reason for their infidelity is different to men's. There are two possible reasons for women's infidelity:

- Although a male might be dominant, his sperm might not be good quality. If a woman has sex with more than one man, the one with the fittest sperm is the one that is likely to fertilise her egg.
- If two men think they are the father of her offspring, there will be two men who will be interested in the survival of her and her young. Therefore, there will be two men who could protect and provide for her.

Xenophobia

When we have to compete for resources, whether it is food, mates, living space or jobs, any people migrating to our territory from elsewhere will increase the competition. We really do not want life to be harder for ourselves by having more people competing, as the resources will not stretch as far and we might lose out. Therefore it is natural for us to hate anyone from outside, and to view them with suspicion, because they will have an impact on how successful we are in obtaining or keeping the things we need to survive. It will make food harder to find, and it will become harder to pass on our genes.

Commentary

- A lot of research, for example Cascardi and Vivian (1995), has shown that the biggest single cause of aggression in a relationship is jealousy.

- Buss (1993) supports the sex difference in jealousy as predicted by evolutionary theory. He found that men are more jealous of their partners having sex with another man, women are more jealous of their partners developing an emotional attachment with another woman.

- Research has compared the T-cell count of primates and found a correlation with the sexual behaviour of each species. Promiscuous species, like chimpanzees, have a high T-cell count to fight possible infection from sexually transmitted diseases. Species that do not have many sexual partners, like gorillas, have a low T-cell count. The more sexual partners an animal has, the more it needs to be protected from infection. Humans have evolved a T-cell count that is consistent with a monogamous lifestyle. This suggests that we have evolved not to be unfaithful, despite its advantages.

- Because a lot of our instinctive behaviour (sexual and aggressive urges) has to be controlled because of the rules of society, it is going to be hard to measure. We hide our real feelings and do not behave as we would like to because it is socially unacceptable or even against the law. So researchers cannot easily observe jealousy or prejudice, or draw conclusions about their causes.

Group displays of aggression

Evolutionary explanation

Because individuals are capable of violence, we can argue that it must be in our nature. However, uncontrolled violence is not the best behavioural strategy in a community because the costs are too high, for example, there is a risk of injury. The best behavioural strategy is therefore to use aggression tactically.

Lorenz referred to ritualised displays of aggression in which two opponents try to make each other believe they would lose if it actually came to a fight. So the potential risk through combat is avoided if the loser backs down and runs away. In this context, the threat of violence can be a very successful strategy in the competition for resources (Clutton-Brock and Albon, 1979).

Maynard Smith and Price (1973) defined an evolutionary stable strategy (ESS) as a type of behaviour that dominates a community to such an extent that it will not change. It is thought that whereas ritualised displays of aggression are an example of an ESS, actual aggression will not be tolerated. In small communities, people who show uncontrolled aggression are feared, and they may be the target of collective action by others (Lee, 1969).

One group display of aggression is the warrior display. This might be in the form of army games or military tattoos. These are shows of strength to inhibit attacks from another nation. During the Cold War, the term 'mutually assured destruction' referred to the fact that both the US and the USSR had enough weaponry to destroy each other if they ever went to war. The theory was that as both nations knew this, both would avoid conflict at all cost. On a smaller scale, the haka is a traditional Maori display of aggression you might see on a rugby field prior to a game. It serves the same purpose of trying to convince your opponent not to bother competing too hard because you are stronger than them.

> **Apply it**
>
> There are social psychological explanations for group displays of aggression such as social identity theory (SIT), relative deprivation hypothesis, scapegoat theory and lynch mobs. These could be used as evaluative commentary.

Commentary

- Frosdick and Marsh (2005) offered support for Lorenz's view that much aggression is ritualised displays. Studying football supporters, they were able to show that although rival supporters taunt each other outside the football ground, they are careful not to let chants and slogans descend into actual physical violence.

- Tajfel and Turner (1979) contradicted the evolutionary approach, suggesting instead that social factors are responsible for group displays of aggression. The social identity theory states that individuals bolster their self-esteem by identifying with groups. This leads to a sense of hostility towards any other out-group.

- One problem with research in this area is interpretation of the findings. The robbers' cave study of Sherif *et al.* (1961) clearly demonstrates group displays of aggression in boys. But how do we know whether they were the result of social factors like the social identity theory or the relative deprivation hypothesis? Or were they caused by an innate mechanism that has evolved to create a hostility towards other groups because it has survival value? The answer is, we cannot know. This makes conclusions difficult to draw, and a resolution of the nature–nurture debate as it applies to aggression is most unlikely.

Thinking about issues and debates

Determinism

If aggression is caused by our genes, biochemistry, or abnormality of our brain structure, then we have no choice about how we behave. If we cannot control our behaviour, then it is determined. This has legal implications for the state with regard to punishing and treating violent people.

Psychology as a science

The evolutionary approach to aggression is quite hard to acknowledge as providing hard evidence. It relies on post hoc reasoning: if a behaviour exists in humans today, it must have evolved due to natural or sexual selection. All behaviours that did not have survival value will have died out. This is a circular argument based on flawed logic, not evidence.

Nature–nurture debate

There is plenty of evidence for the role of biology and social psychological influences on aggressive behaviour. It is therefore quite easy to comment on the implications of research in this area to our understanding of the nature–nurture debate, and how a combination of both provides a more complete explanation.

Issues and debates in aggression research

Socially sensitive research

To argue that behaviour might be determined by factors beyond our control provides excuses for certain crimes. Pointing to the influence of genes, hormones, brain abnormalities or evolution in those who rape or commit murder reduces their guilt. This means research into the causes of aggression will have consequences for society.

Reductionism

In trying to break down aggression into easily understood explanations, we risk over-simplifying a complex pattern of behaviour. We may well find strong evidence for the role of hormones in aggression. But if we ignore the impact of the environment on those hormones in the first place, we only have half an explanation.

Exam-style questions

Example 1

0 1 Discuss explanations of institutional aggression.   *(24 marks)*

Example 2

0 2 Outline and evaluate **one** social psychological and **one** biological explanation of human aggression.   *(24 marks)*

Example 3

0 3 Discuss **one or more** biological explanations of aggression.   *(24 marks)*

Example 4

0 4 Describe research into evolutionary explanations of group displays of aggression.   *(8 marks)*

0 5 Consider the view that aggression is a behaviour that has evolved in humans.   *(16 marks)*

Sample answers

Suggested content for the other example questions for this section can be found at
www.nelsonthornes.com/psychology_answers

Example 3

0 3 | *One explanation of aggression is neurophysiology, the structure of the brain. This explanation states that aggressive behaviour occurs when the structure of the brain is changed, such as damage to the limbic system, or when parts are removed, such as the prefrontal cortex. Neurophysiology says that if the limbic system is more active than the prefrontal cortex, then the limbic system impulses may appear in behaviour, such as aggression.*

A basic outline of neurophysiology, without a lot of detail

One study done to suggest neurophysiology is a viable explanation of aggression was performed by Delgado, who implanted electrodes into the hypothalamus of monkeys, which when stimulated caused the monkey to attack another monkey in the cage with it. This suggests that the limbic system, which contains the hypothalamus, is a cause of aggressive behaviour. Further support can be found from the study of Whitman, who exhibited aggressive behaviour by shooting people from a clock tower. It was found that Whitman had a tumour pressing on his amygdala (another part of the limbic system), changing its structure and possibly causing aggression. These studies suggest the limbic system is a centre for aggressive behaviour. However, Whitman was abused by his father as a child, so this implies that the tumour might not have caused his aggression, but rather a psychological element may be the cause.

This includes some relevant research. It is a nice combination of description (AO1) and evaluation (AO2/3).

These studies suggest the limbic system is the cause of aggressive behaviour, but other studies have evidence to suggest it is the lack of activity in the prefrontal cortex (which controls the urges of the limbic system and keeps them in check) that causes aggressive behaviour to occur. A study done by Raine showed that criminals in prison for violent crimes had much less activity in the prefrontal cortex than criminals incarcerated for non-violent crimes, suggesting that the prefrontal cortex controls aggressive behaviour in people.

Both paragraphs contain evidence from studies and further elaboration of neurophysiology.

This is supported by Delgado's monkeys, because when the monkey with the experimental monkey was dominant, it was not attacked. This suggests that we learn to control our aggression and this can be explained by the development of the prefrontal cortex.

An evaluation of neurophysiology is that it is reductionist. Ignores other biological explanations such as biochemistry and genetics. If we reduce all behaviour to merely brain structures, then we fail to explain the potential influence of the early abuse on Whitman's behaviour. We also fail to explain why social factors (learning their position in the troop hierarchy) stopped the monkeys in Delgado's experiment from becoming aggressive in some conditions but not others.

This attempts to include some remarks about issues and debates. This is good, but not fully expanded.

Another biological explanation of aggression is biochemistry. This suggests we are aggressive due to our hormones, such as high levels of testosterone, or our neurotransmitters, such as low levels of serotonin. A study done by Young supports high levels of testosterone causing aggression. He injected pregnant rhesus monkeys with testosterone and found their babies to be more aggressive when they were born than they would have been without the injection of testosterone.

These paragraphs go through the same procedure with biochemistry. They incorporate a nice balance of description and evaluation.

Another study done to support biochemistry was carried out by Davidson, Putnam and Larson, who found that criminals in prison for violent crimes had lower levels of serotonin than criminals in prison for non-violent crimes. But a study done by Brunner on a Dutch family contradicts this, as he found high levels of serotonin causing aggressive behaviour. This contradiction makes it unclear whether low levels of serotonin cause aggression or not.

An evaluation of biochemistry is that it is deterministic. We cannot control our biology, so we are only hosts for our aggression, because free will doesn't exist. This has all kinds of implications for the law in terms of punishing and treating violent offenders. Furthermore, we do not know if it is the cause or effect: studies only show a correlation between biochemistry and aggression. It might be that biochemical imbalances are responsible for the aggressive actions of people. However, it might be the case that aggressive behaviour has had an impact on our biochemistry. Correlations only show links; they do not prove cause and effect. And yet we know that external factors can influence our hormone and neurotransmitter levels, so considering one without investigating the other seems likely to provide an incomplete explanation of the cause of aggression.

This final paragraph again attempts to incorporate issues and debates, and again it is appropriate use of material, but a little incoherent.

AQA Examiner's comments

Both description and evaluation are reasonable, but not quite effective. This answer would achieve a fairly good basic/reasonable band mark.

5   Eating behaviour

Biological explanations of eating behaviour

You need to know how to

✔ describe how we know when to start and stop eating a meal

✔ explain how we regulate body weight in the long term

✔ explain how and why certain food preferences may have evolved through natural selection

✔ evaluate evolutionary explanations of food preference.

We start meals and then stop eating when we feel full. In most societies, people eat two or three meals a day. Over months and years, adult humans maintain a fairly constant body weight (although there is increasing anxiety over obesity levels, especially in children). These simple observations raise key questions about the biological approach to eating behaviour.

Think about it

It would be simple to say that we start a meal when we feel hungry, and stop when we feel full. However, meals are usually at set times of the day – they anticipate hunger rather than respond to it. This is a cultural aspect of eating behaviour.

Neural mechanisms and eating behaviour

The hypothalamus is a small structure buried deep towards the base of the brain. It plays a key role in controlling many biological and physiological functions, including eating behaviour.

Research studies

In 1942, Hetherington and Ranson showed that damage to part of the hypothalamus caused rats to overeat massively and become grossly obese. They concluded that this area of the hypothalamus, the ventromedial nucleus, was a satiety centre. Its normal function is to stop or inhibit feeding, so when it is damaged eating is completely uninhibited.

In 1951, Anand and Brobeck lesioned (damaged) the lateral area of the hypothalamus in rats. These rats simply did not eat at all (aphagia). They concluded that the lateral hypothalamus was a feeding centre. Its normal function is to stimulate feeding in hungry rats.

The satiety and feeding centres in the hypothalamus make up the dual centre model of feeding. In response to signals of hunger or food intake from the body, they control feeding behaviour.

Evaluation

- The dual centre model is based on the two hypothalamic centres – the lateral and ventromedial nuclei. It is supported by further research showing that electrical stimulation of the hypothalamic centres can stimulate or inhibit feeding.

- Most of the work is done on rats as humans rarely survive accidental damage to the hypothalamus. Findings have to be extrapolated to humans.

Think about it

The feeding and satiety centres in the hypothalamus are central to the regulation of eating behaviour. But they cannot act in isolation. They must have information about the state of the body's energy and food reserves. There must be signals for starting meals, stopping food intake at the appropriate time, and also for regulating body weight in the long term.

- Animals rarely survive lesion and stimulation studies. This raises key ethical issues relating to the stress to the animal balanced against the scientific value of the work.

Signals for starting meals

- Social patterns – we eat at set times.
- Smell and taste of food stimulate the release of enzymes needed to break down food in the digestive system.
- Signals from the stomach – ghrelin travels in the bloodstream to the hypothalamus where it signals the degree of emptiness, a key trigger for feeding behaviour.

Research study

Cummings *et al.* (2004)

Method: Using six participant volunteers, Cummings *et al.* measured blood levels of ghrelin at five-minute intervals between eating lunch and the time when participants asked for their evening meal. Participants also recorded their degree of hunger every 30 minutes.

Findings: Ghrelin levels fell after eating, reaching their lowest point 70 minutes after eating. They then rose steadily, peaking as participants asked for their evening meal. Importantly, there was a high positive correlation between ghrelin levels and the degree of hunger reported by the participants.

Conclusion: Ghrelin levels are an accurate index of stomach emptiness and are closely correlated with feelings of hunger. This supports a key role for ghrelin in signalling hunger to the hypothalamus and triggering feeding behaviour.

Evaluation: This was a very technical study, which was why only six participants could be studied, and they were all male. This small number leads to problems of generalising findings to the wider population and to women.

It was a correlational design, so we cannot draw conclusions about ghrelin 'causing' hunger pangs and triggering feeding behaviour.

However, the findings support previous work on the role of ghrelin in feeding regulation.

Signals for stopping meals

- Presence of food in the stomach.
- Release of the hormone cholecystokinin (CCK) has the opposite effect to ghrelin. Injections of CCK cause a reduction in meal size and appetite in animals and humans (Smith *et al.*, 1982).
- Blood glucose levels. These vary with food intake and can act on glucoreceptors in the hypothalamus to affect appetite. However, the relationship is complicated as some researchers find that blood glucose levels do not vary enough under normal circumstances to be an effective signal.

> **AQA Examiner's tip**
>
> Physiology and neural mechanisms can seem very complicated. Try to keep a clear picture of the dual centre theory, why the hypothalamus needs signals of food intake to perform its functions, and how at least two of these signals work.

Signals that control body weight

Our fat stores are one of the main indicators of body weight. Fatty tissue is made up of special cells called adipocytes. These release a hormone called leptin into the bloodstream, and the amount released is proportional to the fat content of the adipocytes. The hypothalamus satiety centre in the ventromedial nucleus has receptors for leptin, and so it stops food intake as levels of leptin rise. In this way, feeding behaviour, the amount of stored fat and body weight are regulated in the long term. Studies with mice genetically modified to lack leptin show that they rapidly become obese (they are called 'ob' mice). Injections of leptin restore normal body weight, supporting a role for leptin in the control of body weight.

Evaluation

- Neural mechanisms of feeding are complex but are basic to food intake and body weight regulation. Understanding them can provide insights into eating disorders such as anorexia nervosa and obesity.
- The approach is reductionist, focusing only on physiological and neural systems. It ignores higher-level social and cultural factors that can influence our feeding behaviour.
- Much of the evidence comes from studies with non-human animals. This raises the problem of extrapolating results to humans, and also involves ethical issues of working with animals.

Evolutionary explanations of food preference

Food preferences

Today our food preferences are affected by social and cultural factors, but we can still see the influence of our evolutionary past. This is particularly the case with our taste sensitivities. The experience of taste comes from our specialised taste receptors. These make us sensitive to a range of taste qualities:

- Sweet: this quality allows us to identify carbohydrates such as sugars, a key source of energy.
- Sour: identifies foods that have gone off, and may contain harmful bacteria.
- Salt: all cells in the body require salt to function, so it is important to identify foods containing salt.
- Bitter: this is associated with plant chemicals that might be poisonous.
- Umami: discovered relatively recently, these receptors detect a meaty or savoury quality, indicating a good source of protein.

Humans are full omnivores, specialised to eat meat as well as fruits, nuts and plants. We developed meat-eating soon after splitting from the great ape line about 6 million years ago (great apes such as chimpanzees will eat meat if it is available, but they are largely vegetarian). Meat is a rich source of protein and this change in diet allowed the development of a larger brain, basic to the success of humans.

Through evolution other distinctive eating behaviours have emerged:

- Spices such as onions and garlic are used in cooking, especially in hot countries where food goes off quickly. Spices contain chemicals that kill bacteria, so protect people from poisoning.

> **Think about it**
>
> If increasing leptin levels reduces food intake by acting on the hypothalamus, then could leptin be a treatment for obesity? Unfortunately, although leptin can work in some obese individuals, in most cases it is ineffective. It seems that in these cases the hypothalamus is insensitive to the effects of leptin.

> **Think about it**
>
> In today's advanced industrialised societies, food hygiene is very different from a million years ago. However, as with other areas where evolutionary explanations are used, such as human sexual selection and parental investment, it seems that our behaviour is still influenced by our ancient past.

- Fear of new foods ('food neophobia'). New foods may be dangerous, so it did make sense to avoid them. Even today, our liking for new foods increases with familiarity (Frost, 2006).

- Taste aversion learning. All animals, including humans, learn in one experience to avoid foods that make them ill. Garcia *et al.* (1977) made wolves sick with lamb's meat containing a mild poison. Afterwards the wolves avoided live sheep that they would normally attack. Taste aversion learning is a powerful mechanism for keeping animals alive.

- Morning sickness. This is a form of nausea associated with the early months of pregnancy, and drives mothers to avoid some foods, in particular coffee, tea, meat, alcohol and eggs (Buss, 2008). The evolutionary explanation is that each of these foods could damage the developing baby (coffee and tea contain high levels of caffeine, while meat and eggs are likely to contain bacteria).

Evaluation

- The general problem with evolutionary explanations is that they are speculative. It is impossible to test evolutionary hypotheses using scientific experimentation. Instead, the explanations rely on observations of our modern eating behaviour and compare these with speculations about eating behaviour in the era of evolutionary adaptation. They may not be wrong, but they lack direct support.

- Evolutionary explanations are also reductionist as they focus on a limited range of evolutionary factors. They ignore the important role of psychological, social and cultural factors that influence eating behaviour in today's modern world.

- However, they can provide quite convincing explanations of, for instance, the increase in levels of obesity today, by showing how our evolutionary ancient feeding mechanisms cannot cope with the change to a high carbohydrate diet and over-abundance of food.

Think about it

This evolutionary view of morning sickness is known as the embryo protection hypothesis (Profet, 1992). As with all evolutionary hypotheses, it is hard to test directly. However, the fact that up to 75 per cent of pregnant women report significant morning sickness (Buss, 2008), and it seems specific to particular foods, makes it very plausible. It is an excellent example of how evolution has influenced food preferences to protect the species.

AQA Examiner's tip

Make sure that you know and understand the evolutionary background to three or four examples of our food preferences. Remember that our food preferences today are massively affected by social and cultural factors, and examples of these would provide excellent AO2/3 material in questions about evolutionary explanations. Use other explanations as evaluation and develop this by reference to the strength of evidence for other factors and their implications.

Eating behaviour

You need to know how to

✔ describe how factors such as mood, familiarity, culture or advertising influence people's food preferences and attitudes

✔ evaluate the importance of these factors, referring to research evidence

✔ describe explanations of why diets fail and why they sometimes succeed

✔ evaluate these explanations using relevant research evidence.

Food preferences in children

Familiarity

Food neophobia is found in babies and children, but this changes to liking and preference with repeated exposure (Birch and Marlin, 1982). Familiarity is an important part of attitudes to food.

Parental attitudes

There is a significant positive correlation between the diets of mothers and children (Ogden, 2007). Parents, especially the mother, provide key role models for the child.

Research study

Nicklaus *et al.* (2004)

This investigated the correlations between food preferences at age 2 and food preferences at age 22 in a longitudinal study of French children.

Findings: Although there were only low correlations between overall diet at age 2 and adult diet, for about 50 per cent of dietary items there was a clear association between childhood and adult preferences.

Preferences, especially for cheese and vegetables, remained fairly stable between age 2 and adulthood.

Preference for meat decreased in females as they got older, possibly representing ethical and health concerns.

Evaluation: Adult preferences were assessed through questionnaires and interviews. This raises the problem of 'self-presentation', where participants may give 'healthier' answers so they look better in the eyes of the experimenters.

Conclusion: There were clear links between childhood food preferences and adult diet, but there were also changes, showing that childhood experiences are important but not decisive.

Peers and the media

Studies have shown that modelling using admired peers can increase consumption of fruit and vegetables (Lowe *et al.*, 1998). Media advertising also has a powerful influence on the food choices of children.

Food preferences in the adult

Media campaigns

There is increasing awareness of the spread of obesity, often attributed to unhealthy diets. Government campaigns and the efforts of media celebrities such as Jamie Oliver have helped to change attitudes. Unfortunately, the availability of cheap fast food, high in fats and carbohydrates, reduces the effectiveness of such campaigns.

Food and mood

There is a close link between food and our emotional state. Even in babies, sweet foods are effective in reducing distress (Benton, 2002). In times of stress or when we are distressed, there is often an increase in sugar and fat consumption (Gibson, 2006). This is associated with an improvement in mood and an increase in energy (Macht *et al.*, 2003).

Food and culture

There are significant differences in diet across cultures. At the extreme, impoverished societies are grateful for any food they can find. Even in the affluent West, different patterns can be seen (Wardle *et al.*, 1997):

- People in Mediterranean countries eat more fruit and vegetables than those in England and Scotland.
- People in Sweden, Norway and Denmark eat the most fibre while those in Portugal, Spain and Italy eat the least.

These differences are usually due to the availability of particular foodstuffs, but can also reflect cultural influences.

Think about it

As well as providing role models, parents also buy and prepare food for their children. So the child's early experiences are totally under their parent's control. So, if early experiences are critical, parental eating habits will profoundly affect their children's attitudes.

Think about it

Pleasurable feelings are associated with activity in the brain's reward pathways. These pathways use neurotransmitters from the group of endorphins. Drugs increasing endorphin activity in the brain increase the perceived tastiness of food, while sweet foods alone can increase the release of endorphins in the brain (Gibson, 2006). This shows a close link between sweet foods and the mood-regulating systems of the brain.

Think about it

We have already seen with taste aversion learning that animals rapidly learn associations between taste and the consequences of eating certain foods. The same happens with sweet and rewarding foods. We learn from childhood that sweet taste is associated with improved mood and pleasure, so we turn to sweet-tasting foods when stressed or depressed.

Research study

Leshem (2009)

Leshem (2009) compared Bedouin Arab women living in desert encampments with those now living in urban (town) environments, and also with a group of urban Jewish women. In urban settings, there is access to a far greater range of foodstuffs.

Findings: The diet of urban Bedouins was very similar to that of desert-living Bedouins; a much higher intake of carbohydrates and proteins and salt than the Jewish group.

In a later study, Leshem found that the diet of a Muslim community living in the same urban setting as a Christian group was much higher in carbohydrates, protein and salt than the Christian community, although body mass was the same.

Conclusion: Even with equal access to a range of foods, different ethnic groups have different diets, demonstrating the influence of culture and dietary history on food preferences.

AQA Examiner's tip

There is evidence for a range of factors influencing attitudes to food, such as familiarity, parental attitudes, peer and media influences, mood and culture. No one factor is decisive, so you need to be clear that our eating behaviour is the product of many influences. Do not forget that eating has essential biological functions as well.

AQA Examiner's tip

The specification refers to 'factors influencing attitudes to food and eating behaviour'. This is rather vague, but if such a question comes up, you must be prepared with a range of factors whose influence you can outline and evaluate. It is better to cover a limited range effectively than to provide superficial coverage of many factors.

Conclusions

- Research is an important source of AO2/3. Studies have shown that familiarity, parental attitudes, peers and media can all influence food preferences in children, and this has a strong link to adult food preferences.

- Adult attitudes to food are also affected by media campaigns. There is a close link between food and mood, supported by research evidence on the effects of sweet foods on brain pathways of reward.

- Eating behaviour varies across cultures. Although availability of foods is important, research shows that there are significant cultural influences on diet.

- Adult attitudes to food are therefore a complicated mix of early and adult experiences, and social and cultural influences.

Explanations for the success or failure of dieting

At any one time, it is estimated that about 40 per cent of women are dieting to lose weight. It is also known that most will fail, and that up to half will actually put on more weight than before they started dieting (Mann et al., 2007). Why is dieting so hard ?

The boundary model (Herman and Polivy, 1984)

- This model combines both physiology and psychological cognitive processes.

- We have a body weight set-point, determined by our biology, that we try to maintain through what we eat.

- When we diet, we are setting a cognitive boundary that is lower than the body weight set-point.

- The unrestrained eater simply eats until they reach their biological set-point.

- The dieter, or restrained eater, eats until they reach their cognitive boundary.

Research study

Herman and Mack (1975)

This study used 45 female students for a study of taste experiences. They were divided into three groups. One group had no food as a preload before the 'taste test', the second group had one high-calorie milkshake as a preload, the third group had two milkshakes as a preload. All groups were then given tubs of ice cream and they were asked to rate its taste qualities. They could eat as much as they liked in 10 minutes.

After the taste test, they were given questionnaires on attitudes to food and dieting to identify restrained eaters (dieters) and unrestrained eaters.

Findings: Herman and Mack found that unrestrained eaters eat less ice cream in the two milkshake preload condition than in the one or no preload condition. This was predicted, as they should feel fuller after two preloads than after one or zero preloads. However, the restrained eaters (dieters) showed a different pattern. They eat more ice cream after one or two milkshake preloads than after zero preloads.

Conclusions: Unrestrained eaters follow their biological set-point, and eat less after preloads as they are already close to their set-point.

Restrained eaters (dieters) have a cognitive boundary as well. With no preload, they eat ice cream until they reach this boundary, that is, they do not eat very much.

However, in the high-calorie preload conditions, the preloads push them beyond this cognitive boundary. They then have a 'what the hell effect' and eat until they reach their biological set point i.e. more than in the no preload condition.

Evaluation

- The division into restrained and unrestrained eaters was done at the end of the study (to prevent bias in the findings), so within the three preload groups the numbers were not equal. This reduces the reliability of the findings.
- There were individual differences. Some participants may have liked ice cream more than others, and with only small numbers in each group, this may have biased the results.
- It was a laboratory study, giving it good internal validity but low ecological validity. Dieting in the real world may involve more complicated issues.
- Although some studies have found similar effects to Herman and Mack, other findings are inconsistent.
- The 'what the hell effect' can be applied to the real world. It has been used to explain the failure of people to give up alcohol or smoking, as well as the failure of dieting (Ogden, 2007).

Think about it

People diet because they are unhappy with their bodies. This is often associated with lowered self-esteem. We have already seen that food (especially sweet food) is associated with improved mood, so dieters have even more motivation to eat to improve their mood and self-esteem, making dieting even more difficult.

Other factors in dieting

Ironic processes: this refers to the common observation that the more we try not to think about something, the more we think about it. This has been shown with thoughts about sex and white bears (Ogden, 2007). The more dieters try to suppress thoughts about food, the more likely they are to become obsessed with those thoughts and to eat more.

Body weight set-point: the body's physiological processes try to maintain this body weight. If dieting is trying to reduce body weight below this set-point, the body will work against it. This is shown most clearly by the body's metabolic rate. This is the rate at which we burn energy. Dieting reduces the body's metabolic rate, so even though less food is being taken in, less energy is being used, so weight loss becomes even more difficult.

Conclusions

- The boundary model is not reductionist as it combines biological and cognitive factors. However, it relies heavily on laboratory studies with good internal validity and control of variables, but which have weak ecological validity. This means that results may not be generalisable to the real world.

- Cognitive models such as the role of ironic processes are limited as they ignore important biological factors such as body weight set-point. They are also difficult to test scientifically as ironic processes are hard to define and measure.

- Research has shown that diets combined with group and individual support can be effective. This shows that the success or failure of dieting involves an interaction between psychological and social processes, as well as biological factors such as body weight set-point. There is no single dominant explanation.

> **Think about it**
>
> For some people dieting can work, but these people are the exceptions. Studies have shown that key factors include: realistic ambitions; physical exercise (this helps to burn some calories, but more importantly it helps mood and self-esteem); group and individual support to provide reinforcement and encouragement; self-monitoring, such as diary-keeping, which increases the sense of being in control (Powell *et al.*, 2007).

> **AQA Examiner's tip**
>
> There are many factors involved in the success or failure of dieting. The key to effective answers is organisation. Prepare carefully, and know beforehand which points and studies you are going to use. Have some general points of commentary ready for this complicated area. It would also help if you practise writing short clear summaries of, for example, the boundary model and associated research.

Eating disorders

> **You need to know how to**
>
> ✔ evaluate psychological explanations of your chosen eating disorder
>
> ✔ describe biological explanations of your chosen eating disorder referring to neural mechanisms
>
> ✔ describe evolutionary explanations of your chosen eating disorder
>
> ✔ evaluate biological and evolutionary explanations of your chosen eating disorder.

> **AQA Examiner's tip**
>
> You only need to describe psychological explanations of **one** eating disorder: anorexia nervosa (page 65) or bulimia nervosa (page 67) or obesity (page 69). You do not need to know about all of them.

Anorexia nervosa

Anorexia nervosa: symptoms and facts

- Body weight is less than 85 per cent of normal weight for age and height.
- Sufferers have an intense fear of becoming fat.
- There is a distorted perception of body weight and shape.
- Amenorrhoea (loss of three consecutive menstrual cycles in women) may be a factor.
- Ninety per cent of cases are women.

Psychological explanations

Role of the media

Media effects on eating disorders can be explained through social learning theory, the idea that we learn through observing and imitating others. This is particularly effective when the 'models' are prestigious and admired. Direct reinforcement can also be important as the person may be praised by peers for losing weight and looking thinner.

Research findings

- Media images of the idealised woman have become taller and slimmer over the last 50 years. This has been associated with the rise in the number of eating disorders, especially anorexia nervosa (Striegel-Moore and Bulik, 2007).
- Meta reviews show that exposure to media images of thin women increases body dissatisfaction in females (Groesz *et al.*, 2002).
- Becker *et al.* (2002) found that eating disorders were only found in Fiji after the introduction of television and exposure to Western images of women.
- Although media influences are important, only a tiny minority of females exposed to them develop anorexia nervosa. There must be other vulnerability factors.
- Girls internalise media and culturally defined standards of female beauty:
  - in some this leads to extreme dissatisfaction with their own body shape
  - in the very vulnerable this leads to an eating disorder such as anorexia nervosa.
- Females who develop eating disorders tend to be perfectionists with high social anxiety and low self-esteem. These personality characteristics may make them vulnerable to eating disorders. But a genetic factor has also been proposed.

The psychodynamic approach

Bruch (1973) proposed that anorexia develops in girls who are trying to feel independent or autonomous in families that do not allow them autonomy. Eating behaviour is one area the girl can control.

Loss of weight in anorexia nervosa prevents menstruation. Crisp (1980) suggested that the eating disorder is an attempt by the girl to remain pre-pubertal as they fear they cannot cope with adulthood.

The family systems approach of Minuchin *et al.* (1978) sees the eating disorder as an attempt by the child to divert attention away from other family problems, such as the parents' relationship difficulties.

Evaluation

- There is no single explanation for anorexia nervosa. There is strong research evidence for an involvement of the media leading to body dissatisfaction, but only a small minority of women develop anorexia nervosa. There must therefore be additional factors involved, for instance a genetic vulnerability. Any purely psychological explanation is therefore likely to be limited.
- Psychodynamic explanations are difficult to test scientifically and are largely based on case studies, which have low internal validity (control of variables). The success of some forms of family therapy for anorexia nervosa suggests that family dynamics are important. However, it can be difficult to tell whether the eating disorder is *caused* by stressful family dynamics or in fact helps to cause them.

> **Think about it**
>
> Meta reviews combine and analyse the findings from many studies to produce an overall picture of what is happening in a given area of research. Why would we give the results of meta reviews more weight than the results of a single study?

> **AQA Examiner's tip**
>
> In some areas of psychology, we can come up with straightforward conclusions. With anorexia nervosa, this is not possible. Do not be afraid to refer to the complexity of eating disorders, and the fact that they almost certainly represent a mix of social, psychological and biological factors. Remember also that research support, for example for the role of the media, is a highly effective source of AO2/3 marks.

Biological explanations

The evolutionary approach

The 'adapted to flee famine hypothesis' (AFFH) (Guisinger, 2003) is based on the observations that women with anorexia nervosa are more active than usual and also deny being hungry. Guisinger suggests that in the environment of evolutionary adaptation (EEA) humans were hunter-gatherers, moving from place to place as food supplies became exhausted. High activity and insensitivity to hunger would have been adaptive in these conditions when survival depended upon migration.

As with all evolutionary hypotheses, it is speculative and there is no direct evidence for the idea. It is impossible to test scientifically. In addition, it does not explain why anorexia is not as common in men as it is in women, but it does account for some of the symptoms of anorexia.

Genetics

Reseach study

Holland *et al.* (1984)

These investigators used 16 monozygotic (MZ) and 14 dizygotic (DZ) female twin pairs to study the genetics of anorexia nervosa. Whether twins were MZ or DZ was determined by either blood group analysis or by a 'similarity' questionnaire. One of each pair had been diagnosed with anorexia nervosa.

Findings: If one MZ twin had anorexia nervosa, there was a 55 per cent chance of the other twin having it (this is the 'concordance rate'). The concordance rate for DZ twins was 7 per cent.

Conclusions: The differences in concordance rates between MZ and DZ twins is strong evidence for a genetic influence on anorexia nervosa.

Evaluation: There were only a small number of participants (as anorexia nervosa is a rare condition), reducing the reliability of the findings.

Status as MZ or DZ twins was determined by blood tests or questionnaires. These, especially questionnaires, are not perfectly accurate measures.

Concordance for MZ twins was 55 per cent, not 100 per cent, meaning that significant non-genetic factors are involved in anorexia nervosa.

However, subsequent studies have supported a role for genetic factors in anorexia nervosa (Bulik *et al.*, 2006).

Serotonin

Serotonin is a brain neurotransmitter involved in many behaviours, including the control of feeding behaviour. Kaye *et al.* (2005) found evidence for a reduction in brain serotonin activity in anorexia nervosa. However, this reduction could have been caused by the condition itself – significant weight loss alters the body's physiology in dramatic ways.

However, brain scanning studies have found evidence of a reduction in the number of serotonin receptors in the brains of women with anorexia nervosa. This would indicate underactivity of the serotonin system, and, importantly, this was found in participants who had recovered from the disorder. So weight loss associated with anorexia may not have been a factor in causing this serotonin underactivity (Kaye *et al.*, 2005).

AQA Examiner's tip

MZ/DZ twin studies are used in many areas of psychology. If you present such evidence, make sure that you demonstrate your understanding of the reasons for comparing MZ and DZ twins, i.e. explain clearly the implications of concordance rates.

AQA Examiner's tip

Questions will focus on either psychological or biological explanations, but do not forget that you can use the alternative explanations as evaluation. This is particularly effective in the area of eating disorders, as research evidence shows that eating disorders are clearly a combination of psychological and biological factors, and you would be expected to comment on this.

Evaluation

- A range of twin studies provide evidence for a genetic influence in anorexia nervosa.
- Concordance rates for MZ twins are never close to 100 per cent, meaning that non-genetic psychological and social factors also play an important role.
- Neural explanations, such as the role of serotonin, depend upon studies on people with anorexia nervosa or who have recovered from it. A more convincing approach would be to study people before they develop the disorder. However, at the moment it is impossible to predict who will become anorexic.
- Although there is a wealth of research evidence supporting a role for biological factors in anorexia nervosa, the approach is heavily reductionist. It ignores higher-level factors such as the role of the media and personality characteristics in the development of anorexia nervosa.

Think about it

It can sometimes be difficult to bring issues, debates and approaches into your answers. Eating disorders are an excellent area for this. They involve psychological, biological and evolutionary approaches, the issue of nature–nurture, gender differences and biases, cultural differences and biases (most research involves Western advanced societies), applications of findings, e.g. to treatments, free will and determinism, and the reductionism debate. Make sure that you show your understanding of the relevance of any of these that you use.

Bulimia nervosa

Bulimia nervosa: symptoms and facts

- Bulimia nervosa involves repeated episodes of binge eating (eating more in a two-hour period than is usual) followed by purging, exercising or fasting.
- The individual feels a loss of control during binge-eating episodes.
- Cycle of binge/purge occurs at least twice a week for at least three months.
- The individual has high levels of dissatisfaction with body weight and shape.
- The individual's self-esteem is extremely dependent on their body weight and shape.

Psychological explanations

Role of the media

Research into the causes of anorexia and bulimia nervosa is often generic, meaning that it is assumed that similar factors may influence both disorders. This is particularly the case with media influences. The work of Striegel-Moore and Bulik (2007), Groesz *et al.* (2002) and Becker *et al.* (2002) was outlined in the previous section about anorexia nervosa, and their conclusions apply equally to bulimia nervosa. A critical feature of eating disorders is dissatisfaction with body weight and shape, and there is no doubt that media influences contribute to this dissatisfaction. We still have to explain why only a small proportion of people exposed to media influences go on to develop bulimia nervosa.

Personality

Research into the personality characteristics of women diagnosed with bulimia nervosa has identified some factors that may contribute to their vulnerability (Bardone-Cone *et al.*, 2008). These include:

- Body dissatisfaction.
- High levels of perfectionism – having high standards and being heavily self-critical, even over the smallest mistake.

- Low levels of self-efficacy. Self-efficacy is the sense of being able to control one's own life and being confident in one's own abilities.
- The perfectionist sees body dissatisfaction as a 'mistake' that they should be able to control and change. However, low self-efficacy leads to maladaptive coping behaviour in the form of binging and purging.

Family dynamics

Minuchin's family systems approach to eating disorders (Minuchin *et al.*, 1978), reviewed in relation to anorexia nervosa, can be applied to bulimia nervosa. The eating disorder is an attempt by the child to divert attention away from internal family problems.

Evaluation

- There is convincing evidence that media influences contribute to the body dissatisfaction that may lead to eating disorders such as bulimia nervosa.
- There is also evidence that people who go on to develop bulimia nervosa have particular personality characteristics that make them vulnerable to the disorder.
- However, most of this research is carried out in Western affluent societies and conclusions cannot automatically be applied to other ethnic groups and cultures.
- Research usually involves people already diagnosed with bulimia nervosa. We cannot be sure that the personality characteristics are not the *result* of the eating disorder.
- The family dynamics approach is based on case studies. It is hard to test scientifically or to replicate any findings. However, psychotherapy can be a successful treatment for bulimia nervosa, giving some support to the family dynamics approach.

Biological explanations

Genetics

The early study of Kendler *et al.* (1991) on monozygotic and dizygotic twins where one twin had been diagnosed with bulimia nervosa suggested a genetic factor in bulimia. Concordance rates were 23 per cent for MZ twins and 8.7 per cent for DZ twins. Although this suggests a genetic factor, the concordance rate for MZ twins is relatively low. Later research (Bulik *et al.*, 2006) concluded that the genetic contribution to bulimia nervosa was between 50 and 80 per cent.

Although much twin research is based on small numbers (as bulimia is not a common disorder) and is also culturally specific (being based on Western societies), there is general agreement that people who develop bulimia nervosa have a genetic vulnerability. However, MZ concordance rates are nowhere near 100 per cent so there is room for a substantial involvement of non-genetic psychological and cultural factors.

Serotonin

The brain neurotransmitter serotonin is heavily involved in the pathways underlying eating behaviour. Some research has shown low levels of activity in serotonin pathways in people with eating disorders, including bulimia nervosa (Frank *et al.*, 2002; Kaye *et al.*, 2005).

However, it is still difficult to decide whether the serotonin changes *cause* the disorder or occur as a *result* of the disorder. Any changes in the pattern of eating are almost certain to produce changes in brain serotonin activity, but these would not be *causal*. Drug treatments for bulimia are largely ineffective, suggesting that it is not a straightforward problem with serotonin activity.

Apply it

Make a list of evaluative points for biological explanations and elaborate each where possible, citing evidence.

AQA Examiner's tip

Make sure that you revise your knowledge of why MZ and DZ twin studies are so important in the study of genetic factors in normal and abnormal behaviour. If you refer to them in your answers, explain how the concordance rates lead to the conclusions.

AQA Examiner's tip

There is no single agreed explanation for bulimia nervosa, so be prepared to discuss the interaction between all of the different influences. Discussion in questions about either psychological or biological explanations should always include the possible involvement of alternative explanations.

Conclusions

As with anorexia nervosa, bulimia nervosa seems to involve many factors at different levels. A diathesis-stress model would propose that body dissatisfaction arises as a consequence of personality factors and media/social/family influences. For bulimia nervosa to develop, this dissatisfaction needs to be combined with a genetic vulnerability.

Obesity

Definition of obesity

Obesity is defined by the body mass index (BMI). This is calculated by dividing your body weight in kilograms by the square of your height in metres.

- BMI less than 18.5 – underweight
- BMI over 25 – overweight
- BMI over 30 – obese
- BMI over 40 – morbidly obese

Body weight is determined by the energy we take in as food and the energy we expend. Energy expenditure is mainly made up of our metabolic rate (a measure of the activity of all the cells in the body) and physical exercise. We put on weight when energy expenditure is less than the energy we take in. So obesity can involve the amount and type of food we eat, and the amount of physical activity we take.

Psychological explanations

Social and cultural factors

- The increase in the number of working parents means less time for meal preparation and more reliance on fast food. Fast food and soft drinks have a high calorie (energy) content in the form of fats and sugars. Portions have also increased in size (Anderson and Butcher, 2006).
- The increase in time spent watching television, playing computer games and social networking matches the increase in obesity over the last 20 years. Research suggests that an extra hour's viewing each day increases levels of obesity by two per cent (Dietz and Gortmaker, 1985). Besides the lack of exercise, TV viewing is associated with eating more fast foods.
- The food industry is very effective at altering dietary habits, but advertised foods are often high in energy content (fats and carbohydrates) and low in nutritional value.
- There is more reliance on car travel and less emphasis on walking and playing outside.
- Overall, over the last 20 years there has been a general increase in energy input in the form of high-calorie foods, and a general reduction in physical activity. This is a recipe for weight gain and increased levels of obesity.

Evaluation

- Changes in dietary habits and physical exercise over the last 20 or 30 years cannot be studied in a purely scientific way. It would be unethical to systematically study the effect of high-calorie diets in humans over years. This means that data are largely correlational, and cause and effect relationships cannot be identified. So we cannot say, for instance, whether dietary change is more significant than reduced physical exercise.

> **AQA Examiner's tip**
>
> Where statements in the text are followed by a particular reference to research studies, do not forget that these studies are a key source of AO2/3 material for the explanation, hypothesis or theory concerned.

■ However, changes in diet and exercise over the last 20 years do correlate highly with increased levels of obesity, and fit in well with the energy-in energy-out model of obesity.

Biological explanations

Evolutionary approaches

In the environment of evolutionary adaptation (EEA) it would have been adaptive to store energy in the form of fat as efficiently as possible. Food supplies would have been unpredictable and so fat reserves would have been critical in survival. It has been proposed that we evolved a 'thrifty gene' that allows us to store fat efficiently (Wells, 2006).

This adaptation operates today, a time when, at least in prosperous countries, food is readily available. So our drive to store more food than we need operates in overdrive and leads to increased levels of obesity.

Evidence in favour of this hypothesis is that the Pima Indians of Mexico, living in a harsh environment, had little or no obesity. However, increased exposure to western high-fat diets has led to an epidemic of obesity. Their thrifty gene is taking advantage of the regular availability of energy-rich diets to store more fat than they need (Poston and Foreyt, 1999).

Genetic and neural factors

Twin studies of obesity have found a concordance rate of around 50 per cent for MZ twins, showing some genetic influence but also suggesting a major role for non-genetic factors.

Leptin is a hormone released from fatty tissue that travels to the hypothalamus in the brain. It acts as a signal of the body's fat reserves – as these increase, leptin levels rise and signal the hypothalamus to inhibit feeding. Leptin acts as a satiety signal. Genetically modified mice lacking the leptin gene become obese, and this can be reversed by injections of leptin. This could be a model of human obesity, but unfortunately most obese people have normal levels of leptin.

However, some obese people may have an insensitivity to leptin, perhaps with reduced numbers of leptin receptors in the hypothalamus.

In general, only about 10 per cent of cases of obesity seem to be related to clear genetic abnormalities. But twin studies do support genetic influences on obesity, and further research is likely to uncover some of these influences.

Physiological factors

Obesity and weight regulation involve general physiological factors as well as genetic and neural influences.

For some time it was thought that in obesity the basal metabolic rate (BMR: the rate at which we burn up energy) was lower in the obese. Less energy was used in cell metabolism, less food was burned up and more was stored as fat, contributing to obesity. But research shows that in fact the BMR in obese individuals is within the normal range.

However, there is some evidence for an involvement of the BMR. In people of normal weight, the BMR increases as they put on weight, as the body tries to burn off the excess. In obese participants, this increase in BMR does not seem to occur (Mobbs *et al.*, 2005). Failing to burn off excess fat would contribute to weight gain and obesity.

> **Think about it**
>
> Evolutionary explanations of behaviour are always difficult to test directly, so they can seem very speculative. The evolutionary fossil record can give us some idea of life 100,000 years ago, while studying living hunter-gatherer societies is thought to provide insights into life back in the EEA. But the lack of direct evidence will always be a problem for the evolutionary approach.

> **AQA** Examiner's tip
>
> Eating disorders are complicated. The specification states that you can be asked for at least two psychological and two biological explanations of one eating disorder. You can use research evidence for biological explanations to evaluate the psychological approach, and vice versa. So plan carefully, and use supporting/contradictory evidence.

Evaluation

Feeding behaviour is tightly bound up with our biological need for a balanced diet. This biological background, including feeding centres in the hypothalamus, adipose (fatty) tissue and leptin release, and basal metabolic rate, mean that we cannot ignore the biology of obesity.

- There is speculation that the thrifty gene may contribute to obesity levels.
- There is research evidence from twin studies for a genetic influence on obesity.
- There is little evidence for a general role for leptin in obesity.
- There is research evidence showing abnormalities of the BMR in obesity, as obesity may be related to a failure of the BMR to increase as weight increases.

> ### Think about it
>
> There is evidence that both psychological and biological factors play a part in the development of obesity. One difference from, for example, anorexia is that we can see a clear influence of social/cultural changes in diet and physical activity on obesity. Where does that leave biological factors?

Thinking about issues and debates

The biological approach to eating behaviour is *reductionist*. It focuses on explanations at the level of brain centres, neurotransmitters and hormones, and ignores higher-level influences such as familiarity, learning, and social and cultural factors. Many studies involve non-human animals, raising problems of *extrapolating* results from animals to humans.

The evolutionary approach is *reductionist* in that it reduces complex human eating behaviour to a relatively simple set of evolutionary principles. It ignores the clear influence of social and cultural factors on our eating behaviour. It is also impossible to test using scientific experiments, but relies instead on the study of current eating behaviour and speculations about how these relate to the environment of evolutionary adaptation.

The study of influences on children's eating behaviour involves the *behaviourist* approach and learning through direct reinforcement, and *social learning theory* via modelling and imitation. There is also strong evidence for *cultural influences and differences* in eating behaviour. Findings are culturally limited as research is largely based in Western societies.

Issues, debates and approaches in eating behaviour

The study of eating disorders is largely Western-based, and so it is culturally limited. Results may not be generalisable to other cultures. It also focuses on eating disorders in females. Although such disorders are not as common in males, there is a relative lack of research into male eating disorders.

The study of eating disorders involves a range of different approaches. These include *biological* (physiological, neural, evolutionary) and *psychological* (behavioural, social learning theory, cognitive, psychodynamic). *Social* and *cultural* factors are particularly important in explanations of obesity. Explanations focusing on biological factors are *reductionist* as they ignore the important role of higher-level influences such as psychological, social and cultural.

Explanations for dieting involve an interaction between *physiological* and *cognitive* approaches. However, many studies are laboratory-based, with good internal validity (control of variables) but low ecological validity, meaning that results may be hard to generalise to the real world. Studies are usually carried out in Western affluent societies, showing a *cultural bias*. Results from studies of other cultures may be different.

Exam-style questions

Example 1

| 0 | 1 | Outline factors influencing attitudes to food and eating behaviour. *(4 marks)* |

| 0 | 2 | Outline and evaluate **one or more** psychological explanations of one eating disorder. *(4 marks + 16 marks)* |

Example 2

| 0 | 3 | Discuss the role of neural mechanisms in controlling eating **and/or** satiation. *(24 marks)* |

Example 3

| 0 | 4 | Outline and evaluate **one or more** psychological explanations of **one** eating disorder. *(24 marks)* |

Example 4

| 0 | 5 | Discuss explanations for the success and failure of dieting. *(24 marks)* |

Eating behaviour

Sample answers

Suggested content for the other example questions for this section can be found at
www.nelsonthornes.com/psychology_answers

Example 4

0 5

Dieting involves restricting food intake to reduce weight. It can also be combined with exercising. Dieting is very common in Western societies at least – about 40% of the female population are trying to lose weight. This essay will first discuss the factors which lead to the failure of dieting and secondly, what we know about successful dieting.

Dieting often fails. There are both biological and psychological explanations for this. One biological explanation is the boundary model. This model argues that each person's body has a 'set point' and weight does not fluctuate very much above or below this (homeostasis). When a person goes on a diet, they set themselves a cognitive limit (for example eat 1000 calories) which is less than the body would like. If they go over the cognitive limit (for example eating 1200 calories) they think 'what the hell' and then carry on eating so the diet fails.

● Reasonable. Some omissions in this description.

This model has received support from studies of restrained eaters. Herman and Mack 1975 studied 45 women. Some were on diets (restrained eaters) and some weren't. One group were given one milkshake and another group had two milkshakes (the preload) then they were given access to different kinds of ice cream. The women not on a diet who had had two milkshakes didn't eat much ice cream as they were already full. But those on a diet who had had two milkshakes ate more ice cream. They had already broken their diet, thought what the hell and continued to eat.

● A short summary of this study in support. Generally accurate.

The boundary model helps to explain why dieting fails, because restricting food is going against the body's natural urge to eat. Dieting is different to trying to give up smoking or drinking alcohol because you have to eat: you can't give it up completely. The model takes into account both biological factors (the set point) and psychological factors (setting a calorie limit) so it cannot be criticised for being reductionist. But most of the experiments like Herman and Mack's are laboratory based and these may be unrealistic and fail to show how people manage dieting/eating in real life. A different explanation of dieting failure is given by the evolutionary approach. When we reduce calorie intake, the body responds by assuming we are in famine and reduces its metabolic rate. This would have been useful for survival in the past but it isn't good for dieting as the body burns up food more slowly.

Nice conclusion and analysis, addiction is referred to.

Reference to issues and debates though this needs elaboration.

A small amount of methodological critique.

When you stop dieting, the body piles the weight back on as fat to store for lean times. The evolutionary approach helps to understand how and why dieting is so difficult. But it is also rather deterministic and suggests we are doomed to fail at diets. This isn't always true and people can and do lose weight as the next section of the essay will show. A final explanation of why diets fail is that people go on and off them, they lose weight, and then go back to eating the same rubbish as before and it's not a surprise that they put it back on. These approaches show why diets often fail. ——— ● Another block of AO1

However, it IS possible to lose weight – although maybe not just by dieting. One factor that makes it successful is telling other people you are dieting and getting social support. Lots of studies have shown that going to WeightWatchers will help as you can get positive reinforcement from other people. This is linked to the behavioural approach and it contradicts the idea that diets are doomed to fail. Other studies have shown how it is better to increase activity rather than simply restricting eating. This is best done by changing your lifestyle (walk to work, take the stairs not lift) rather than going on then off a diet. Permanent lifestyle changes are stressed as the way to maintain weight loss by the NHS so they must work.

AQA — Examiner's comments

AO1 is reasonable with two explanations (boundary model, evolutionary approach) in a fair amount of detail. This answer would achieve marks in the basic/reasonable band. AO2/3 is reasonable. The essay is focused and has a clear line of argument. There is some reference to appropriate issues and debates, but more detailed consideration of issues, debates and approaches is needed to make this answer effective.

6 Gender

Biological influences on gender

You need to know how to

✓ explain the terms 'sex' and 'gender' and the difference between them

✓ describe evolutionary explanations of gender development

✓ evaluate evolutionary explanations and the role of genes and hormones in gender development

✓ explain what is meant by, and the main characteristics of, gender dysphoria

✓ use the biosocial approach to critique biological and social explanations of gender development.

The evolutionary approach

- This approach argues that gender differences occur because of selective pressures in the past that shaped different behaviours in men and women.

- The important time period is believed to be the environment of evolutionary adaptation (EEA), between about 40 thousand and 10 thousand years ago, when our ancestors were hunter-gatherers.

- Gender differences in behaviour were produced by two complementary processes – natural selection and sexual selection. Natural selection is the selection of behaviours or bodily features that allow an animal to compete successfully for food and shelter and to survive. Sexual selection is the selection of behaviours that allow an animal to compete successfully for mates and to reproduce. These processes ensured that behaviours that helped survival and reproduction for our ancestors were kept in the gene pool.

- Trivers (1972) suggested that gender differences came from differences in parental investment. This is investment by the parent that increases the offspring's chance of survival at the cost of the parent's ability to invest in other offspring. The qualities and behaviours that led to reproductive success were different for males and females.

- These differences continue to exist in today's world due to genome lag, although the modern environment is very different from the EEA.

AQA Examiner's tip

Make sure that you are clear about the difference between sex and gender and use the terms correctly in the exam. The term 'sex' refers to bodily aspects of being male or female, such as having a penis or vagina. 'Gender' refers to behaviour, which can be masculine, feminine or have features of both (androgyny). These terms are used incorrectly in real life much of the time!

Parental investment and gender differences

	Parental investment	How reproductive success is achieved	Behaviours that lead to reproductive success
Males	Limited: Men produce millions of sperm with little effort and can fertilise many women. In theory, a man can father thousands of children.	Having sex with as many fertile females as possible	Behaviours and traits that enable males to compete for access to females by fighting, such as aggression, dominance and competitiveness, will be selected. Flashy displays of resources and strength to attract females will also be selected. Sexual opportunism will be advantageous. These behaviours are thought of as masculine.
Females	Substantial: Women produce one egg a month. Each offspring involves nine months of pregnancy, then childbirth and care after birth for survival. A woman can only produce a few children.	Ensuring the survival of the few precious offspring that are produced	Behaviours that ensure the survival of young will be selected. Females who are helpful, sensitive to others' needs, gentle, warm and compassionate will leave behind more surviving offspring. Females who are choosy about mate selection and unwilling to engage in casual sex will produce more surviving offspring. These behaviours are thought of as feminine.

Evidence for the evolutionary explanation

- Differences in size and weight. On average, human males are about 1.15 times larger than females. This suggests that size and weight were characteristics that enabled men to compete successfully for access to females in the EEA. Size differences between males and females are shown in many other species.

- Differences in aggression. Males show greater amounts of aggressive behaviour across almost all cultures and are more likely than women to be convicted of violent crimes. This suggests that male aggression may have a genetic basis. Aggression has clear links to testosterone, a male hormone. When women undergo sex changes to become male they receive testosterone, a male hormone. Following hormone treatment, they report an increase in aggressive feelings (Van Goozen *et al.*, 1994).

- Differences in sexual behaviour. Clark and Hatfield's 1989 study shows how men and women have different attitudes to casual sex. Seventy-five per cent of male students agreed to have sex with an attractive female stranger on an American campus. No females agreed to have sex when propositioned by an attractive male.

Think about it

Two characteristics that are stereotypically masculine are independence and forcefulness. Why might these behaviours have been selected for men? Two feminine characteristics are the ability to sympathise and loyalty. What advantage could these behaviours have brought for survival and reproduction in the EEA?

Think about it

There are differences in body size and testicle size between gorillas, chimpanzees and humans.

Male gorillas are much bigger than females, but they have small testicles. This suggests that male gorillas fought between themselves for access for females and aggressive behaviour was selected.

Male chimpanzees are a similar size to female chimps, but they have very large testicles. This implies that they did not fight physically (size has not been selected), but production of large amounts of sperm was an advantage. This suggests that competition took place through the amount of sperm produced – and female chimps were promiscuous.

Human males are a bit larger than females and have medium-sized testicles. What does this suggest about competition between males?

Apply it

If you are also revising the chapters on aggression and relationships, you can borrow some of the material to use as evidence here. For example, you could use the studies of human reproductive behaviour on page 34. Just remember to keep the focus on gender in your essays – how and why differences in behaviour between males and females have evolved.

Problems with evolutionary explanations of gender

- Evolutionary accounts cannot be tested using scientific methods as it is not possible to go back to the EEA to see how people behaved.
- Female choosiness can be explained by cultural pressures. In most parts of the world, female chastity is coerced using many different strategies. It may not be an adaptation at all.
- Evolutionary psychology assumes that male/female differences were *designed* to solve the problem of reproductive success. However, it is not always clear that traits are adaptations that led to success. For example, promiscuity may not lead to increased reproductive success for males, as offspring were less likely to survive in the EEA when males did not stick around (Sternglanz and Nash, 1988).
- The evolutionary account of gender differences explains unacceptable behaviours like rape as 'natural'. Thornhill and Palmer's book *The Natural History of Rape* (2000) claims that rape is an evolved tactic that enables males who cannot reproduce with consent to be successful by resorting to sexual violence. This ignores the fact that many rape victims are of non-reproductive age (e.g. young children or older women), disproving the claim that it aids reproductive success.
- According to Hagen (2002) evolutionary psychology is becoming out of date and ignoring advancements in archaeology and anthropology. Although there are some indisputable features of the EEA (women got pregnant and men did not), evolutionary psychologists need to update their understanding based on recent discoveries.

The biological approach

The evolutionary approach argues that differences between males and females are inbuilt and coded in genes. The biological approach builds on this to examine the importance of genes and hormones in relation to male and female behaviour. Genes dictate the biological sex of the baby and control the production of sex hormones before and after birth.

- The sex of a baby (female or male) is established at conception when the sperm fertilises the egg.
- An embryo has 23 pairs of chromosomes, each one made up of one from the father and one from the mother.
- The 23rd chromosome establishes the sex of the baby. If an X chromosome is supplied by both parents, the baby will be a girl. If a Y chromosome is supplied by the father's sperm, the baby will become a boy.
- The release of hormones begins between four and eight weeks after conception in both sexes and is controlled by the gene on the twenty-third chromosome.
- In boys, the testicles begin to produce the hormone testosterone. Testosterone affects the part of the brain called the hypothalamus. It enlarges areas called INAH 1, 2 and 3, known overall as 'the sexually dimorphic nucleus', making these larger and denser. This is not obvious in brain scans until boys are around six years old.
- In girls, the ovaries begin to produce female hormones. The release of these hormones is slight and they have little effect on the hypothalamus. The sexually dimorphic nucleus remains smaller and the number of cells is less dense.
- Not everyone is born clearly male or female with the usual twenty-third chromosome pattern of XX or XY. Chromosomal abnormalities include 'super males' who have an XXY pattern. They are taller than normal and were thought to be more aggressive until evidence contradicted this claim. About one in 500 males have an XXY chromosome pattern (Klinefelter's syndrome). They have enlarged breasts and a womanly shape and they are often infertile.

AQA Examiner's tip

Your essays gain better marks for evaluation if you can elaborate and explain the points that you make rather than listing them. Practise writing an evaluation section using three of the points about problems with evolutionary explanations of gender shown here, but explain them with your own examples to make them come to life.

Commentary

- Generally there is strong link between genetic sex and feelings of masculinity or femininity. Most men are biologically male and feel masculine.

- Some people are born 'inter-sex', meaning they have features of both male and female anatomy (e.g. an ovary and a testicle). They often receive treatment to 'align' them to their preferred gender.

- The conditions above and inter-sex states show that genetic sex is more complicated than simply having two categories of male and female. For this reason, genes are no longer used to determine the sex of sportspeople, for example in the Olympic Games.

- The experience of gender dysphoria (see page 80) causes problems for the genetic explanation. Some people are genetically one sex but 'feel' like they are the other sex (e.g. a female who has always felt male). They refer to themselves as being trapped in the wrong body. Cases of gender dysphoria show that gender is more complicated than being purely produced by genetics. If gender dysphoria was related to anomalies in genetic sex, it would remain consistent throughout life.

Apply it

Use the internet to find out about the case of Caster Semenya, the runner whose status as a female athlete was questioned in 2009. What types of gender verification tests were carried out on Semenya and what did they show?

Look at the section on the biosocial approach to gender development on pages 79–80. Write a short summary that you could insert into a biological essay as a critique of the genetic argument.

Key research

Sex hormones and gender

Animal studies: Young (1966) administered male hormones to one group of pregnant rats and female hormones to another to see whether hormone exposure influenced the behaviour of the offspring. In the first group, female offspring that had been exposed to large amounts of male hormones showed typically male mating behaviours, attempting to mount their partners from behind. In contrast, male offspring exposed to high levels of female hormones showed the characteristic behaviour of female rats, adopting the crouching lordosis position. This suggests that hormones influence sexual behaviour (in rats at least).

Case studies: Hines (1994) examined a group of girls and boys aged 3–8 who had congenital adrenal hyperplasia (CAH), a condition in which they were exposed to high levels of male hormones in the womb. They were compared with a control group who had not experienced high levels of hormones. There were minor differences between the two groups. The CAH girls tended to prefer playing with boys rather than other girls. In a second study, Hines compared 25 CAH adults with their unaffected relatives and found that the women remembered playing more boyish games. In both samples, the CAH males did not differ from those without CAH. This study suggests that hormone exposure has only mild effects on behaviour.

Correlational studies: There are various bodily markers that indicate pre-natal exposure to hormones. One of the most extensively studied is 2D:4DR, the relative lengths of the second and fourth fingers. Rommsayer and Troche (2007) measured 2D:4DR in more than 700 students. They also asked each participant to complete an inventory (Bem's SRI) that measured masculinity and femininity. They found that men whose SRI showed that they were feminine had a finger pattern that was similar to females. However, other studies have contradicted this (Troche, 2007) and these findings remain controversial.

AQA Examiner's tip

Make sure that you can summarise research studies succinctly and accurately. You should always draw a conclusion from any study that you include in your essays by ending with 'this shows that' or 'this supports/contradicts the claim that'.

Commentary

- The claim that testosterone enlarges three areas of the brain is not universally supported. Swaab and Fliers (1985) argued that the SDN was 2.5 times larger in males from their sample of 31 people. However, Le Vay (1991) has argued that the differences between men's and women's brains are less marked and exist in only one area of the brain – INAH 3. The extent of brain differences is still disputed.

- Young's rat experiment implies that hormone exposure had a strong effect on behaviour. Rats given hormones showed reproductive/mating behaviours usually associated with the opposite sex. However, the case study evidence from Hines suggests a much less important role for hormones in human behaviour. There were few differences between hormone-exposed females and non-exposed females except the preference for more physical, tomboyish games.

- Why might these studies contradict each other? Animal experiments allow for precise control and manipulation of an IV (in this case, the amount of hormones has been varied), but the findings should not be generalised to people. Rats and humans are both mammals, but there are important differences. People are more complicated than rats. People have a far greater ability to think about behaviour and choose to act in certain kinds of ways in response to learning and social pressure.

The biosocial approach to gender development

The biosocial approach to gender originally put forward by Money and Ehrhardt (1972) argues that gender development results from the interaction between biological and social factors.

According to the biosocial approach:

- Biological factors include genes and hormones: genetic sex (based on the pattern of XY or XX chromosomes) controls the production of hormones, notably testosterone. Testosterone acts by masculinising the brain. Hormone exposure leads to the development of male or female characteristics in the newborn baby.

- Social factors begin at birth with labelling of a baby as male or female. These factors include socialisation through the immediate environment (parents, peers) and the wider culture. Labelling leads to different paths of socialisation for girls and boys. The paths vary depending on the cultural views of sex roles, masculinity and femininity.

- Initial predictions by Money and Ehrhardt suggested that the gender of a child could be changed through socialisation if the change took place before the age of around 2–3 years (i.e. a boy could be turned into a girl and vice versa). The case study of Bruce Reimer contradicted this idea as Bruce reverted back to a male identity after puberty.

- More recent refinements of biosocial theory (e.g. Urdy, 2000) suggest that biology sets the limits to the flexibility of gender by affecting how sensitive the child is to female or male socialisation. This helps to explain the case of Bruce Reimer better as the initial exposure to androgens meant that he was not as amenable to female socialisation processes.

- According to the biosocial approach, a girl with congenital adrenal hyperplasia (CAH) who is exposed to high levels of testosterone is likely to be less sensitive to female socialisation processes. A boy who has not been exposed to normal amounts of testosterone may be less sensitive to male socialisation. Parents often work very hard to socialise their

Think about it

The biological approach takes the nature side of the nature–nurture debate, assuming that differences between men and women are largely inbuilt and arise from biological differences. The evidence for this position is weak in humans. It is much more likely that human behaviour is produced by an interaction between biological and social factors (the biosocial model).

AQA Examiner's tip

If you are asked to discuss the role of hormones in gender, make sure that you can refer to different types of evidence (e.g. animal studies, case studies, correlations). Using different types of evidence gives you plenty of opportunities for methodological critique. You can show off your understanding of how science works and gain AO2/3 marks.

Apply it

Research and make a note of some further evaluative points about the biosocial approach to help in an essay question on the topic.

AQA Examiner's tip

The biosocial approach to gender is a valuable evaluation tool for both biological and social explanations. Rather than taking a side in the nature–nurture debate, it acknowledges that both make important contributions to the development of gender. Urdy's account also provides a mechanism to explain why gender socialisation processes may have limited effects on some children. The biosocial approach can explain many of the findings of studies of atypical hormone exposure in young children.

children and encourage them to show masculine/feminine behaviours when the child does not show them naturally.

■ The biosocial theory is helpful in explaining how biological and social factors interact together to influence the development of gender. This approach allows for both nature and nurture to play their part in the development of gender. It helps to explain how nature (biology) sets limits on socialisation processes.

Gender dysphoria

Gender dysphoria (the belief that you are trapped in the wrong body and should be a member of the other sex) is a core symptom of gender identity disorder (GID). GID is a clinical condition that occurs in about one in 11,000 people. In order for it to be diagnosed, the person must feel discomfort with their biological sex and feel psychologically as if they are a member of the opposite sex.

Key study

Research into gender dysphoria

Gender dysphoria can start in young children, although current evidence suggests that many grow out of it by the age of 18. Drummond studied 30 girls referred to a gender disorder clinic aged 2–3 for showing persistent cross-sex identification and behaviour. They were followed up at ages 7 and 18 and asked about their preferred gender identity. At 18, 88 per cent of the girls had lost the symptoms and were contented with their female identity. Twelve per cent wanted to undergo gender alignment surgery to their preferred gender.

There is continued debate about causes and origins. Some theorists blame parenting style (Bradley and Zucker, 1992). There is little real evidence that it is biological in origin as yet.

There is also debate regarding treatment and whether children should be encouraged to conform to gender stereotypes.

Social influences on gender

The behavioural approach to gender

According to the behavioural approach, gender roles are learned through socialisation and upbringing. There are two important types of learning:

- Learning through operant conditioning: providing rewards (positive reinforcement) for some kinds of behaviour, such as playing with cars, and discouragement (e.g. teasing) for others, such as playing with dolls.

- Social learning: observation of same-sex role models and imitation of their behaviour when it is seen to bring rewards (vicarious reinforcement). In young children, the main role models are parents and older siblings. Later they observe peers and friends who also act as role models. Social learning also occurs through wider agents of socialisation, for example television, films, magazines and the music industry. Television is an important agent of socialisation for children. Some of these programmes are careful not to present gender stereotypes, but others are less concerned about this.

Apply it

Make sure that you are clear about the mechanisms involved in reinforcement and social learning and can provide relevant gender examples for each of them. Use the correct language to impress the examiners.

Key research

Reinforcement of gender roles by parents and peers (Lytton and Romney, 1991)

Method: Meta-analysis of 175 studies. There were almost 28,000 participants in total.

Findings: There were no differences in the amount of communication or interaction that parents had with boys and girls. In North America, boys were encouraged to take part in outdoor tasks and girls were encouraged to take part in indoor activities. In Western countries other than the US (e.g. the UK, France) boys were more likely to be physically punished (smacked) than girls. Fathers were more likely than mothers to treat boys and girls differently.

Other studies show punishment and negative reinforcement are used to dissuade children from playing with gender inappropriate toys games:

- Siegel (1987) found that fathers are more likely to 'correct' boys when they play with girls' toys than vice versa.

- Archer and Lloyd (1982) found that three-year-olds will tease friends who play with toys that are seen as 'gender inappropriate'.

- Langlois and Downs (1980) found that teasing was most likely to occur when boys played with girls' toys.

Think about it

Why do you think boys are more likely to be teased than girls for gender inappropriate play? Is it worse for a girl to be called a tomboy or a boy to be called a sissy? Why?

AQA Examiner's tip

Make sure that you know about one piece of evidence in reasonable depth (e.g. Lytton and Romney) and a couple of others in brief. This will enable you to demonstrate both breadth and depth in your essays, which is important if you want to achieve a mark in the top band.

Key reserach

Social influences on gender (Fagot, 1992)

Fagot compared the gender stereotypes of two groups of children brought up in different kinds of families.

Twenty-seven families were classed as egalitarian families. Childcare, housework and paid work were shared between both parents. Forty-two were classed as traditional families. Fathers went out to work and mothers took charge of the childcare and housework.

When the children reached the age of four, they took part in 'gender labelling tasks' in which they were asked about various jobs (e.g. taking out the rubbish or cooking). Children in traditional families produced more stereotypical answers, showing children may absorb the behaviours demonstrated by role models.

Other studies have shown how children are surrounded by gender stereotypes at school, in TV programmes and in magazines:

- Colley (1994) has shown how the sex of teachers correlates with children's perception of subjects. Science and maths are more likely to be taught by men, and children often view these as subjects for boys. In contrast, geography and sociology are more likely to be taught by women and are often perceived as 'girlie' subjects.

- Morgan (1982) found that children who watched more TV had stronger stereotypical views about gender (a positive correlation).

- Pierce (1993) showed how stories in magazines aimed at teenage girls emphasise relationships with boys and portray girls as dependent, emotional, clingy and unable to make their own decisions.

Commentary

There is considerable evidence that reinforcement plays an important role in shaping children towards gender appropriate behaviour (e.g. studies by Siegal, Lytton and Romney, and Fagot). These studies show that boys are far more likely to be 'shaped' directly than girls. Parents and friends use negative strategies like teasing to discourage feminine behaviour/play in boys.

Durkin (1995) and Harris (1998) argue that peers play more of a role than parents in shaping gender appropriate behaviour.

It is difficult to measure the effects that watching television or reading magazines have on the development of gender roles. Correlational studies (e.g. Morgan, 1982) do not tell us that watching TV causes children to develop stereotyped views, just that the two go together.

Reinforcement and social learning are concepts from the behavioural approach. Behavioural explanations tend to assume that gender roles are learned passively. One criticism of this approach is the tendency to overlook children's ability to think things out for themselves. Some children resist pressures to conform to gender roles and develop more androgynous behaviour.

The behavioural approach emphasises nurture in the development of gender. However, it overlooks the part played by biology, notably the role of hormone exposure shown in Young's 1966 study with rats (see page 78)

AQA Examiner's tip

You can use biological evidence (e.g. Young's study of rats and hormones) to evaluate the behavioural approach. It shows that gender is not purely developed by socialisation and that biology also plays a role. You can also use the evidence presented here to critique the biological explanation of the development of gender.

Apply it

Construct a short paragraph on the behavioural approach which you can use to criticise the biological explanation of gender. It should start with: 'The biological explanation is contradicted by evidence that shows that gender roles are learned through reinforcement and observation. For example, Fagot found that …'.

Culture and gender development

People's culture has an impact on gender roles. This may change over time and vary between cultures. Cross-cultural studies can help us tease out the roles played by biological factors and socialisation (nature and nurture):

- If gender development is largely under the control of biological factors (hormones), then gender roles should be broadly similar across cultures.
- If it is mainly socialisation/upbringing, as the behavioural approach suggests, gender roles may vary across cultures.
- If gender is produced by the interaction of biological and cultural factors, some aspects of gender should be culturally universal but others are likely to differ based on socialisation.

Key study

The six-culture study of socialisation (Whiting and Whiting *et al.*, 1988)

Method: Whiting and Whiting *et al*. carried out a cross-cultural study in which gender was one of the variables investigated. They observed children in their natural environments, with parents, siblings and friends. The six cultures that they studied included two that were relatively affluent (the US and Japan) and four developing countries (Kenya, India, the Philippines and Mexico).

Findings: There were some key differences between boys and girls that were the same across all six cultures. Girls showed more nurturing behaviours and boys showed more dominance.

However, girls and boys were socialised differently from each other:

- Boys spent more time with their fathers and girls with their mothers.
- Boys were encouraged to achieve and become more independent than girls.
- Girls were socialised into nurturance and obedience.

The differences in the treatment of boys and girls were fairly small in the US, Kenya and the Philippines.

The differences in the treatment of boys and girls were substantial in India, Mexico and Japan. In these countries, girls were given more household tasks and expected to care for younger siblings. Boys were more likely to spend time outside and were given tasks such as feeding/herding animals, often carrying out these jobs with peers.

AQA Examiner's tip

You can link this study to how science works. In studies where the independent variable (in this case, culture) occurs naturally, it is impossible to infer that it causes changes in the dependent variable (gender roles). Many other factors, in this case upbringing and socialisation practises, also influence gender development.

Think about it

Whiting's study shows how both biology and upbringing play a role in gender development. It indicates some differences between girls and boys that occur across cultures and these may be biological in origin. However, it also shows how differences in socialisation can magnify these. In countries where children are treated very differently (e.g. India) these differences are much greater than in countries where they are treated similarly.

Commentary

There is considerable evidence for the claim that young boys show higher levels of competitiveness, aggression, dominance, and rough-and-tumble play than girls (Ember, 1981). The same patterns have been found in playground observations in countries as varied as Switzerland, Ethiopia and the US (Omar, Omark and Edelman, 1975). This suggests that some gender differences are biological.

Whiting and Whiting's study indicates that boys and girls are socialised differently and different qualities are encouraged. Bee (1995) argues that girls and boys show different qualities because of the way they are brought up. For example, girls show greater nurturance than boys because they are taught to be responsible at an early age as a result of having to care for younger siblings.

Psychological explanations of gender

Cognitive developmental theory

Cognitive explanations of gender argue that children do not come into the world with masculine and feminine behaviours as babies. Instead, they develop gender roles as their understanding of the world develops over the first few years of life. Cognitive theories focus on the child's thinking and their understanding of what it is to be male or female, a boy or a girl.

■ Kohlberg's theory provides a framework and shows how children's understanding of gender increases with age.

■ Martin and Halverson's theory builds on Kohlberg's, but argues that gendered behaviour begins at a much earlier age than Kohlberg thought, probably as young as two or three years old.

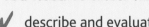
Key theory

Kohlberg's cognitive developmental theory (1966)

Kohlberg's theory argues that children develop an understanding of gender in three stages that are loosely linked to age. At each stage, the child's understanding becomes more sophisticated as their ability to think develops. This runs parallel with the other kinds of understanding. Kohlberg believed that boys and girls only begin to show differences in behaviour when they understand that gender is constant and cannot change, somewhere around the age of six to seven.

Kohlberg's three stages of understanding are as follows.

Stage 1: Gender identity. By the age of two to three and a half, children can correctly identify themselves as a boy or girl when asked. However, they do not understand that this is permanent.

Stage 2: Gender stability. At about four or five, the child knows that they are a boy or girl and that their sex will not change. A boy knows that he will continue to be a boy and will not grow up to be a mummy.

Stage 3: Gender constancy. Between four and a half and about seven the child learns that other people's sex does not change even with changes in appearance. A long-haired man is still a man, not a woman. A woman who shaves her head does not become a man. This is linked to the child's general understanding of the world and is known as 'conservation'.

Once the child has worked out that gender is constant, Kohlberg believed that they begin to show distinct differences in behaviour. Boys become masculine and girls become feminine.

Commentary

- Kohlberg's theory accurately identified the ages at which children gain different kinds of understanding, and many studies (e.g. McConaghy, 1979) have supported this.

- Kohlberg's claim that children's thinking becomes more complex and sophisticated is widely accepted. Children start with simple ideas about gender and build on these as their thinking develops.

- There is some evidence for Kohlberg's claim that children who have achieved 'constancy' pay close attention to same-sex role models. Slaby and Frey (1975) studied two to five-year-olds. Some had achieved the stage of gender constancy and others had not. They were shown two films using a split-screen TV. One was of a man changing a tyre and the other was of a woman baking a cake. Children who had achieved constancy spent more time watching the same-sex model (boys watched the tyre changing and girls watched the baking). Children who had not reached the stage of constancy were equally interested in both films.

- Ruble (1981) examined children's responses to adverts for toys on television. He found that children who had reached constancy were able to read between the lines and identify the subtle gender messages in toy advertising.

- Kohlberg's claim that gender develops when the stage of constancy is reached is disputed by other theories and contradicted by evidence. Martin and Halverson's gender schema theory suggests that children start to pay attention, to same-sex models much earlier than Kohlberg thought. According to this theory, children construct simple schemas by around the age of two. These drive the child's attention, making them tune into their environment and pay attention to same-sex role models in a very specific way.

> **AQA** **Examiner's tip**
>
> One great way to evaluate a theory is to present a contradictory account and show how evidence supports it. The knack is not to simply describe the second theory (remember that you cannot get marks for that), but to use it to show how it provides a better explanation.

Gender schema theory

Key theory

Gender schema theory (Martin and Halverson, 1981)

Martin and Halverson agree with Kohlberg that gender roles are driven by cognition (what the child thinks). But they argue that the process of gender development starts much earlier than Kohlberg thinks. They suggest that behaviour is driven by schemas – basic sets of knowledge about something. According to gender schema theory, gender development starts when children are about two years old and they put themselves into the category of boy or girl.

Once children have worked out which group/category they belong to, they focus their attention on that group (the in-group). They ignore anything that they label as belonging to the other group. Boys seek out information about the behaviour of boys – what toys they should play with, what games they should play, which clothes they should wear. They actively ignore anything that they see as being for girls.

Over time, children's schemas about gender become more complex, taking in a wider range of ideas about what is right for males or females. This includes school subjects, sports and even cars.

Key study

Campbell *et al.* (2004)

In 2004, Campbell *et al.* studied 56 toddlers who were just over two years old. They returned to visit them again when they were three. In each visit, the children were asked to pick out specific pictures from a larger set in a picture book. This activity was designed to assess the information in the children's current gender schema at each age.

The children were asked to pick out three things related to their own sex:

- 'Find me a picture of a girl (or boy).' This was the simple gender labelling task.

- 'Find me a girl's toy (or boy's toy).' This task was designed to see whether the child's schema contained information about the kinds of toys that were suitable for their own group.

- 'Find me a game for girls (game for boys).' This task was designed to see whether the child's schema contained information about games that were suitable for their own group.

At two years, about half of the children could correctly pick out the same-sex child, showing that they had developed a basic gender schema. They were unable to complete the second and third task. When Campbell re-tested the toddlers, almost half of the children could pick out a football as being suitable for a boy or the brush and comb set as being suitable for a girl. This study shows how the child's gender schema rapidly becomes more complex and detailed, as Martin and Halverson predict.

Commentary

- Martin and Halverson suggest that children are tuned in to gender from a very young age. This claim is supported by Campbell's study (above). Poulin-Dubois (2002) demonstrated how two-year-old girls were able to choose gender stereotypical dolls who would be shaving (male) or vacuuming (female).

- Gender schema theory sees the child as actively constructing their understanding of gender through their interaction with the environment. It therefore takes into account the importance of role models as well as cognitive development.

- Gender schema theory also helps to explain why young children have rigid ideas about gender. This is because they only pay attention to information that fits in with their schema and ignore information that contradicts it.

- Gender schema theory does not explicitly consider where schemas come from. A study by Tenenbaum and Leaper (2002) has pointed to the significant similarity between parents' schemas and their children's views about gender. Put simply, parents who hold gender stereotypical views have children who absorb these attitudes and probably take them for granted.

Thinking about issues and debates

Approaches

The gender section of the course is based around three approaches:

- biological (the role of genes, hormones and evolution)
- behavioural (the role of learning from parents, peers and culture)
- cognitive (the sense made by the child of the gendered world they see around them).

The biological and behavioural approaches contradict each other in important ways.

Nature and nurture

The biological/evolutionary approaches emphasise the role of nature.

The evolutionary approach suggests that behaviours are in the gene pool today (nature) because of the advantages they brought in the past. The biological approach emphasises the role of hormones (nature) in gender differences.

In contrast, the behavioural approach emphasises the importance of nurture (upbringing) and the learning of gender through reinforcement and role models.

The biosocial approach brings these two approaches together suggesting that nature (biology) sets limits, but that culture and upbringing influence gender within these limits.

The cognitive approach does not fit clearly on one or other side of the debate but assumes that children's reasoning is the basis for gender.

Approaches, issues and debates in gender

Socially sensitive research

The claims of the biological and evolutionary approaches can be seen as socially sensitive as they imply that men's and women's roles are pretty fixed and inflexible and that differences cannot be changed. This has implications for women and men at home and in the workplace.

The evolutionary approach suggests that men are programmed to be unfaithful as this leads to reproductive success and that rape is a natural adaptation designed to increase reproductive success. What makes these claims socially sensitive?

Free will and determinism

Another theme running through the chapter is fixity and change. Are gender roles set in stone or can they change?

The biological approach sees gender differences as pretty inevitable due to their biological origin. This is an example of biological determinism.

The behavioural approach allows slightly more room for change: different rewards, reinforcements and role models could theoretically alter how children are socialised. It is less deterministic but still argues that children are pretty passive and are shaped by rewards and punishments.

The cognitive approach allows for greatest free will (agency) as children develop their gender schemas based on what they see. This potentially allows for some change in gender roles.

Exam-style questions

Example 1

| 0 1 | Outline **one** psychological explanation of gender development (e.g. Kohlberg's theory or gender schema theory). |
| | *(8 marks)* |

| 0 2 | Evaluate the explanation you described in 0 1 . *(16 marks)* |

Example 2

| 0 3 | Discuss the role of genes **and/or** hormones in gender development. *(24 marks)* |

Example 3

| 0 4 | Outline and evaluate evolutionary explanations of gender development. *(24 marks)* |

Example 4

| 0 5 | Discuss the role played by social influences (e.g. parents, peers, schools and/or media) on gender. *(24 marks)* |

Gender

Sample answers

Suggested content for the other example questions for this section can be found at
www.nelsonthornes.com/psychology_answers

Example 4

0 5 *Children start to show gender roles at quite a young age, sometimes around three years when they begin to choose certain toys and games which are suitable for boys or girls.*

There are different explanations of gender development. The social explanation is based on the behavioural approach and it argues that children 'learn' gender from their parent, peers, TV, etc. There are two ways gender can be learned. The first is through rewards and punishments (operant conditioning): parents might tell their daughter she looks pretty when she wears a dress (a reward) but tease her (a punishment) if she prefers dungarees. Parents might try to dissuade their son from playing with dolls by teasing him.

A clear link to the underlying approach.

Quite clear coverage of reinforcement using appropriate language.

The second social influence on gender is the observation and imitation of role models. Children are exposed to role models in real life by watching their parents and on TV. They pay attention to and copy same-sex models, so girls might model themselves on Girls Aloud and boys on footballers.

Weaker coverage of imitation and social learning. A bit more detail and reference to vicarious reinforcement would be useful.

There is quite a lot of evidence which shows that social influences are important. For example, Lytton and Romney found that parents treat boys and girls differently, giving them different jobs to do around the house; boys are more likely to be punished. Their study was a meta-analysis using lots of different pieces of research so it had a very large sample size which makes it more likely to be reliable. Other studies such as Fagot have shown that friends will tease children for 'cross gender' play from as young as three years old. Some psychologists such as Durkin think that peers are more important in reinforcement than parents.

Not the correct name here, but the study is accurate and there is a useful critical comment at the end of the section.

It is likely that observation and role modelling is more important in gender development than reinforcement. This is because the influence of parents gets less when children go to school, but children spend lots of time watching television which shows stereotypical gender roles. Morgan found that children who watch more time have stronger stereotypes, although this study was correlational making it hard to establish that watching TV causes stereotypes. Fagot compared two types of families – those with traditional roles and those where parents shared work and child care, and found that children from traditional families had stronger stereotypes. Both of these studies suggest that children pick up their ideas about gender from the role models they are exposed to.

However, biological psychologists don't agree that gender roles are wholly produced by upbringing or nurture. They argue that hormones and genes (biology) play an important role in the development of gender. Studies such as Young's animal experiment show that exposure to testosterone led female rats to behave in a masculine way. There have also been case studies (such as Hines) which show that girls exposed to high levels of testosterone behave more boyishly. These studies suggests that gender roles are at least influenced by biology and social influences are not the only cause. The biosocial approach argues that nature and nurture work together to produce gender so it is not a matter of either/or but how much part they both play.

Another problem for the behavioural approach is the existence of androgyny. Some people adopt a non-gendered or androgynous lifestyle in which they avoid being masculine or feminine (sex typed). This suggests that people can choose how they want to behave rather than simply copying the role models available. One problem with behavioural approaches is that they ignore the importance of cognitive factors in the development of gender but they are very important.

A good comment trying to weigh the importance of different influences and the assertion is justified.

A nice conclusion at the end of the paragraph.

Introducing another approach is a good way of developing AO2. This is neatly linked to issues and debates too.

AQA Examiner's comments

AO1 good reasonable-band response. AO2 just makes it into the higher band. A good selection of material with a clear argument. Overall this answer would achieve marks on the border of the reasonable and higher bands.

7 Intelligence and learning

Theories of intelligence

> **You need to know how to**
> ✔ describe the psychometric approach to intelligence
> ✔ describe and evaluate psychometric theories of intelligence
> ✔ describe and evaluate information-processing theories of intelligence.

The psychometric approach

There are two facets of the approach, firstly the development of instruments to measure abilities and individual differences and secondly the development of theory about the measurements.

Binet introduced the notion of mental age and this was used to calculate intelligence quotient (IQ). Tests to measure IQ include the Wechler Adult Intelligence Scale (WAIS) and Raven's progressive matrices.

Psychometric or factor theories of intelligence

Psychometric theories of intelligence are based on the factor analysis of results from a variety of psychometric tests (such as tests of verbal abilities, numeracy, etc.). Factor analysis is a technique for examining whether the scores from various types of tests all correlate or whether there are no links between test scores. Those tests that show a high correlation are thought to be measuring one factor. The psychometric theories vary in the number of factors that they use to describe intelligence.

Spearman – one factor

Spearman suggested that all intelligent behaviour is highly correlated and therefore is the result of one general intelligence factor labelled 'g'. The idea that one single factor is behind all intelligence has been the centre of a major debate in psychology. Some still believe that 'g' is a valid concept, but others do not believe that the complexity of human intelligence cannot be encompassed in a single factor.

Thurstone – seven factors

Thurstone's factor analysis of intelligence test data suggested that there are seven primary abilities or factors. These are: verbal comprehension, verbal fluency, number, perceptual speed, spatial realisation, memory and inductive reasoning. Later researchers have suggested they may be part of one general factor (i.e. they are linked together).

Carroll – hierarchical model

The Carroll three-stratum model combines elements of both Spearman's and Thurstone's theories. Carroll suggests that the top of a hierarchy of intelligence is one general factor but that under this there are eight broad factors. The eight broad factors, such as 'general memory and learning', determined ability of specific factors.

Evaluation of psychometric theories

The psychometric approach to intelligence has led to one of the most widely used and powerful groups of tests in psychology, the IQ tests. However, all of the psychometric theories use factor analysis to determine which factors constitute intelligence and there are a number of problems of using factor analysis to develop theories of intelligence. These include:

■ Factor analysis can be done in a number of ways. Some methods will identify fewer factors, others will identify more (hence the differences in the theories).

■ Factor analysis only *describes* relationships between test scores, it does not *explain* them.

■ The output from factor analysis depends upon the data fed into the analysis. Therefore, if only data about academic abilities are fed into the analysis then the factors identified can *only* be academic. If data about other abilities, such as interpersonal skills or emotional intelligence, are not included they will not emerge as a factor.

Information-processing theories of intelligence

Sternberg's triarchic theory

Sternberg (1985) put forward a triarchic theory, based on information-processing ideas, that tries to give a fuller picture of intelligence. The triarchic theory consists of three interrelated components.

■ Componential sub-theory is concerned with the mental mechanisms or information processes that underlie intelligent behaviour. It is the analytical component of intelligence.

■ Experiential sub-theory is concerned with how experience affects intelligence. The same problem does not need the same level of use of the information processing components because of differences in previous experience. It is the creative component of intelligence.

■ Contextual sub-theory is concerned with intelligence in the context of culture and environment. The internal component of intelligence, componential, constantly interacts with this, external, component. It is the practical component of intelligence.

Evaluation of the triarchic theory

The main strength of the theory is that it brings various elements of intelligence (analytic, creative and practical) together. The theory shows how internal information processing mechanisms can be used to deal intelligently with the external world. Evidence suggests it is valid in a number of settings (i.e. schools and workplace). However, as it encompasses so many ideas some researchers suggest it lacks coherence. The emphasis on information processing tends to ignore any biological element of intelligence. Unlike some other theories, it does not explain why some individuals are gifted or impaired in a particular intellectual ability.

> ### Apply it
> Research and find more evidence regarding Sternberg's triarchic theory of intelligence to help your evaluation of it.

Gardner's theory of multiple intelligences

Gardner (1983) believed that a single factor of intelligence (or 'g') does not exist. He suggested that there are different types of intelligence that are independent from each other. People differ in the types of intelligence they show. He originally proposed that there are seven types of intelligence but later added an eighth.

Gardner's intelligences

Type	Description	Exemplified by
Linguistic intelligence	The ability to learn language and express ideas using language (both written and spoken).	Poets such as Emily Dickinson
Logical-mathematical intelligence	The ability to perform mathematical operations. Also the ability to reason and think logically.	Scientists such as Albert Einstein
Musical intelligence	The ability to produce, appreciate and perceive elements of music such as pitch and rhythm.	Composers such as Igor Stravinsky
Bodily-kinaesthetic intelligence	The use of mental abilities to control the body and solve physical problems.	Athletes or dancers such as Martha Graham
Spatial intelligence	The ability to perceive spatial information and interpret 3D space that cannot be seen.	Architects or artists such as Pablo Picasso
Intrapersonal intelligence	A form of self-knowledge used in understanding oneself and one's motivations and emotions.	Writers or psychologists such as Jane Austen
Interpersonal intelligence	The ability to understand other people's motivations, emotions and intentions.	Politicians such as Mahatma Gandhi
Naturalistic intelligence	The ability to recognise and categorise patterns in nature. Awareness of subtle changes in nature and environment.	Environmentalists or naturalists such as Charles Darwin

Evaluation of the theory of multiple intelligences

Evidence	Problems
Gardner used evidence from a wide range of sources to look at the idea that there are a number of independent intelligences and used some as criteria for different types. These include: • They are selectively affected by brain damage. • They are shown by people with exceptional abilities in one area such as savants or prodigies. • They have a different evolutionary history. • They have a different developmental history. • There is evidence from experimental psychology. • There is evidence from psychometric tests. Further support for Gardner's theory is that it has been very influential in education.	Other abilities, such as face recognition, show the same criteria used by Gardner to indicate an independent intelligence but are not included. If we were to adopt Gardner's criteria, the list is potentially huge and could include such diverse abilities as 'humour intelligence' or 'olfactory intelligence'. Some researchers believe that Gardner confuses intelligence with abilities and talents. There is some evidence from psychometric studies that the types of intelligence are not independent. Although Gardner's theory has been influential in changing educational practice, its impact has not been well evaluated.

Animal learning and intelligence

You need to know how to

✔ describe classical and operant conditioning

✔ evaluate the role of conditioning in non-human animal behaviour

✔ discuss social learning in animals and whether animals show Machiavellian intelligence

✔ evaluate evidence of self recognition in animals.

How do animals learn about their environments? How do they learn where to find food, avoid predators and return to shelter? There are two theories of how animals learn – classical conditioning and operant conditioning.

Classical conditioning

Key study

Pavlov (1927)

Pavlov was investigating the salivation reflex in dogs when he noticed a change in the dog's behaviour. In the beginning of the study, the dogs only produced saliva when they had food in their mouths. This is a reflex action that is not learned. However, after a while he found that the dogs were producing saliva *before* they had food in their mouths. They produced saliva in response to the sight and sounds of food being prepared. This change in behaviour showed some form of learning.

Pavlov investigated this systematically and found that if he paired giving the food with the sound of a bell a number of times, eventually the dogs would produce saliva just to the sound of the bell. He gave names to identify the general procedure of classical conditioning. The original salivation reflex was not learned or conditioned. He therefore called the food an *unconditioned stimulus* and the salivation an *unconditioned response*. Producing saliva to the sound of a bell is not a reflex but is a learned or conditioned behaviour. He therefore called the bell a *conditioned stimulus* and the salivation in this case the *conditioned response*.

General process of classical conditioning

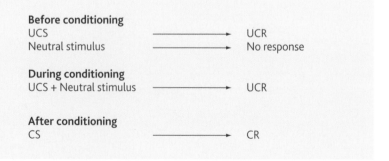

AQA Examiner's tip

You can use a diagram in your exam answer to explain classical conditioning. To gain credit it would need to be accurate and detailed.

This general process applies to all classical conditioning and many new stimuli can be linked to reflexes in this way.

Extinction and spontaneous recovery

In Pavlov's experiment, the dogs did not salivate to the sound of a bell for very long. When a conditioned stimulus is presented repeatedly without the unconditioned stimulus the conditioned response soon dies out or shows extinction. Sometimes the response comes back again and this is known as spontaneous recovery.

Generalisation and discrimination

Pavlov trained his dogs with a particular bell, but he found that other bells with similar tones also produced salivation. Showing a conditioned response to a stimulus like the conditioned stimulus is called stimulus generalisation. The opposite can also happen. Animals can be trained to respond to a narrower and narrower range of stimuli, and this is called stimulus discrimination.

Operant conditioning

One of the problems of classical conditioning is that animals do not learn a new response. In effect they learn to produce a reflex to a new stimulus. However, much animal learning is concerned with changing voluntary behaviour. Skinner (1938) showed how voluntary behaviour could be learned with operant conditioning.

Key study

Skinner (1938)

Skinner developed a simple, automated apparatus for studying the learning of voluntary behaviour, which became known as the Skinner box. The box was a plain environment that contained few stimuli except a light, a lever and a food hopper. When an animal, such as a rat, was placed in the box it typically showed a variety of behaviours. Eventually the rat would push the lever as it explored the box. When it did so, it was given some food. This made the pushing of the lever more likely to happen again.

Skinner found that learning of voluntary behaviour was due to the consequences of the behaviour. Any behaviour that was rewarded, or reinforced, was more likely to be repeated. In the Skinner box, the food acted as a reinforcement and made lever pushing more likely.

The ABC (Antecedent, Behaviour, Consequence) of operant conditioning

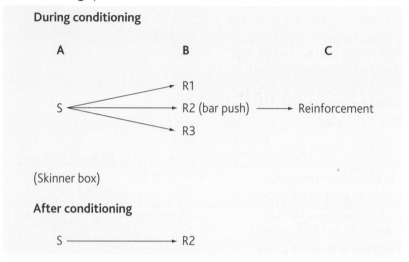

During conditioning

| A | B | C |

S — R1
— R2 (bar push) → Reinforcement
— R3

(Skinner box)

After conditioning

S ————————→ R2

Positive and negative reinforcement

Reinforcement can be positive or negative. Positive reinforcement occurs when a behaviour is followed by a pleasurable consequence. Negative reinforcement is when a behaviour results in the removal of, or avoidance of, unpleasant stimuli. For example, if a rat learns to jump from one side of a cage to another to avoid a mild electric shock, then the avoidance of the shock acts as a negative reinforcement.

Schedules of reinforcement

Skinner found that reinforcement does not have to be given each time an animal performs the desired behaviour. Reinforcement can be given in different schedules that change both the response and extinction rate.

The effect of schedules of reinforcement on response and extinction rates

Think about it

The schedules of reinforcement found in Skinner boxes may seem remote from real animal and human behaviour, but it is not. Look at the following examples of human reinforcement and decide which schedule they represent. Then look at the response and extinction rates in the table.

- Weekly pay
- Winning on a slot machine
- Being paid on commission

Schedule of reinforcement	Description	Effect on response rate and pattern	Effect on extinction rate
Continuous reinforcement	Reinforcement follows every single appropriate response.	Response rate is low but regular.	Extinction is very rapid.
Fixed ratio (FR)	A reinforcement is given after a fixed number of responses (e.g. one reinforcement is given after 10 responses).	Response rate is very high. There tends to be a lull after a reinforcement followed by rapid responding.	Extinction is fast.
Variable ratio (VR)	A reinforcement is given after a number of responses, but that number varies each time around an average value (e.g. one reinforcement is given after eight responses and another after 12).	Response rate is very high and steady.	Extinction is slow. VR tends to be the most resistant to extinction.
Fixed interval (FI)	A reinforcement is given after a fixed period provided the response is made at least once during the period (e.g. reinforcement is given every 40 seconds).	Response rate is low. There tends to be pause after each reinforcement with an increase in responding towards the end of an interval.	Extinction is fast.
Variable interval (VI)	A reinforcement is given after periods that vary around an average time provided the response is made at least once during any period (e.g. reinforcement is given after 30 seconds in one period and 50 in another).	Response rate is moderate. The pattern is more steady than FI, but there is some increase in responding as time since the last reinforcement increases.	Extinction is slow.

Primary and secondary reinforcement

A primary reinforcer is a stimulus that reinforces behaviour naturally. These are linked to biological needs and include food, water, avoidance of pain, and so on. Secondary reinforcers do not naturally act as reinforcers, but if they are linked to a primary reinforcer they can act as a reinforcer by themselves.

The role of classical and operant conditioning in the behaviour of non-human animals

Role in behaviour	Problem
Classical conditioning explains how animals learn to react to a new stimulus. Evidence suggests that it is involved in predator avoidance (e.g. learning of fear responses) and in foraging and diet selection (e.g. avoidance of bad food).	Classical conditioning does not explain differences in learning between species. Some species learn to avoid food sources very quickly, but others do not. It is easier to teach animals to avoid some stimuli than others. In classical conditioning, no new behaviour is learned. Animals only learn to produce an existing behaviour (e.g. fear) to a new stimulus.
Operant conditioning explains how new voluntary behaviours are learned and therefore how animals learn about new sources of food, water, etc. It also explains how animals can learn complex behaviour and sequences of behaviour. Laboratory studies also show how subtle changes in the environment (such as reinforcement schedules) can have dramatic effects on response rates and resistance to extinction.	Operant conditioning does not explain the role of cognitive factors in learning such as insight learning or learning by observation. It also fails to take into account animals' evolutionary history. It is much easier to teach one species one type of response than another (i.e. to run to avoid a shock rather than push a lever). It is also easier to teach one behaviour to one species rather than another. Operant conditioning theories of learning tend to emphasise external factors such as reinforcement rather than internal factors such as motivation.

Social learning

Many animals live in social groups and it is possible that individuals within the group do not learn everything by conditioning but by imitating the actions of others. This could be useful in a number of ways:

- Using imitation to solve problems. A famous study of a troop of macaque monkeys suggested that the behaviour of one monkey (washing sweet potatoes left in the sea by researchers) was soon imitated by others (Kawai, 1965). In the wild, some groups of chimpanzees have learned to crack open nuts, but others have not. There is evidence from captive chimpanzees that this complex behaviour, which requires the use of tools and precise manipulation, is learned by juveniles imitating adults.
- Imitation of diet. Rats are wary of new food sources. However, if they have contact with a rat that has eaten one food, when given the choice of two foods they choose the one eaten by the other rat (Galef, 1988).

Self-recognition

Self-recognition demonstrates intelligence because it implies understanding of the concept of self as being separate from the rest of the world. Humans have this ability and can recognise themselves in a mirror, but what happens when animals are shown their reflection in a mirror? Many species treat the image as a rival or threat. However, many of the great apes do not and eventually use the mirror image to groom themselves. In a study of self-recognition, dye was applied to one eyebrow

Think about it

Look at the short video called 'Brilliant Pink' on the website for the gorilla that uses sign language, Koko (www.koko.org).

- Does Koko seem to show self-recognition?
- Is this type of observational evidence conclusive?
- How could you test this experimentally?

and the opposite ear of chimpanzees. When shown their reflection in a mirror, the chimpanzees touched these areas far more than in the control (or baseline) condition. More recent evidence suggests that elephants may also be capable of self-recognition (Povinelli *et al.*, 1997).

Machiavellian intelligence

Social animals have to deal with others in the group. One sign of intelligence would be shown by the manipulation of other group members. This type of intelligence has been labelled Machiavellian intelligence. There is observational evidence of wild animals showing that they may manipulate others by using deception. For example, a juvenile baboon was observed sitting next to an adult who had dug up a root. The juvenile let out a scream and its mother, a dominant member, attacked the other adult. The juvenile then ate the root (Byrne and Whiten, 1988). However, this evidence is anecdotal and there are many ways of explaining it.

Evaluation

Much of the evidence of animal intelligence is ambiguous. There are usually several interpretations of the behaviour shown by the animal. The evidence in the natural environment is observational and therefore does not establish cause and effect. The experimental evidence from laboratory studies places animals in unnatural situations and often demands unnatural behaviour from them, so it may not be relevant to normal behaviour.

Human intelligence

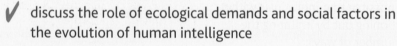

You need to know how to

✔ discuss the role of ecological demands and social factors in the evolution of human intelligence

✔ discuss intelligence testing and environmental and genetic factors associated with intelligence test performance

✔ discuss the role of culture in intelligence test scores.

Humans have evolved in a very short time (in evolutionary terms) to have large brains and an extraordinary level of intelligence. This raises a number of questions. Firstly, what is the relationship between brain size and intelligence? Also, what caused the rapid development of human brain size and intellect?

Human evolution

Humans are a species in a family of species called hominids that include the great apes. In considering the evolution of human intelligence, we should be aware of the environment of evolutionary adaptation (EEA) of our hominin and, eventually, human ancestors. The conditions were very different to those that humans live in today.

Brain size and intelligence

Brain size does seem to be related to intelligence. However, absolute brain size is not necessarily a measure of an animal's intelligence. For example, some whale species have a brain that is four or five times larger than the brain of humans. Large animals need large brains to control all the muscles and physiological processes in the body. Intelligence is governed by what proportion of the brain is 'left over' after controlling the body.

This can be assessed by the encephalisation quotient (EQ). EQ is calculated by comparing the ratio of the body to brain size across a range of similar species. The average EQ is 1. Any figure less than 1 indicates a lower-than-average brain size, whereas any figure above 1 suggests a higher-than-average brain size for the species. Chimpanzees, a highly intelligent species, have an EQ of 2.5, which suggests that they have a brain that is two-and-a-half times bigger than other mammals of the same size. Humans have an EQ of 7, the highest value of any species.

Relatively large brains do confer the advantage of increased intelligence. However, they also incur costs. Brains use a disproportionate amount of energy (the human brain uses 20 per cent of our energy but is only 2 per cent of our body weight).

Apply it

There has been a long-standing debate about whether brain size in humans is related to intelligence levels as measured by IQ tests. Use a search engine to explore some of the evidence and arguments around this debate.

Remember that the information you will be studying is largely correlational. What is one of the major problems of correlational data?

The role of ecological demands in the evolution of human intelligence

There are a number of ecological demands on hominins that may have caused the rapid evolution of human brain size and intelligence.

Factor	Evidence
Diet. As hominins moved from forests to grassland their diet changed from fruit and nuts to a more varied diet that included meat. Meat is a concentrated source of energy that may have allowed the expensive brain to grow.	There is a positive correlation between diet quality and brain size in primates. There is archaeological evidence that meat played an increasingly important part of hominin diet.
Foraging demands. The increasingly varied diet of hominins meant that finding food required more intelligence (increased memory demands, spatial awareness and the need to use tools).	The changes in tooth structure and tool sophistication in early hominins correspond to the increase in brain size.
Climate. The cooling of the environment led to both long-term changes and short-term seasonal variations in temperature and rainfall. One way of adapting to such changes is to increase intelligence.	There is evidence that EQ corresponds to the degree of seasonal variation in temperature.
Bipedalism. Being bipedal may have developed in order to increase field of vision in grassland, but it also leaves the hands free to manipulate and use objects. This requires greater intelligence.	Fossil evidence shows the development of the hands, and archaeological evidence shows ever greater tool sophistication.

Problems of ecological explanations of evolution of human intelligence

The climate change that led to changes in hominin diet and foraging affected all species in Africa at the time. Therefore, the major question that all of these factors fails to address is why it was *only* the hominins that showed a rapid increase in brain size and intelligence. Hominins do not have a unique EEA that can account for their unique intelligence. The other feature of the evidence above is that it is correlational. Just because two factors occur at the same time does not mean one caused the other.

The role of social factors in the evolution of human intelligence

If the evolution of increased brain size and intelligence is not due to ecological demands, perhaps the driving force behind it was social in origin. Humans are a social species, and living in large groups introduces demands on intelligence.

Factor	Evidence
Social complexity. Living in large groups has great advantages (for hunting, predator avoidance, etc.) but it also introduces demands on intelligence. Socially complex societies require memory of other group members (who are rivals, who are friends?) and the need to understand others.	Evidence from other groups of species suggests that there is a positive correlation between group size and EQ. Archaeological evidence suggests that hominins lived in ever more complex and large groups.
Sexual selection. The choice of mates for certain features affects the evolution of both physiology and behaviour in animals. It has been suggested that hominins started to make mate choice on the basis of intelligence, resulting in an ever more intelligent population.	It is very difficult to find any direct evidence of mate choice. It may be that the emergence of culture, which has no obvious extrinsic value, is a result of the sexual selection pressure to demonstrate intelligence.
Language. In many primate groups social cohesion is maintained by grooming. However, this is time consuming and limits group size to about 50. Hominin groups were about 150 in number. This is too big for physical grooming, so perhaps language developed to maintain cohesion.	There is a link between hominin group size and brain size and other features that are associated with language production.

Evaluation

The social explanations suffer from problems similar to those that affect the ecological explanations:

■ What was unique about the social complexity of early hominins that caused an increase in intelligence in them but not other great apes?

■ Of all the species in history, why should only hominins choose to select mates based on intelligence?

■ The evidence is correlational and does not show cause and effect. For example, did language develop as a result of increased intelligence, or did hominins need greater intelligence because they developed language?

Ecological dominance-social competition model

Both the ecological and social explanations of the evolution of human intelligence fail to explain why human evolution seems to be unique (Flinn, Geary and Ward, 2005). The ecological dominance-social competition model suggests that it was a unique combination of the two that led to the rapid evolution of human intelligence. The model suggests that hominins were the first species to achieve some degree of dominance over ecological factors. As a result, the population grew and the evolutionary pressure was now within groups and between groups of hominins. Greater intelligence was required to compete with others, resulting in an upward spiral of intelligence. This resulted in the highly intelligent modern humans.

This model is an elegant explanation of why our evolution is unique and is seen by some as the most comprehensive theory about the evolution of human intellectual abilities.

Intelligence testing

The original intelligence tests were based on norms obtained for particular age groups. Individuals could be compared to these norms to find their mental age. IQ is chronological age, divided by mental age, multiplied by 100. This way of defining and testing IQ works only for children who develop greater skills as they get older. However, the mental age of late adolescence and adulthood does not change with increasing age. Modern IQ test scores are therefore based on the normal distribution of IQ scores from very large samples.

There are two main problems of intelligence testing:

- There is not one generally agreed definition of what intelligence is (see the first part of this chapter, Theories of intelligence) so different tests may be measuring different abilities.
- At best, IQ tests measure a *sample* of a person's intelligence, not all of it.

There is debate about whether the differences found in IQ scores are caused by genetic factors or environmental cultural factors.

Genetic factors and intelligence test performance

One possible source of the differences in IQ scores could be genetic factors. However, it is not possible to manipulate the genes or environment of people. Therefore, evidence of genetic factors comes from correlations or natural experiments.

AQA Examiner's tip

Remember that the discussion about the contribution of genetic versus environmental factors is about the contribution to differences in intelligence, not total level of intelligence or all intelligent behaviour shown by people. The discussion is about the relative contribution of each factor to the *differences* in scores as measured by tests.

Evidence	Problems
Family studies generally show that individuals with a closer genetic relationship have better correlation of IQ levels.	This evidence does not establish whether genes are the cause of the better correlation. Individuals with close genetic links tend to share the same environment.
Twin studies act as a natural experiment because there are two types of twin – monozygotic (MZ) and dizygotic (DZ). Both types of twin share similar environments as they are brought up by the same family at the same time, but they differ in their genetic similarity. Many studies show that MZ twins show greater similarity in their IQ scores than DZ twins. This is the case when they are reared together and when they are reared apart.	MZ twins are treated as being more alike than DZ twins and therefore may be more similar because of environmental factors. Many of the studies of twins reared apart were of twins raised by different people in the same family, and they had lots of contact. Twin studies may lack population validity because they are not typical of the whole population.
Adoption studies compare the IQ scores of adopted children to both adoptive and natural parents. Most studies show a greater similarity to biological parents, suggesting a genetic component in intelligence test scores.	The policy of selective placement (placing children in backgrounds similar to those they came from) means that it is difficult to separate biological and environmental factors.

Environmental factors and intelligence test performance

Environmental factors can be biological or social.

Evidence	Problems
There is evidence that a number of environmental biological factors can influence intelligence. For example, exposure to some toxins such as lead can cause a reduction in intelligence levels in children. Similarly, an adverse prenatal environment caused by maternal behaviour such as smoking or drinking alcohol is linked to lower IQ levels and cognitive impairment. Some factors, such as breastfeeding, have been linked to increased IQ scores.	It is difficult to separate the effects of biological factors in the environment from other socioeconomic factors. For example, most researchers agree that malnutrition is associated with lower IQ levels. However, it is difficult to know whether the effect is caused by malnutrition itself or the social conditions that are linked to the malnutrition.
Many studies suggest that IQ levels tend to decrease with birth order (i.e. on average, first born have higher IQ levels than second born, and so on). This may be linked to levels of parental attention. Children who have been in school longer than those of a similar age have higher IQ scores, and the IQ scores of children tends to drop after the long summer break.	It is almost impossible to isolate one social variable from another. Therefore, although many social factors may affect intelligence test performance, it is difficult to measure the impact of any of them.
Environmental enrichment programmes can act as a natural experiment for the role of social stimulation. Enrichment programmes are typically aimed at children from financially deprived backgrounds and give the children a pre-school boost in intellectual stimulation. Comparisons of children who were on such programmes with those who were not suggest that environmental enrichment improves intellectual outcomes.	Environmental enrichment programmes typically have an immediate impact on intelligence test performance, but few studies have demonstrated a lasting impact. For example, IQ may be higher than comparable children not on the programme while still pre-school, but this difference is no longer evident after several years of schooling.

Culture and intelligence

There are cultural differences in the concept of intelligence. Intelligent behaviour in one culture or context is not regarded as intelligent in another. For example, in Western individualistic societies the emphasis in on individual skills such as problem solving, but in some collectivist cultures in Africa and Asia the emphasis is more on social skills (Sternberg and Kaufman, 1998). Sternberg (2004) argues that it is not just what is *regarded* as intelligence that differs, but intelligent behaviour in one context or culture is not in another.

Thinking about issues and debates

Nature and nurture

One of the major debates about intelligence centres on whether differences in test scores are due to genetic or environmental factors. This debate has been one of the fiercest in psychology because it has implications for many socially sensitive questions such as what are the causes of gender and ethnic group differences in intelligence test performance.

Cultural bias

The theories of intelligence and the tests of intelligence presented here all stem from Western conceptions and research. Although there is evidence to show that ideas about intelligence differ across cultures, there is still very little emphasis on alternative views.

Issues and debates in intelligence research

Psychology as science

Some of the topics discussed here are difficult to study in a traditionally scientific way. For example, many of the theories of what could have caused the evolution of human intelligence are supported by some circumstantial evidence. However, it is rarely possible to develop falsifiable tests of the theory.

Ethical issues

Some of the animal studies in this section have raised ethical concerns. For example, to ensure that the rats used in the Skinner box were motivated by food rewards, they were first starved to 60 per cent of their normal body weight. The study of human intelligence is socially sensitive.

Exam-style questions

Example 1

0 1 Describe **one** theory of intelligence. *(8 marks)*

0 2 Discuss genetic influences on intelligence test performance. *(16 marks)*

Example 2

0 3 Discuss the role of **two or more** factors in the evolution of human intelligence. *(24 marks)*

Example 3

0 4 Discuss the influence of environmental factors in intelligence test performance. *(24 marks)*

Example 4

0 5 Outline the role of operant conditioning in the behaviour of non-human animals. *(8 marks)*

0 6 Evaluate evidence for intelligence in non-human animals. *(16 marks)*

Sample answers

Suggested content for the other example questions for this section can be found at
www.nelsonthornes.com/psychology_answers

Example 4

| 0 | 5 |

Operant conditioning is learning by rewards and punishments. It is one of three ways in which animals (and people) learn. The other two ways are classical conditioning and social learning.

Not well focused on question here – scene setting does not get marks

Operant conditioning was first investigated by Skinner. Skinner put hungry cats or rats into a 'Skinner box 'where they would try to escape. The rat would try out lots of different behaviours and one typically would include pressing a lever which led to a food pellet being delivered to a hopper. Quickly, the rats learned to press the lever to receive food every time they were put in the box.

Skinner also investigated different kinds of consequences or reinforcements; behaviour which led to a reward (positive reinforcement) would be repeated. Behaviour which led to something nasty would be less likely to be repeated. So if a cat ventured into the neighbour's garden and was fed, it would repeat the behaviour. If it was attacked by the resident cat, it would be unlikely to go back (punishment).

Generally accurate and reasonably detailed

Operant conditioning is important in allowing animals to learn about important aspects of the environment such as finding food or shelter. However, it is learning by trial and error and it may be that social learning is less costly for the animal.

| 0 | 6 |

How can you tell if animals are intelligent? Many people think their dogs or cats are clever, but what kind of evidence would you need to prove they are? Psychologists have used different kinds of tests to establish animal intelligence including studies of self-recognition (can they recognise themselves in a mirror) and evidence of social learning which is learning by imitation and modelling similar to Bandura. One of the difficulties of the topic is that people do not agree on what intelligence is.

Useful critical statement

There are quite a lot of examples of social learning involving animals. One study, examining macaque monkeys, found that one monkey, Imo, started washing her sweet potatoes in the sea as the salt made them taste better.

This behaviour was quickly imitated by others (Kawai, 1965) suggesting intelligence. However, some critics have argued that the behaviour may not have been social learning or intelligence at all but simple operant conditioning – the better-tasting potatoes were a reward. This would be less clever than social learning. Either way, it seems pretty clever for the monkeys to have worked it out! Primates are probably one of the cleverest of species: after all, some people argue that apes should have human rights.

First piece of evidence and a little commentary. This is a legitimate criticism but it is not well expressed

There is also quite a lot of evidence suggesting that other animals/ mammals like rats are intelligent: for example, a rat will choose foods which they have seen another rat eat (Galef, 1988). This is clever because it has less danger attached than learning by trial and error. Social learning is part of the behavioural approach and it ignores differences caused by genetics. Some studies have shown that you can breed maze bright and maze dull rats suggesting that there are differences within species as well as between them.

Some consideration of why behaviour is considered intelligent here

A creditworthy point with some reference to approaches

Studies of self-recognition might provide better evidence for animal intelligence. The argument here is that if an animal recognises itself in the mirror then it must be clever. Studies have tested this in lots of different species usually putting some lipstick on the face of the animal and seeing if they touch the spot in the mirror or on their own face. Lots of animals have shown the ability to do this including chimpanzees and elephants. However, pigeons are also pretty good at it (and they are not clever, although Skinner taught them to play ping pong) and this suggests that experience with mirrors, like in caged birds, can ruin this as a test. It is difficult to carry out research with animals as studies rely on observation and obviously – animals can't talk.

AQA — Examiner's comments

In the answer to question 05 the candidate has presented an account that is generally accurate and reasonably detailed. They could have covered negative reinforcement or schedules rather than the small amount of evaluation at the end. This answer would achieve a good basic/reasonable-band mark.

In the answer to question 06, the three pieces of evidence, some commentary and basic reference to issues and debates would be worth a mark in the basic/reasonable band.

Basic/reasonable band mark overall.

8   Cognition and development

Development of thinking

You need to know how to

✔ describe theories of cognitive development including those of Piaget and Vygotsky

✔ evaluate theories in relation to evidence

✔ understand how these have been applied to education.

AQA   Examiner's tip

A lot of terminology is used in this section to describe the ideas about how children's cognitive development occurs. If you are able to use these key terms, it demonstrates your knowledge to the examiner. This alone may lift your AO1 mark from basic to reasonable, or from reasonable to effective.

Theories of cognitive development

Key theory

Piaget's theory of cognitive development

Piaget was struck by the way children's abilities seem to develop at approximately the same ages. For example, they will take their first steps, say their first words, and develop object permanence at around 10 months old. They will be capable of performing logical operations like conserving and decentring at around seven years. This made him think that cognitive development occurs as a process of maturation, i.e. children will not be able to perform certain tasks until they are old enough. This is known as the readiness approach. He outlined four stages of development through which all children progress (see below).

He believed that children are like little scientists – they find out about the world by experimenting on it, not by being told about it. He called this 'discovery learning'.

For any object or situation a child will have a schema (a well-defined sequence of physical or mental actions) that tells them what to do. It is a little pocket of information that can be physical (like sucking when anything is put near its mouth) or mental (like recognising what the word 'mummy' refers to). As the child encounters new objects or concepts, they will try to incorporate them into their existing schemata. If they can do this without the schema changing, it is known as assimilation. If the schema has to be modified to deal with the new object, it is known as accommodation. If the child cannot assimilate or accommodate the new object, they will be in a state of disequilibrium until they can discover what to do with it.

Apply it

There are several types of conservation tasks, including number, volume, weight and length. Children find some easier to understand than others, so the process of being able to conserve does not happen suddenly. Familiarise yourself with the procedures for each one of these conservation tasks.

Piaget's four stages of cognitive development

The sensorimotor stage (0–2 years)	This stage is divided into six sub-stages. The child's knowledge of the world is based only on their senses. The only schemata that the child has when they are born are a few reflexes, and their thinking is egocentric. During this stage the child will develop object permanence.
The pre-operational stage (2–7 years)	There are two sub-stages in the pre-operational stage. The child has developed language, and can represent their world with symbols. They are still egocentric and their thinking will also demonstrate animism and artificialism. The child cannot yet perform conservation tasks.
Concrete operational stage (7–11 years)	The child can now conserve, so they understand class inclusion and know that number, weight and volume stay constant and decentre, so they become less egocentric. Mental operations can be performed, and logical problems can be solved, but only if they relate to real objects.
Formal operational stage (11+ years)	The child can now use abstract reasoning to solve hypothetical problems.

Evidence for Piaget's theory

- Piaget has conducted many experiments on children of different ages to demonstrate how their thinking changes as they grow older. These experiments support the stages of development that he outlined.
- He demonstrated an infant's lack of object permanence by covering a toy with a cloth. As the children stopped reaching for it, this proved they had no mental schema that things continue to exist even when they are out of sight.
- His mountains experiment proved that young children are egocentric, as they cannot visualise the scene from another's (the doll's) perspective.
- His conservation experiments showed that children under seven fail to realise that the quantity of an object remains the same even though its appearance changes.
- The previous two experiments prove that children's thinking changes fundamentally at around seven years old.
- The task of working out which variables affect the swing of a pendulum has been used to show that children's cognitive abilities progress further at around 11.
- The fact that all children reach developmental milestones at around the same time and pass through the stages in the same order despite cultural differences, suggests Piaget was right to think that a process of maturation was involved.

Criticisms of Piaget's theory

- Piaget underestimated the ages at which children progress from one stage to the next. This is largely due to flaws in his experimental procedures.
- Bower and Wishart (1972) showed that infants acquired object permanence younger than Piaget suggested by turning off the lights rather than covering the toy with a cloth.
- Rose and Blank (1974) argued that the pre-transformation question in the conservation experiments misled children, causing their incorrect answers.
- McGarrigle and Donaldson (1974) altered the appearance of objects in a more meaningful way for the children and also found that they could conserve at a younger age than Piaget claimed.
- Hughes (1975) used his policeman doll experiment to show that children can decentre younger than Piaget suggested.
- Gelman (1979) showed that four-year-olds can adjust their speech when talking to two-year-olds and blindfolded people to accommodate their different needs. Piaget's theory would not predict this.
- Dasen (1994) argued that there are cultural differences in how children pass through Piaget's stages.
- A point made by Meadows (1995) is that Piaget ignored the influence of other people on a child's development.

Key theory

Vygotsky's theory of cognitive development

Vygotsky saw children as apprentices, who learn about the world by interacting with experts. He suggested that all learning is social in nature, because children learn in informal situations even more than at school from teachers. They see how parents and other family members (the experts) solve problems, and by interacting with those around them children internalise these problem-solving skills and develop their own cognitive abilities.

Language is crucial in cognitive development. According to Vygotsky, it serves two purposes: social speech and intellectual speech. Social speech is useful for asking questions and understanding answers. Intellectual speech is thinking aloud. When young, children voice what they are thinking, but when they get to around seven or eight years old they internalise their thoughts, which enables them to move from simple to complex reasoning tasks. Intellectual speech means they can solve problems alone, when prior to this they had to rely on the help of others.

Vygotsky saw how children could perform much better with the help and guidance of experts than they could alone. He referred to the gap between what a child could do alone and what they could potentially do with help as the zone of proximal development (ZPD). This was the potential of the child.

Scaffolding relates to the help children receive from parents and other experts around them. When the child is learning something new or difficult, the help they receive is quite substantial. But as the child develops their abilities, the help they receive is varied and then withdrawn until the child can complete the task entirely alone. The scaffolding supports the child's progress through its ZPD, bridging the gap between their current level of development and their potential.

Evaluation of Vygotsky's theory

A lot of evidence from studies shows that Vygotsky's ideas were correct. This evidence suggests that his theory was valid.

- Nunes (1992) studied Brazilian street urchins, revealing their mathematical skills developed from interacting with adults as vendors. They had no formal schooling but had learned via culture and context, highlighting the social nature of learning.
- Greenfield and Lave (1982) found evidence of the same process in Mexican girls learning to weave by watching and interacting with adults. The women provided easy tasks first, and then harder ones as the girls became more adept.
- Wood and Middleton (1975) observed mothers teaching their four-year-old children to complete a jigsaw puzzle. They identified five types of scaffolding used. The most helpful was that which adapted to the child's successes and failures.
- Moss (1992) similarly identified three types of scaffolding naturally used by mothers when helping their children to construct a tower from building blocks.
- Berk (1994) found that 60 per cent of six-year-olds spend time talking to themselves while solving maths problems. He also found that those who talked to themselves the most performed better the following year. This supports the idea that language is a cognitive tool.

Despite the plentiful support for this theory, one way in which it is lacking is that it fails to take any account of biological factors that might have a bearing on cognitive development.

- Vygotsky himself did not make a clear distinction between different types of social interaction (e.g. general encouragement versus specific instructions) although others have studied this.
- His ideas about the importance of language contradict Piaget's ideas. Piaget thought that language reflected cognitive ability, whereas Vygotsky thought it improved cognitive ability.

- Whereas Piaget thought that children discover things for themselves, Vygotsky emphasised the role experts play in children's cognitive development.
- Like Piaget's theory, however, Vygotsky's ideas have had many implications in education.

Piaget's theory of cognitive development applied to education

The readiness approach: children can only progress from one stage to the next when they are mature enough to deal with new concepts. There is an order in which they must learn things, according to which stage they are in. For example, concrete before abstract problems.

Discovery learning: children learn from exploring and interacting with their environment. This means the teacher needs to create disequilibrium in the child by setting challenging tasks, then giving the child the opportunity to solve the tasks themselves.

The role of the teacher: to understand which stage of development children are in, to set tasks they find intrinsically motivating, and to facilitate the progress from one stage to the next.

Commentary

- The first problem of trying to apply Piaget's theory to education is that he underestimated children's abilities. This means that they will be able to progress at a younger age than Piaget suggested.
- He downplayed the role of language in education. Others have indicated that language and social interaction are crucial in developing children's cognitive skills. Piaget disagreed with this.
- In a review of five studies, Brainerd (2003) found that discovery learning was less successful than guided learning in teaching conservation concepts.

Vygotsky's theory of cognitive development applied to education

Language and social interaction: these are important components in the development of children. This means that guided learning plays a fundamental role in education. 'What a child can do with assistance today, they can do by themselves tomorrow.'

Peer mentoring: children learn from 'experts', who can be anyone with more knowledge than them. In a formal environment, there will be older or more advanced children who can act as experts. The more advanced child will also benefit from passing on their knowledge to the younger or less able ones (Tzuriel and Shamir, 2007).

The zone of proximal development: teachers need to be aware of the child's current ability and their potential. They can then provide activities that will continually stretch the child, but not so far that it is beyond the child's ZPD.

Scaffolding (Vygotsky's idea, developed by Bruner): children require the help of others (e.g. teachers) to reach their potential. The help they receive is most effective if it is pitched just above the child's current ability, and varied or withdrawn in line with the advances the child makes.

Commentary

- Evidence has shown that Vygotsky was correct in suggesting that teachers are able to assist performance, and thus development through scaffolding.
- Wood and Middleton (1975) found that mothers offered different levels of help to their children when they were doing puzzles. This is

Examiner's tip

Remember that a perfectly acceptable way of gaining AO2 marks is to compare one theory with another theory. As you will have read, the last three points in the list do just that. They compare and contrast Vygotsky's theory of cognitive development with that of Piaget.

Apply it

There are a lot of similarities between the theories of Piaget and Vygotsky. Construct a grid with a column for Piaget and one for Vygotsky. Down the side, write key ideas that appear in either of their theories and tick the Piaget and Vygotsky columns if they include it. This helps you to remember when an idea is relevant to just one or both psychologists, e.g. 'Language is important for cognitive development in children': Vygotsky – tick, Piaget – no tick.

the strategy that Vygotsky suggested was most effective in developing children's abilities.

- Gardner and Gardner (1969) have shown the success of instruction in the development of cognitive functioning in chimpanzees.

Development of moral understanding

You need to know how to

 describe Kohlberg's theory of moral understanding

 discuss this theory in relation to evidence.

Key study

The development of moral understanding (Kohlberg, 1963)

In order to investigate how moral understanding develops, Kohlberg posed 10 moral dilemmas to a cross-section of American boys aged 7, 10, 13 and 16. Each moral dilemma presented a situation in which a person or persons acted in a morally questionable way. The boys were then asked to comment on the behaviour of each character. Kohlberg analysed these quantitative data and classified the answers into three levels of moral reasoning that formed the basis of his theory (see below).

Perhaps the best-known of Kohlberg's moral dilemmas is the story of Heinz:

In Europe, a woman was dying of cancer. A drug that might save her had recently been developed by a doctor who lived in the same town. The doctor was charging $2,000 for the drug, even though it only cost him $200 to make. The woman's husband, Heinz, could not afford $2,000. He asked everyone he knew if he could borrow the money, but he was still unable to get enough. He asked the doctor if he would sell him the drug cheaper, or let him pay later, but the doctor refused. Heinz could not think how to pay for the drug, so he broke in and stole it.

After hearing this story, the boys would be asked if Heinz had done the right thing, and to explain their reasoning. Kohlberg found that as the boys got older, their moral understanding became more sophisticated, but he did not tie their development to specific ages like Piaget's theory of moral development had. What he concluded was that 7-year-olds were dominated by level one reasoning, but by 13, the majority had reached level two (see the table overleaf).

AQA Examiner's tip

When evaluating a theory like Kohlberg's, you can use his own studies as supporting evidence. But remember, if you are asked to discuss a theory, do not *describe* the study. You use a study to show that the conclusions support the theory or that the methods employed by the researcher were flawed, which might invalidate the theory (all of which is AO2/3).

AQA Examiner's tip

You do not need to learn the detailed content of the dilemmas. One of the dilemmas is described here for context.

Kohlberg's theory of moral development

- Children's morality is characterised by having rules imposed on them by authority figures. This is the pre-conventional level of morality. As they mature, they internalise the laws and regulations of their social group. This is the level of conventional morality. Finally, the level of post-conventional morality occurs when individuals are able to use their own principles to make moral judgements.

- Within each level, there are two stages. Kohlberg suggested that a person's reasoning will be consistent across different situations. That means, if they answer one of the moral dilemmas with an answer typical of stage four reasoning, they will answer all the rest using stage four reasoning too.

- Kohlberg did not believe that an adult will inevitably pass through all six stages of moral development. Most people stick at level two. When he studied adults in their thirties, Kohlberg only found 10 per cent of people demonstrate level three reasoning, and very few people at all reach stage six.

Kohlberg's levels of moral development

Level 1: Pre-conventional Moral rules are imposed by authority figures (i.e. adults)	**Stage 1**: Punishment and obedience orientation	Behaviour is based on the avoidance of punishment. It is morally wrong if you receive punishment for it.
	Stage 2: Individualism, instrumental purpose and exchange	What is good is determined by what brings rewards from others (adults).
Level 2: Conventional The moral rules of the social group (civil or religious laws) are accepted and internalised	**Stage 3**: Mutual interpersonal expectations (good boy orientation)	The child internalises the ideas of right and wrong from its social group. A behaviour is good if others approve of it and it makes you well liked.
	Stage 4: Law and order orientation	Focus shifts from the family to wider society. Moral behaviour is determined by obeying the law.
Level 3: Post conventional Moral judgement is based on one's own values and principles	**Stage 5**: Social contract orientation	Although laws are still respected, the individual knows that sometimes they do not protect human rights. Morality is therefore determined by democratically accepted principles.
	Stage 6: Universal ethical principles	The individual acts in accordance with their own beliefs and conscience, regardless of the majority view.

Evaluation

As Kohlberg used his own study for support, any flaws in his method would have an impact on the validity of his theory:

- The moral dilemmas are hypothetical scenarios. People may not think or act in the same way if faced with the actual situation themselves. Santrock (1975) found that whether children would cheat or not in reality could not be predicted by their level of moral reasoning.

- People do not act consistently. In one situation, they may use stage five reasoning, but in another they may use stage four reasoning. This was demonstrated by Denton and Krebs (1990) with students, whose reasoning changed in different contexts.

- Kohlberg's dilemmas require people to compare two negative events (e.g. death of wife versus breaking the law). Eisenberg argued that a better understanding of moral development would be to use pro-social scenarios, such as getting a child to choose between their own needs and the needs of others.

It has been suggested that Kohlberg's theory is ethnocentric (i.e. the conclusions were drawn without actually testing them but by using research based on one culture):

- Because the participants in Kohlberg's studies were American, it has been argued that the moral levels are based on the idealised views of an industrialised society. In other cultures, putting the laws of society above one's own values is considered to be morally superior.

- Isawa (1992) showed that although Americans and Japanese display the same stage of reasoning in the Heinz dilemma, their explanations for their reasons are culturally determined.
- Kohlberg referred to universal principles, but research has suggested that moral understanding is not universal. Snarey and Keljo (1991) found that post-conventional morality occurs mainly in industrialised societies, and much less in rural communities.

Kohlberg has also been criticised for his theory being androcentric (i.e. based only on an investigation of male behaviour):

- The first participants of Kohlberg's studies were all male. This might have been why his research tends to show that women are morally inferior. This clearly indicates alpha bias.
- Gilligan (1992) argued that Kohlberg took a male view of morality, and ignored the way women are more concerned with care than justice. Because his view was oriented towards the male perspective, women will inevitably underperform by his standards.

Development of social cognition

> **You need to know how to**
>
> ✔ discuss how children develop a sense of self, including the theory of mind
>
> ✔ discuss the development of children's understanding of others, including perspective taking (Selman)
>
> ✔ describe and evaluate biological explanations of social cognitions, including the role of the mirror neuron system.

The development of the sense of self

How children progress to having a sense of self is a combination of nature and nurture, that is, innate abilities and interaction with the environment.

- Fantz (1961) showed that neonates have an innate preference for looking at faces. Several studies have shown that from a few days old, they are able to distinguish their mothers from other women. This suggests that children are innately capable of recognising differences in people.
- Infants imitate gestures that they see others performing. (The fact that other primates also do this suggests a biological aspect to this behaviour.)
- Through constant observation of and interaction with parents, children learn to direct their gaze where others are gazing or pointing. They also learn to direct others by gazing and pointing themselves.
- The development of object permanence at around 10 months old (see page 107) helps the child to realise that other things continue to exist in their own right, even when they are out of the child's own field of perception. This will help the child to see itself as separate from other people and objects.
- The development of language helps children to distinguish themselves from others by creating a way of referring to themselves and others. So by 18 months old, the child will be able to use personal pronouns like 'me' and 'you', 'my' and 'her' (Clarke-Stewart *et al.*, 1985).

- By two years old the child will have developed a sense of self. They will be able to point to themselves in photographs, refer to themselves (e.g. 'That is me'), and know how they can influence others for their own purposes.

Key study

Self-recognition in children (Lewis and Brooks-Gunn, 1979)

Red dye was put on infants' noses by their mothers while pretending to clean their faces. When the infants were shown a mirror, they showed no sign of self-recognition. If they had recognised themselves, they would have realised that the red dye on their noses was odd, and investigated it. Lewis and Brooks-Gunn found that from 15 months old, children will try to rub off the red dye because they realise it should not be there. In other words, they know what they look like and recognise when there is something unusual about their appearance. This study has also been conducted on other animals. Only the great apes and, interestingly, elephants have demonstrated behaviour that suggests self-recognition.

Theory of mind

Once children have developed a sense of self, they know that they are different from others. Much later, children come to realise that others may think of them differently to how they think of themselves. This understanding, that others have different thoughts and perceptions from themselves, is known as the theory of mind. It is not until the child is around four years old that they will fully grasp the idea that other people know things that they do not, and that they may know things that others do not. This was found by Wimmer and Perner (1983) in a study in which chocolate is hidden from a doll, and the child is asked what the doll will do. This is why two-year-old children will answer a question over the phone by nodding instead of speaking – they do not understand that the person on the other end of the phone does not know what they are doing. This mistake is tied to the inability to decentre (Piaget).

A study by Baron-Cohen et al. (1985) showed how theory of mind is absent in most autistic children.

Key study

The false belief task (Baron-Cohen, Lesley and Frith, 1985)

This study was an extension of Wimmer and Perner's (1983) unexpected transfer task given to children. In the Baron-Cohen et al. version a scenario is put to the children and then they are asked three questions.

There are two dolls, Sally and Ann. Sally put a marble into her basket, then went out to play. Ann took the marble from the basket, while she was outside, and put it into a box.

The three questions are:

1 When Sally comes back in, where will she look for the marble? (The belief question)
2 Where is the marble really? (The reality question)
3 Where was the marble in the beginning? (The memory question)

If you have a theory of mind, you will realise that you know something that Sally does not (i.e. the marble has been moved from where she left it). So your answer to the first question will reflect what Sally knows, not what you know.

Baron-Cohen *et al.* presented this scenario not just to normal 4- and 5-year-old children, but also to 11-year-old children with Down's syndrome and 12-year-old autistic children. They found that all the children in all three groups answered questions two and three correctly. There were differences with the answer to the first question however: 85 per cent of the normal children and 86 per cent of the Down's syndrome children got the question correct, but only 20 per cent of the autistic children got it right. These figures represent the percentage of each group of children that had developed a theory of mind.

Think about validity

What is the point of investigating the behaviour or capabilities of children who have an abnormal development? Ask yourself the same question about studies using non-human animals. Does this serve any useful purpose in our investigations of the sense of self? Maybe it helps us to unravel the nature–nurture debate. Commentary like this will gain you evaluative (AO2/3) credit.

Evaluation of research into the theory of mind

■ There is a lot of support from studies of different types that have all indicated there is some sort of developmental milestone that leads children to a theory of mind when they get to around four years old.

■ It has further been shown that the abilities children display earlier in their development can indicate whether they will attain theory of mind earlier or later than normal, or not at all. Baron-Cohen *et al.* (1996) gave five theory of mind tests to 16,000 18-month-olds. Nearly all children who failed the tests were diagnosed with autism before they were four.

On the other hand, the accuracy of this milestone has been questioned by some psychologists who have highlighted problems with the procedures used in some studies:

■ Siegal and Beattie (1991) argued that the question, 'Where will Sally look for her marble?' could be interpreted by young children to mean 'Where should Sally look for her marble?' This means that children could achieve a theory of mind at an earlier age than research has shown, but the way the question was asked was linguistically ambiguous to the children.

■ In a similar demonstration of theory of mind (known as the appearance reality task), Saltmarsh, Mitchell and Robinson (1995) showed that how the task is presented will have an impact on whether children seem to have a theory of mind or not.

Selman – perspective theory

Robert Selman argued that for effective social communication, it is important for people to be able to take other people's perspectives (to understand how other people view a situation differently). This, like the theory of mind, is not something that children can do at a very young age, but it develops as they get older. Unlike the theory of mind, Selman (1976) suggested it is a gradual process that takes many years to develop. By presenting social dilemmas to children and assessing their answers, he was able to outline a series of five stages for the development of perspective taking. The dilemmas involved scenarios like having to make a choice between disobeying your father and helping a friend or rescuing a cat from a tree.

Selman's stages of development

Stage	Age	Stage name	Stage description
1	3–6 years	Undifferentiated perspective-taking	Children do recognise that the self and others are different, with different thoughts and feelings, but they are not able to distinguish between their thoughts and those of others.
2	5–9 years	Social informational perspective-taking	Children understand that others may have a different perspective because they have access to different information.
3	7–12 years	Social reflective perspective-taking	Children develop the ability to see things from others' viewpoints, including seeing their own thoughts from another person's perspective.
4	10–15 years	Third-party perspective-taking	Children are able to remove themselves mentally from a two-person situation, and understand how it appears from the perspective of a third 'onlooker'.
5	14 years–adult	Societal perspective-taking	The individual now understands that the view of a third party can be influenced by a variety of factors, like cultural norms.

Evaluation

- There are a number of studies that support the view that children develop an increasingly sophisticated ability to take someone else's perspective, including a five-year longitudinal study by Gurucharri, Phelps and Selman (1984). Later research also shows there is good reliability for the evidence gained from such studies.

- Considering the usual criticism of the lack of validity of people's responses to hypothetical dilemmas, Selman *et al.* (1983) compared the responses of a group of girls with their actual behaviour in a social situation. They found that those who had better perspective-taking skills communicated more effectively in a group discussion, which is what would be predicted.

- On the other hand, Kurdek (1977) claimed that perspective-taking is a complex social skill, not capable of being neatly displayed in a table of five stages.

- Jarvela and Hakkinen (2003) make the point that Selman's stages are not able to explain the new kinds of relationships people have with the use of modern technology now. It is quite likely that the normal dynamics of social exchanges do not apply. Internet exchanges are not as personal as face-to-face exchanges. Consequently, Selman's model may have limited usefulness.

Two contributing factors to a child's ability to understand the perspective of other people are their cognitive development and their early family experiences.

- Keating and Clark (1980) examined the relationship between perspective-taking and Piaget's stages of cognitive development. They found that pre-operational children fit into the first of Selman's stages, those in the concrete operational stage are in stages two and three, and those who have reached the formal operational stage are in Selman's stages four and five. This reinforces the view that the ability to understand others might be a maturational process tied in with cognitive development.

- Children who have been badly treated are less empathetic than normal (Bolger, Patterson and Kupersmidt, 1998). It is thought that this is due to their poor ability to take others' perspectives. This in turn might be because they have observed socially inadequate behaviour in their parents (who are their primary role models) and because they have not had a very high level of verbal communication from their parents.

Biological explanation of social cognition

Psychologists have attempted to determine whether there is a biological basis for social cognitions. They have done this by studying the brain functioning of normal people and those who have abnormalities that impact on their social behaviour. The aim has been to discover which structure or structures may be involved. In normal people, the use of brain scanning has revealed the significance of certain areas of the brain which play a role in social cognition. In people suffering from some sort of psychopathology, evidence has also come from changes in behaviour following operations, and from post mortems.

Evidence from normally functioning brains

- The amygdala, which is a structure found in the limbic system, has been shown to be important in recognising and interpreting emotions in others. This needs to function properly if we are to be able to understand the feelings of others.

- The frontal cortex is involved in our social decision-making. It is active when we are problem-solving and working out behavioural strategies.

- Ley and Bryden (1979) presented images of faces to the right and the left hemispheres of the brain separately with the method used to test split-brain patients. They found that the right hemisphere is better at judging emotions than the left.

Evidence from abnormally functioning brains

- Scott *et al.* (1997) reported the case of a woman known as D.R., who sustained bilateral damage to her amygdala. Following this, she was unable to distinguish people's emotions either from their facial expressions or the tone of their voice.

- A lack of activity in the amygdala has been revealed in psychopaths, who demonstrate a lack of empathy and failure to recognise suffering in others. This is thought to be the cause of their harming people apparently without good cause.

The role of mirror neurons in social cognition

Key study

Analysis of the motor cortex of macaque monkeys (DiPellegrino *et al.*, 1992)

In 1992, research by DiPellegrino *et al.* into the brains of macaque monkeys identified what they called mirror neurons. They made the following discoveries:

- When a monkey made a goal-directed movement, like reaching for a peanut, 17 per cent of the neurons in the F5 region of the motor cortex fired.

- If the monkey observed another monkey making the same movements, the same neurons would fire. (This was discovered by accident.)

- This would also happen if the monkey observed a human reaching for a peanut.

- But neurons would not fire if the monkey observed just random movements. The movements had to be goal directed; (e.g. reaching for a peanut, not just waving the arms about).

- The observer monkey did not need to see the movements of another monkey in order for the mirror neurons to fire; they would also fire if it heard the goal-directed activity, that is, the cracking of the nut.

AQA Examiner's tip

When you come to evaluate evidence such as that presented here, remember to comment on the method used. Some methods produce more valid findings than others. The strength of evidence such as this is that it is high in credibility due to the use of objective scientific methods. Brain scanning and post-mortems, which can clearly identify malfunctioning areas, are not open to interpretation in the same way that observational research is.

It would seem that the function of mirror neurons is twofold. If neurons fire when we perform an action and when we observe others performing the same action, it seems that they must play a role in the imitation of others – a key part of social learning theory. Secondly, they must facilitate the understanding of others' actions, or empathy.

Evidence supporting the mirror neuron system

- Rizzolatti *et al.* (2006) found that if we observe others in pain, the same parts of our brain are active as when we are in pain ourselves.
- It has also been found that there is less activity in the mirror neuron system in people who score low on measures of empathy (Gazzola *et al.*, 2006) and in autistics (Oberman *et al.*, 2003).
- Lacoboni *et al.* (2005) showed that context is important in the activity of mirror neurons. This implies there is an understanding of the meaning of behaviour, it is not just imitation that is happening.

Criticisms of the motor neuron system

- The accuracy of studies on monkeys cannot be replicated on humans. To study human brains EEG and fMRI machines are used, which record activity in areas of the brain, not single cells.
- It is hard to generalise from a simple species to a more complex one, as social cognition is more developed in humans, e.g. the ability to deceive others.
- Social cognition is a broad area. It is unlikely that a single part of the brain is responsible for all social behaviour.
- Biological explanations are by their nature reductionist. They overlook social psychological explanations of behaviour.

Thinking about issues and debates

Gender bias

Accusations of gender bias have been aimed at theories of moral development produced by both Kohlberg and Gilligan. This was due to their selection of participants and choice of moral dilemmas in each of their studies. This bias inevitably raises issues of validity regarding the application of their theories to both sexes.

Determinism

Piaget's views about cognitive development are quite pessimistic in that he believed that children's cognitive development is limited (or determined) by their ages. He found it hard to accept that children could develop faster than maturity would allow, with the consequence that there would be no point trying to advance them through special tuition. Clearly this has implications for the role of education.

Issues and debates in cognitive development research

Socially sensitive research

Kohlberg's assessment of what constitutes higher-level moral reasoning has been criticised as having a Western view. As a consequence of this, we may regard collectivist cultures as being morally inferior. His research using moral dilemmas involved an imposed etic. But what Kohlberg reasoned was conventional morality might just as easily be seen as higher reasoning by other cultures.

Psychology as a science

As thought is an abstract concept, investigating how children think raises problems with operationalising the variables. With controlled experiments, however, Piaget has yielded results that are thought to be valid. He was able to imply how children's thinking changes with age by constructing clever problems for them to solve. However, children are not as good at explaining themselves, so his use of interviews may have provided results that were not entirely valid.

Exam-style questions

Example 1

0 1 Describe **one** theory of cognitive development. *(8 marks)*

0 2 Consider ways in which research into cognitive development has been applied to education. *(16 marks)*

Example 2

0 3 Outline and evaluate Vygotsky's theory of cognitive development. *(24 marks)*

Example 3

0 4 Discuss research into the development of moral understanding. *(24 marks)*

Example 4

0 5 Discuss the development of children's understanding of others, including perspective-taking. *(24 marks)*

Cognition and development

Sample answers

Suggested content for the other example questions for this section can be found at
www.nelsonthornes.com/psychology_answers

Example 3

| 0 | 4 |

> Kohlberg's theory of moral development comprises three levels, each with two stages. Like Piaget, he thought that children's moral understanding becomes more sophisticated as they get older, but unlike Piaget, he didn't tie his stages to particular ages. He called the first level the pre-conventional level. In this level children are concerned firstly with avoiding punishment (stage 1) and then with obtaining rewards (stage 2). The second level is the conventional level of morality, and sees the child firstly influenced by the need to gain social approval (stage 3) and then by following the law and other rules (stage 4). The third level is the post-conventional morality, and the person's reasoning is dominated by democratically accepted principles (stage 5) and his or her own values and conscience (stage 6).
>
> There is support for this model. Kohlberg presented boys with moral dilemmas such as the story of a man who decided to steal a drug to save his wife's life. That meant breaking the law, and the boys had to decide if he had done the right thing. He used their answers to develop his theory.
>
> But there are criticisms of Kohlberg's work. The fact that he only used boys in his study has led people to argue that his study and his theory are gender biased. Using the boys' answers and constructing a theory means that it won't apply to girls. Indeed using the sort of moral dilemmas Kohlberg used shows women have a lower level of morality than men. Gilligan has studied morality in women, using dilemmas that have greater significance to them than men. She found women are just as moral as men, which means Kohlberg's criteria were androcentric. This makes his model unethical because it could be harmful to women.
>
> It has also been argued that this theory is ethnocentric. It is based on a Western view of what is moral. In collectivist cultures it is thought that putting the state higher than yourself is the most moral. Kohlberg values individual principles as higher, and this is disputed in different parts of the world.

This is an accurate but brief description of a model. Further description (AO1) is needed though, either from a second model or at least one study.

This paragraph makes a good point related to an issue. The reference to ethics needs elaboration.

Good. It is useful to point out that it only becomes gender biased if the theory based on boys is applied to girls.

This section would be improved if there was more detail about the difference between the Kohlberg and Gilligan dilemmas.

This paragraph also relates to an issue, although quite briefly. A sentence explaining what is meant by imposed etic would gain further evaluative (AO2/3) credit.

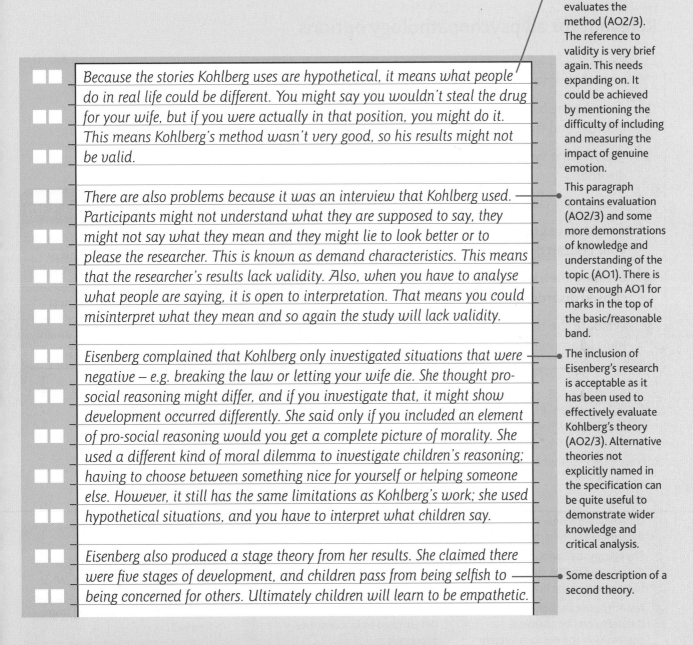

Because the stories Kohlberg uses are hypothetical, it means what people do in real life could be different. You might say you wouldn't steal the drug for your wife, but if you were actually in that position, you might do it. This means Kohlberg's method wasn't very good, so his results might not be valid.

This paragraph evaluates the method (AO2/3). The reference to validity is very brief again. This needs expanding on. It could be achieved by mentioning the difficulty of including and measuring the impact of genuine emotion.

There are also problems because it was an interview that Kohlberg used. Participants might not understand what they are supposed to say, they might not say what they mean and they might lie to look better or to please the researcher. This is known as demand characteristics. This means that the researcher's results lack validity. Also, when you have to analyse what people are saying, it is open to interpretation. That means you could misinterpret what they mean and so again the study will lack validity.

This paragraph contains evaluation (AO2/3) and some more demonstrations of knowledge and understanding of the topic (AO1). There is now enough AO1 for marks in the top of the basic/reasonable band.

Eisenberg complained that Kohlberg only investigated situations that were negative – e.g. breaking the law or letting your wife die. She thought pro-social reasoning might differ, and if you investigate that, it might show development occurred differently. She said only if you included an element of pro-social reasoning would you get a complete picture of morality. She used a different kind of moral dilemma to investigate children's reasoning; having to choose between something nice for yourself or helping someone else. However, it still has the same limitations as Kohlberg's work; she used hypothetical situations, and you have to interpret what children say.

The inclusion of Eisenberg's research is acceptable as it has been used to effectively evaluate Kohlberg's theory (AO2/3). Alternative theories not explicitly named in the specification can be quite useful to demonstrate wider knowledge and critical analysis.

Eisenberg also produced a stage theory from her results. She claimed there were five stages of development, and children pass from being selfish to being concerned for others. Ultimately children will learn to be empathetic.

Some description of a second theory.

AQA ~ Examiner's comments

Overall, the evaluation is reasonable. Several points are made, but they do not go into a lot of detail. This answer would achieve a mark in the basic/reasonable band.

9 Psychopathology

Explanations, diagnosis and treatment – an overview

Relevant for all psychopathology options

> **You need to know how to**
>
> ✔ describe the biological and psychological models of mental disorder and the explanations they put forward
>
> ✔ describe the systems used to diagnose and classify mental disorder
>
> ✔ describe the clinical characteristics of **your chosen disorder**
>
> ✔ discuss issues relating to diagnosis and classification of **your chosen disorder**
>
> ✔ evaluate the explanations and models in relation to **your chosen disorder**
>
> ✔ evaluate the therapies for **your chosen disorder** in terms of their appropriateness and effectiveness.

> **AQA Examiner's tip**
>
> You only have to study *one* disorder in detail, *either* schizophrenia *or* depression *or* obsessive-compulsive disorder (OCD) *or* phobic disorders. Whichever you study, you must also be familiar with the material on pages 122–4 since it is relevant to them all.

In psychology, there are many different perspectives that explain behaviour in different ways. When considering psychopathology, these are often divided into biological and psychological perspectives. They focus on different processes when explaining behaviour, as shown below.

Biological	Psychological
Genetics: behaviour is determined by inherited genes	Behavioural: behaviour is determined by learning
Physiology: behaviour is determined by the structure and functioning of the brain	Cognitive: behaviour is determined by thought processes
Neurochemicals: behaviour is determined by chemical processes in the nervous system	Psychodynamic: behaviour is determined by unconscious processes

> **Think about it**
>
> These perspectives all consider the determinants of behaviour. What implications does this have for the idea of behaviour resulting from free will?

This means that for each mental disorder there will be several explanations, each of which may have something to contribute to a full understanding of the disorder. Research evidence therefore needs to be considered carefully to see which is most relevant to each case or type of problem. In the key study below, for example, both genetic and environmental factors were found to be influential in causing psychopathology.

Key study

Ingraham *et al.* (1995)

- The Israeli high-risk study is a longitudinal investigation started in 1964; this report in 1995 looked at participants when they were in their early 30s.

- The study compared 50 children who were deemed to be genetically vulnerable to schizophrenia (the 'high-risk' group) with 50 controls who were not.

- Both groups contained children brought up in a kibbutz (a large communal dwelling where parenting responsibilities are shared) and children brought up in towns with their parents.

- Schizophrenia was only found in the high-risk group. Town or kibbutz rearing had no effect, indicating that genetic factors are the most influential in schizophrenia.

Although the initial independent variable (IV) for this study was vulnerability to schizophrenia, analysis of the data showed information about some other disorders:

- Major affective disorder (depression) was more common in the kibbutz high-risk group, indicating that genetic vulnerability may need to be combined with particular environmental conditions in order for problems to show themselves.

- More personality disorders were found in the high-risk group.

It was concluded that genetic and environmental factors both contribute to psychopathology.

The differences between them mean that the biological and psychological perspectives will be associated with different ways of treating mental disorder, as shown below.

Biological	Psychological
Drug therapy	Behavioural therapy
ECT	Cognitive-based therapy
Psychosurgery	Psychoanalysis and insight therapies

Just like the explanations, the therapies have to be evaluated by research, and in this case they are assessed for their appropriateness (which disorders they are suited to) and effectiveness (whether they result in a 'cure' or not). These clinical studies often obtain different results, so the studies themselves must be checked to ensure that they have been carried out properly. Important questions about research into treatment outcomes are:

- Does the research compare similar groups of people?
- Might there be an investigator effect?
- Might previous treatment have had an effect?
- Are the results due to a placebo effect?
- How can effectiveness be measured?

In order to deal with mental disorders effectively, it is considered by the biological model that the disorders must be diagnosed as problems and classified into groups or syndromes.

AQA Examiner's tip

Make sure that you know which behavioural therapies are based on classical conditioning and which are based on operant conditioning. Check that you understand the differences between the two types of learning.

Apply it

Look up the difference between single- and double-blind procedures. How might these be useful in investigating psychopathology?

There are two main classification systems in current use. These are the *ICD* (latest version *ICD-10*) and the *DSM* (latest version *DSM-IV-TR*). The main issues with these are that they should be *valid* and *reliable*. Validity requires that they must identify syndromes that are clearly different from one another (descriptive validity) and which have different prognoses/ response to treatment (predictive validity). Reliability requires that clinicians should be able to agree on the diagnosis if they follow the guidelines given in the manuals.

Recently there have also been concerns that the systems used in the West may not be free from cultural bias. Other systems, such as that used in China, contain different syndromes. One of the most common diagnoses, for example, is neurasthenia or nerve weakness, which is not recognised as a syndrome in the West.

> **Think about it**
>
> Not everybody agrees with this approach to mental disorder, which emphasises identifying syndromes and then putting each person into one (or more) of these groups. What problems do you think it might cause?

Key study

Rosenhan (1973)

Method: Eight volunteers gained admission to psychiatric hospitals with a diagnosis of schizophrenia after they claimed to be hearing voices. They were not in fact suffering from any mental disorder, and were referred to in the study as 'pseudopatients'.

- After admission, they behaved normally.

- They spent an average of 19 days in hospital, despite the nurses and other patients reporting that they showed no signs of abnormality.

- They were discharged with a diagnosis of 'schizophrenia in remission'.

- Case notes revealed that normal behaviours such as writing notes and walking up and down corridors were interpreted as pathological or nervousness.

- The psychiatrists also showed abnormal responses (such as failing to answer questions) to the pseudopatients' attempts to initiate contact.

In an extension to the study, staff at a teaching hospital were told to expect some pseudopatients to arrive. Staff were asked to rate 193 patients to indicate whether or not they considered them to be genuine or whether they thought they might be pseudopatients. Forty-one of these were considered likely to be pseudopatients by at least one staff member, even though all of the patients were genuine. This again shows difficulties with differentiation between genuine patients and pseudopatients.

Although this study is now very dated and the classification and diagnostic systems have since been improved, it does suggest that differentiating the normal from the mentally disordered is not always easy. However, the use of deception has been criticised. The faking of symptoms means that it was hardly a fair test for the clinicians involved. The most useful aspect of the study has been the demonstration that behaviours may be interpreted differently once a label has been applied, and that label can be hard to shake off once applied.

> **AQA** Examiner's tip
>
> The Rosenhan (1973) study can be used to show the problems associated with labelling people as mentally disordered. Claims that it demonstrates problems with reliability and validity are harder to justify. It can also be used to discuss the ethics of research, in particular the use of deception.

Schizophrenia

Clinical characteristics

Schizophrenia is a disorder that may involve both positive symptoms (additional behaviours such as disorganised speech) and/or negative symptoms (loss of behaviours, as shown by social withdrawal). Key symptoms are distorted thinking, impaired emotions, distortion of reality and poor interpersonal skills.

The diagnostic criteria include interference with thoughts, delusions, hallucinations, neologisms, catatonia and negative behaviours. Some of these must be present for at least a month and must not be attributable to any medical conditions or to drug use.

Issues with classification and diagnosis

Perhaps because of the characteristics of schizophrenia, classification and diagnosis have proved to be far from easy. There are problems with both reliability and validity. The main issues are:

- Differences between the *DSM* and *ICD*. Earlier versions of these systems differed quite a lot, but those in current use are much more similar.
- The main difference is that the *DSM* requires problems to have been evident for at least six months and the *ICD* specifies just one month.
- Clinicians may use a variety of clinical instruments designed for particular use with schizophrenia. So participants in research studies may be chosen on the basis of different criteria.

Differentiating schizophrenia

Differentiating schizophrenia from other disorders (such as personality disorders) is not always easy. This is particularly the case as patients may have more than one disorder (co-morbidity). For example, schizophrenia and depression are often found together.

Sub-types of schizophrenia

It is possible that there are sub-types of schizophrenia. Differences in response to treatment, as well as in the way the disorder presents itself, suggest that there may be more than one type of schizophrenia. Those suggested include paranoid, catatonic, hebephrenic, undifferentiated and residual.

Labelling and stigmatisation

As the Rosenhan study shows, those labelled as schizophrenic may well be treated differently by others. This is unlikely to be a positive outcome of diagnosis, and therefore leads to ethical considerations as well.

AQA Examiner's tip

Clinical characteristics will never be allocated more than 5 marks in the exam but you could be asked to write a 24-mark essay on issues of classification and diagnosis.

AQA Examiner's tip

Although 'schizophrenia' means 'split mind' you must not confuse it with the idea of a 'split personality', which is usually associated with multiple personality disorder. The two are quite different syndromes.

Think about it

What is meant by 'neologisms' and 'catatonia'?

Why would it be difficult to assess someone for these two behaviours which are associated with schizophrenia?

Apply it

Look up the differences in behaviour between the main sub-types of schizophrenia. When you revise the explanations and treatments, think about how these may apply to some sub-types more than others. What does this suggest?

Biological and psychological explanations

As mentioned above, psychologists use many ways of explaining behaviour. The information below gives some examples of biological and psychological explanations that have been applied to schizophrenia.

Biological explanation	Evidence or example	Evaluation	Conclusion
Genetic: inherited disorder	Cardno *et al.* (2002) (twin study): MZ twins are more similar than DZ. Tienari (1991) (adoption study): schizophrenia is found in adopted children separated from schizophrenic mothers.	Problems with sample size, diagnostic criteria and measurement Many schizophrenics do not have a family history of disorder. Identical twins are not always concordant.	There is a genetic component, but inheritance is complex and other factors must be involved.
Biochemical: dopamine hypothesis links schizophrenia with increased dopamine	Effects of drugs that alter dopamine levels; behaviour changes as predicted from theory. PET scans and post-mortems of schizophrenics show changes in levels of dopamine and increased levels of receptors.	Drugs do not affect all individuals in the same way. Previous use of drug therapy may have caused the changes observed in patients.	Dopamine is involved, but it may not be a complete explanation.
Neuroanatomy: abnormal brain structure	Buchsbaum (1990): reduced blood flow in frontal lobes. Andreasen *et al.* (1990): enlarged ventricles.	Not found in all schizophrenics. Problem of cause and effect. Contradictions in research.	Research is hard to interpret so we cannot be sure at this stage whether this is a cause.

Psychological explanation	Evidence or example	Evaluation	Conclusion
Family models: disturbed communication (Double-bind theory and expressed emotion theory)	Brown 1972: more relapse in families with high expressed emotion Israeli high-risk study (see page 123): at-risk more likely to develop schizophrenia if also exposed to bad parenting	Disturbed communication is hard to measure. Many studies are retrospective.	Unlikely to be the sole cause but may affect the vulnerable
Cognitive models: impaired attention	Poor performance on information-processing tasks such as reaction time.	More an account of symptoms than an explanation of why the problems develop	Gives an outline of processes that may underlie problems, but it is not a full explanation
Neuropsychological models: look for physiological basis of cognitive deficits	Frith (1992): faulty filter between conscious and preconscious; linked to dopamine Helmsley (1993): stored schemas and current sensory input confused due to hippocampal abnormality	Has shown differences in cerebral blood flow in schizophrenics while doing cognitive tasks.	Lack of supporting evidence Ignore environmental factors

AQA Examiner's tip

When you point out that concordance rates are never 100 per cent in genetic studies, make sure that you link this to monozygotic twins. These are the only individuals who are genetically identical and in whom 100 per cent concordance might be expected for genetically determined characteristics.

AQA Examiner's tip

You may wish to introduce the nature–nurture debate when discussing these two types of theory biological and psychological explanations. However, be careful that you do not imply that biological approaches are totally reliant on nature. There are plenty of biological defects that are caused by disease or accident so, in this case, nurture can also be involved.

Key theory

Double bind

Bateson *et al.* (1956) first suggested that schizophrenia might be the result of being caught in 'double-bind' situations, e.g. repeated experiences where someone receives contradictory messages from a family member. These involve the following features:

- two or more persons (one of whom is designated as the 'victim')
- repetition of the situation
- the threat of punishment if something is done or not done
- a second, conflicting threat, often non-verbal
- a further threat that prevents the victim from simply leaving and ignoring the first two, or making any comment that might help to clarify the situation.

This could then lead to various types of schizophrenic behaviour depending on how the child dealt with the double-binds. One individual may become excessively suspicious and always looking for hidden meanings (paranoia). Another may try to ignore their surroundings (catatonia), or they may accept everything at face value or react in an emotionally inappropriate manner (hebephrenia).

There is no single explanation for schizophrenia; many have some support. The model that draws them together is the diathesis–stress model, which links vulnerability with life stressors. In the case of schizophrenia, a biological vulnerability could result in physiological weakness, leading to an inability to process information normally. The addition of disrupted family communications could then be enough to lead to the development of schizophrenia.

Therapies for schizophrenia

Given the range of explanations for schizophrenia, it is hardly surprising that there is also a wide range of biological and psychological therapies.

Think about it

What are the ethical implications of the family model of schizophrenia?

Would these ethical implications extend to treatment?

AQA Examiner's tip

Think about the links between the therapies and the explanations we considered earlier. It is worth pointing out that explanations do not always lead to viable therapies, and that where therapies work it does not necessarily support the corresponding explanation. Consider the treatment aetiology fallacy, for instance – if a drug works, it does not necessarily mean that the disorder was caused by the absence of the drug.

AQA Examiner's tip

Although you do not have to remember all of the drug names in this table, it will help your AO1 marks if you are able to give examples and explain how they work.

These are summarised below.

Therapy	Example	Evaluation (pluses are strengths and minuses are weaknesses of the therapy)
Biological: antipsychotic drugs	Chlorpromazine, Clozapine	+ Control positive symptoms – Do not affect negative symptoms – Only work as long as drug is taken regularly – Not effective for all patients – Produce unpleasant side effects – Difficult to get dosage right
Psychological: psychodynamic therapy	Psychoanalysis (Rosen, 1947)	– Inappropriate because patients cannot communicate well – May make patients worse
Psychological: social interventions	Milieu therapy Social skills training	+ Introducing social stimulation results in improvements on wards (Wing and Brown, 1970) – Must be maintained or patients deteriorate
Psychological: cognitive-behavioural therapy (CBT)	Coping strategy enhancement (CSE)	+ Alleviates positive symptoms + More effective coping skills (Tarrier *et al.*, 1993)
	Beck and Ellis	+ Reduces delusional symptoms (Kuipers *et al.*, 1997)
	Integrated psychological therapy (IPT)	+ Reduces hospitalisation and psychopathology scores (Brenner *et al.*, 1992) – Does not eliminate schizophrenic thinking
Psychological: family intervention	Family relationship therapies	+ Reduces relapse rate + Improves compliance with medication + Reduces family expressed emotion (EE) ratings

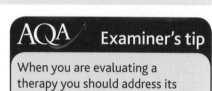

AQA Examiner's tip

When you are evaluating a therapy you should address its appropriateness and effectiveness.

Depression

Clinical characteristics

Depression is a mood disorder that also affects physical condition, behaviour and cognition. It includes major depressive disorder (covered here) and also bipolar disorder and other disorders. The symptoms must be present for at least two weeks to fit the diagnosis of major depressive disorder (MDD). The main symptoms are as follows.

AQA Examiner's tip

Clinical characteristics will never be allocated more than 5 marks in the exam but you could be asked to write a 24-mark essay on issues of classification and diagnosis.

Emotional
Low/irritable mood
Loss of pleasure in activities

Physical
Weight loss or gain
Insomnia or hypersomnia
Fatigue/loss of energy

Behavioural
Restless or slowed down

Cognitive
Feelings of guilt/worthlessness
Poor concentration/indecisive
Thoughts of death/suicide

Issues with classification and diagnosis

As with schizophrenia, there are many issues with classification and diagnosis of depression. Validity, reliability and cultural bias are all relevant here, and there is the additional possibility of gender bias. The main problems are:

- Mood variations are normal, making it difficult to decide where to place the cut-off point for a diagnosis of depression.
- Symptoms can vary widely, so that two people with the same diagnosis may appear to be very different.
- There are several possible sub-types, some of which may not be valid (e.g. seasonal affective disorder or SAD, where sufferers become depressed at certain times of the year – usually in the winter).
- Depression may be co-morbid with other syndromes such as schizophrenia.
- It may also be secondary to physical illness, such as cancer.
- Children are hard to diagnose as they may show the problem in a different way.
- GPs are likely to be the first to see people with depression, because they are more accessible. However, GPs may not be trained in the diagnosis of depression.
- People from other cultural backgrounds may present with different symptoms – for example, physical symptoms may predominate.
- Depression is twice as common in women as in men, which may be partly due to diagnostic biases.

AQA Examiner's tip

If you are asked to outline the characteristics of depression, be sure to include a mention of the emotional changes shown above, as these are key features of the disorder. Note that saying a characteristic is a 'depressed mood' will gain no marks, use 'low' or 'irritable mood'.

Apply it

How many reasons can you think of for the difference in the rate of depression found for men and women? (Try to consider both biological and psychological factors.)

What implications does this have for theoretical explanations of depression?

Biological and psychological explanations

Biological and psychological explanations can both be supported.

Why biological?

- Symptoms often include physical changes.
- The disorder runs in families.
- Some drugs are effective as treatment, while others can induce depression.

AQA Examiner's tip

You need to know what the following terms mean: monoamine; cortisol; frontal lobes; limbic system; EEG; neuro-imaging; post-partum depression; premenstrual depression.

Why psychological?

- Life events often precede the onset of depression.
- Not all sufferers have a family history of depression.
- Psychological treatments can be effective.

Biological explanations of depression

Explanation	Evidence/example	Evaluation	Conclusion
Genes	MZ twins showed 46 per cent concordance, DZ showed only 20 per cent (McGuffin *et al.*, 1996).	Concordance rates are never 100 per cent. Social environments are also similar.	Genes may contribute a predisposition, but they are not likely to be the sole cause of depression.
Biochemical	Amine hypothesis (low activity of monoamines as the cause of depression) is supported by drug treatments.	Drugs affect amines immediately, but mood changes take longer.	Amine changes may be the result of depression not the cause. Several biochemicals may be involved.
	High cortisol levels are found in depressed people.	Newer drugs do not increase amine levels, suggesting that amines may not be the only chemicals involved. Cortisol levels do fall when depression lifts. These levels are also found in anxiety disorders.	It is not clear whether changes in cortisol levels are the cause or the effect of depression. These changes are not exclusive to depression, so only provide a partial explanation.
Neuroanatomical	Amine pathways between frontal lobes and limbic system may be damaged in post-stroke depression (Starkstein and Robinson, 1991).	There is support from EEG and neuro-imaging studies.	There may not be a causal connection between the damaged sites and the depression.
Female hormones	More females than males suffer from depression.	Not all women suffer post-partum or premenstrual depression. Women have more problems if combined with social difficulties (Gotlib *et al.*, 1991).	Findings about the effects of hormones are inconsistent. Premenstrual depression is not fully accepted as a syndrome in the *DMS-IV*.

Psychological explanations of depression

Explanation	Evidence/example	Evaluation	Conclusion
Psychoanalytic	Oral fixation (dependent personality) plus loss in later life can result in depression (seen as turning anger inwards).	Stresses role of early experience. Links to depression have been found with both dependent personality and parental loss. Depressed people do show more anger than others, but it is not turned inwards as predicted by the theory.	Evidence is not convincing so generally this explanation is not highly regarded.
Behavioural	Lack of positive reinforcement from others is observed in depressives (Lewinsohn, 1974).	Support from Coyne (1985) Lack of social skills could explain why depression occurs in families, providing an alternative to the biological/genetic view. Depression may lead to lack of social skills rather than vice versa. It is hard to explain why depression arises initially.	Little support has been found for this explanation.
Cognitive-behavioural	Learned helplessness (Seligman, 1975) in animals shows that a passive response can be learned to painful stimuli.	Animal studies may not be relevant to human behaviour. But Hiroto and Seligman (1975) have shown the same effect in humans (see the key study below for details).	Useful concepts, but origins of maladaptive style or learned helplessness are not explained. These may be effects rather than the cause of depression.
	Maladaptive attributional style, self-blaming and hopelessness may develop as a result of failure (Abramson et al., 1978).	Therapies directed at attributional style are found to be effective . Cannot account for gender differences or for different types of depression.	
Cognitive	Cognitive distortions, biases and negative schemas are found in depressed persons (Beck, 1967).	Therapies are very helpful. Not established that negative thinking precedes depression.	Distortions may maintain the disorder rather than initiating it.
Stressful life events	Majority of depressed persons experience one or more life events shortly before diagnosis (Brown and Harris, 1989).	Retrospective studies may not be accurate. Life events have different impacts on people. Many have negative life events without becoming depressed.	This is best linked to the diathesis–stress model to incorporate the idea of vulnerability.

Key study

Hiroto and Seligman (1975)

Aim: This study looked at the effects of inescapable aversive stimuli on 96 undergraduate participants. The stimuli included loud noises and unsolvable problems. The tasks presented were simple instrumental learning as well as solving anagrams. The authors hypothesised that the aversive events would create a state of learned helplessness that would transfer and affect behaviour across the range of tasks used.

Findings: Both types of task were affected by both types of inescapable aversive stimulus.

Conclusion: Just as in animal studies, the participants had learned to be helpless – that response was futile. It was further theorised that learned helplessness may provide a model for depression, as it seems to produce the same symptoms.

AQA Examiner's tip

You may wish to introduce the nature–nurture debate when discussing these two types of theory (biological and psychological). However, be careful that you do not imply that biological approaches are totally reliant on nature. There are plenty of biological defects that are caused by disease or accident so, in this case, nurture can also be involved.

Therapies for depression

As with most other mental disorders, both biological and psychological therapies have been developed to treat depression. In practice, they may well be used together for maximum effect, but they are considered separately below.

Think about it

What are the ethical issues associated with the use of these biological therapies?

Can the ethical 'costs' outweigh the benefits? Give examples.

Biological therapies for depression

Therapy	Example	Evaluation
Chemotherapy	MAOIs – increase noradrenaline and serotonin	Life-threatening side effects possible
	Tricyclics – raise noradrenaline and serotonin levels	Effective, fewer side effects
	SSRIs – raise serotonin levels	Possible links to suicide but no obvious side effects
		Generally, these drugs do not work for all individuals, effects are not immediate and they need to be taken indefinitely.
ECT	Sackheim and Rush (1995) found this very effective in severe cases.	How it works is still unknown
		Side effects such as brain damage and memory loss are a cause for debate.
		Ethical considerations
Other	Phototherapy for seasonal affective disorder (SAD – depression that occurs at certain times of the year, mainly in the winter)	Effective but limited applicability
	Physical exercise	Effective in conjunction with other interventions

Psychological therapies for depression

Therapy	Example	Evaluation
Cognitive-behavioural therapy	Beck's CBT – challenging negative thinking	Reduces depression and prevents relapse (Kuyken *et al.*, 2007)
		Best used in conjunction with medication (Keller *et al.*, 2000)
		Not effective with all clients (Simons *et al.*, 1995)
		May induce dependency
		Requires client to cooperate
Psychoanalysis	Brief psychodynamic psychotherapy	May not be effective for everyone (Holmes, 1999)
	Sullivan's interpersonal psychotherapy (IPT)	As effective as cognitive and drug therapy (Elkin *et al.*, 1989)

Key study

Kuyken *et al.* (2007)

Aim: To assess the effectiveness of CBT in treating depression.

Method: This study took the form of a literature review, and the effectiveness section incorporated meta-analyses as well as individual studies.

Findings: CBT, used on its own, produces significant improvement in symptoms, at least comparable to those observed with medication and other psychotherapies. It was found to be equally effective when administered in group settings, and the effects persisted for several years afterwards. Recovery was associated with changes in the functioning of key areas of the brain (e.g. the limbic system). This provided evidence of the links between psychological processes and brain functioning.

Further points were:

- The behavioural component alone (attempts to change behaviours) seemed to be just as useful as full CBT (e.g. attempts to change behaviour and negative thinking).

- CBT worked best with clients who engage fully with homework.

- Results were dependent on therapist competence, with therapists who had been rated as more competent producing better outcomes.

- CBT worked better with people suffering only from depression and was less effective with patients who had other disorders as well (co-morbidity).

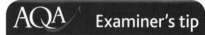

AQA Examiner's tip

When you are evaluating a therapy you should address its appropriateness and effectiveness.

Phobic disorders

Clinical characteristics

Phobias occur when anxiety is associated with a particular type of situation or stimulus. They are identified by:

- disproportionate fear and anxiety
- recognition that this is unreasonable but an inability to control it
- avoidance of the situation, which then interferes with everyday life
- duration of six months or more in under-18s (*DSM* only)

The symptoms seen will include:

- anticipatory fear
- increased arousal
- breathing problems
- increased muscle tension
- sleep disturbances
- possible blushing and trembling.

There are different types of phobia, such as:

- specific phobia (fear of a particular object/situation)
- social phobia (fear of social/public gatherings)
- agoraphobia (fear when away from home).

Issues with classification and diagnosis

- It is not easy to distinguish normal from pathological anxiety.
- Different individuals will show different combinations of symptoms.
- Anxiety may be associated with other mental disorders (e.g. depression) or with medical conditions.
- Different types often co-occur, indicating that the categories may not be valid.
- Correct diagnosis is essential if the most appropriate treatment is to be provided.
- Sufferers may be unwilling to seek help or admit to problems.
- There are cultural variations in the way the disorders are expressed.
- *DSM* and *ICD* differ in some respects so diagnoses can depend on which you use.
- Cut-off points are difficult to establish – when does fear become excessive?
- Some phobias can be confused with other disorders. For example, social phobia and avoidant personality disorder have some similarities. Avoidant personality disorder involves fear of rejection, over-sensitivity and feelings of inadequacy, which tend to make socialising difficult.
- Phobias can co-occur (e.g. social and agoraphobia) making it hard to identify the primary disorder for treatment purposes.
- Cultural differences are evident in the nature of phobias, e.g. *taijin kyofusho* is the Japanese form of social phobia. It involves social avoidance based on the fear of offending others through the appearance, smell or movement of the body.

AQA **Examiner's tip**

Clinical characteristics will never be allocated more than 5 marks in the exam but you could be asked to write a 24-mark essay on issues of classification and diagnosis.

AQA **Examiner's tip**

You can mention the different types of phobia when outlining characteristics, but make sure that you explain why they are examples of phobia.

Apply it

In your Student Book or elsewhere, look up more information about the disorders that could be confused with phobias. See whether you can identify the similarities and differences.

Explanations of phobias

Phobias have been explained using both biological and psychological approaches. A combination of the two seems to be the most useful.

Psychological explanations

Explanation	Evidence/example	Evaluation	Conclusion
Psychodynamic (displaced repressed feelings)	Freud – Little Hans' phobia of horses is linked to his fear of his father.	Case study evidence is not reliable. Hans' phobia could be explained in behavioural terms (see below).	Minimal support
Behavioural/learning theory (classical and operant conditioning)	Little Hans' phobia may be explained by a frightening experience with a horse, resulting in conditioning.	Frightening experiences are not always involved. Frightening experiences do not always lead to phobias. Phobias do run in families to some extent.	Cannot explain all phobias
Learned preparedness (Seligman, 1971 – we are biologically prepared to react anxiously to stimuli that threaten survival)	Fear is more easily acquired to stimuli that were present in prehistory (primitive stimuli), e.g. snakes (Marks, 1977).	Support from: • Ohman *et al.* (1975) – conditioned response is easier to acquire to primitive stimuli. • Cook and Mineka (1980) – similar findings in animals.	Well-supported theory
Modelling (learned through observation, imitation and vicarious conditioning)	Monkeys were found to model behaviour of fearful parents (Mineka *et al.*,1984).	Phobias are not always based on observation. Observation does not always lead to phobias.	Experimental support but cannot explain all phobias
Cognitive-behavioural model	Familiarity, observation and expectations all influence chances of learning phobic behaviours (Davey, 1997).	Some success for threat devaluation therapy, offering support for the cognitive-behavioural model (Davey, 1999). This still depends on conditioning through experience (criticised above).	More detailed than behavioural model. Cognitive factors may play a role.

Biological explanations

Explanation	Evidence/example	Evaluation	Conclusion
Genetic inheritance (possibly affecting autonomic lability or temperament)	Higher concordance in MZ than DZ twins (Skre *et al.* 2000) Increased occurrence in relatives of sufferers (Ost, 1992)	Few studies; conflicting findings Modelling may account for family similarities.	Possible genetic component, but not fully understood
Lack of GABA leads to increased arousal	Benzodiazepines reduce anxiety and act on GABA receptors.	Effect of drug is only temporary.	Limited evidence to date Cause and effect uncertain
Neuroanatomy (the amygdala in particular – a brain structure linked to emotional response)	PET scans show increased blood flow in the amygdala of sufferers.	Successful treatment with drugs or CBT decreases this blood flow (Furmark *et al.*, 2002). Not all phobics show this increased blood flow.	As above

Therapies for phobias

Given the range of explanations that give rise to the therapies for phobias, it is hardly surprising that both biological and psychological therapies have been applied in order to treat the disorder. Examples of both are shown below.

Biological therapies for phobias

Therapy	Example	Evaluation
Drugs	Benzodiazepines	Effectiveness uncertain (Taylor, 1994) Can lead to tolerance/dependence
	SSRIs	Effective for social phobia and some agoraphobia cases Not addictive Only have an effect after six weeks

Psychological therapies for phobias

Therapy	Example	Evaluation
Psychodynamic	Free association and dream analysis used to uncover repressed conflicts	Time consuming, expensive No evidence of effectiveness
Behavioural therapies	Systematic desensitisation (Wolpe, 1958) Flooding Modelling	80 per cent of clients improve using exposure techniques (Marks, 1990). Commitment required, so some drop out
	Social skills training (SST)	Works best in conjunction with other therapies
Cognitive-behavioural therapies	Threat devaluation (Davey, 1999)	Best used in conjunction with exposure techniques Reduces effects of social phobias and agoraphobias (not specific phobias)

Key study

Wolitzky-Taylor *et al.* (2008)

The study was a meta-analysis of data from 33 studies of treatment outcomes for specific phobias.

Findings: Exposure therapies (which are behavioural therapies), were found to be more effective than other treatments, placebo treatment and no treatment groups. In vivo exposure (using real objects/situations) was found to be better than imaginal exposure (asking patients to imagine the objects/situations) initially but not at longer-term follow-up. Placebos had significantly more effect than no treatment at all. More treatment sessions produced more favourable outcomes. No differences were observed according to type of phobia.

Conclusion: Exposure is the best treatment for specific phobias.

> **AQA Examiner's tip**
>
> When you are evaluating a therapy you should address it's appropriateness and effectiveness.

Obsessive-compulsive disorder

Clinical characteristics

As the name implies, this disorder involves:

- obsessions (recurrent intrusive thoughts) and
- compulsions (repetitive mental or physical activities that cannot be omitted).

The diagnostic criteria are that obsessions, compulsions or both:

- must be present on most days over a two-week period
- interfere with functioning and cause distress
- are not the result of other mental disorders.

> **AQA Examiner's tip**
>
> Clinical characteristics will never be allocated more than 5 marks in the exam but you could be asked to write a 24-mark essay on issues of classification and diagnosis.

Issues surrounding classification and diagnosis

- It is not easy to distinguish normal from pathological anxiety.
- Different individuals will show different combinations of symptoms.
- Anxiety may be associated with other mental disorders (e.g. depression) or with medical conditions.
- Different types often co-occur, indicating that the categories may not be valid.
- Correct diagnosis is essential if the most appropriate treatment is to be provided.
- Sufferers may be unwilling to seek help or admit to problems.
- There are cultural variations in the way the disorders are expressed.
- Many normal adults experience unwanted thoughts and carry out some repetitive behaviours resembling compulsions. This makes the cut-off point for diagnosis hard to determine.
- Sufferers may not always be willing to admit to their problems.
- OCD can be co-morbid with depression, making the primary disorder, which should be treated first, hard to determine.
- OCD can resemble schizophrenia.
- OCD may contain sub-types which require different treatment, but these have yet to be identified.

Explanations of obsessive-compulsive disorder

Biological and psychological explanations have both been supported.
Examples of each are outlined below.

Biological explanations of OCD

Explanation	Evidence/example	Evaluation	Conclusion
Genetics	MZ twins show greater concordance than DZ twins (Billett *et al.*, 1998). Relatives of cases show a slightly increased risk (Black *et al.*, 1992).	Family studies show only a slight increase in risk. Possible gene identified – sapap3 (Feng *et al.*, 2007) Animal research may not be applicable to humans	There are only a limited number of well-controlled studies Sapap3 study is promising, but replication of results needed
Biochemical (serotonin deficiency)	SSRIs reduce OCD symptoms.	Improvement is only about 50 per cent (Insel, 1991). Not all patients benefit. Serotonin levels do not differ between OCD patients and controls (Pigott *et al.*, 1996).	Cannot be sole cause of OCD May be an example of the treatment aetiology fallacy
Neuroanatomical factors	Basal ganglia abnormality (Max *et al.*, 1994) Orbital frontal cortex (OFC)-caudate nucleus-thalamus dysfunction (known as the cortico-striatal circuit)	Basal ganglia is no different in OCD and control patients (Aylward *et al.*, 1996). SSRIs inhibit overactivity in OFC. OCD patients have less grey matter in OFC (Menzies *et al.*, 2007).	Findings not yet consistent enough

Psychological explanations of OCD

Explanation	Evidence/example	Evaluation	Conclusion
Psychodynamic	Freud: anxiety results from aggressive impulses generated during toilet training in the anal stage. Anal personality results in OCD.	No evidence of greater toilet-training problems in OCD patients (Milby and Weber, 1991). Some patients do have anal personality traits – but not all. Not all anal personalities develop OCD.	Little evidence
Behavioural	Classical and operant conditioning link compulsions with anxiety reduction.	ERP (Exposure and response prevention) therapy is quite effective. This does not explain obsessions. This does not explain initiation of behaviour.	May explain maintenance of compulsions
Cognitive-behavioural	Catastrophic interpretations of intrusive thoughts, and their suppression, leads to OCD (Rachman, 1997).	Intrusive thoughts increased when patients were asked to suppress them (Salkovskis and Kirk, 1997).	Does not explain why OCD patients have such problems with intrusive thoughts compared to controls

Key theory

Rachman (1997)

Rachman argued that intrusive thoughts are quite normal. Misinterpretation of these thoughts as very important, revealing or catastrophic is what turns them into obsessions in some people, making them become more intense, long-lasting and distressing than normal. For example, thoughts of harming a relative may be interpreted to mean that the person is capable of murder. Such patients feel that their thoughts are very revealing about their inner characters, and so they try to neutralise or atone for them. Others try to block them out or avoid the relevant situations.

The thoughts may be triggered by external stress, and misinterpretation is enhanced by the cognitive biases shown by OCD patients. Firstly, they show responsibility bias – they think that they can be responsible for events which are clearly beyond their control (the well-being of relatives some distance away, for instance). Secondly, they suffer from thought-action fusion, which is the tendency to assume that thinking of things will make them happen. Both will contribute to anxiety.

The vulnerability factors were said to be depression, anxiety, cognitive biases and elevated moral standards. Therapy therefore needed to focus on removing the misinterpretations and reducing avoidance behaviour.

Think about it

As we shall see, psychological therapies have been found to be very effective in treating OCD. What does this tell you about the biological explanations outlined above?

Therapies for OCD

Recent approaches to treatment of OCD have focused on the use of drugs, often in association with psychological therapy of some kind. The main possibilities are shown below.

Biological therapies for OCD

Therapy	Example	Evaluation
Drugs	Clomipramine SSRIs (selective serotonin re-uptake inhibitors) reduce symptoms (Rauch and Jenike, 1998) in children and adults.	Clomipramine was found effective by Thoren *et al.* (1980). Antidepressants that do not affect serotonin have no effect. Possible side effects Relapse is likely if medication is stopped. ERP is more effective than Clomipramine (Foa *et al.*, 2005).
Psychosurgery	Anterior cingulotomy is used on cortico-striatal circuit. TMS (Transcranial magnetic stimulation) is used on supplementary motor area.	Safer than many other procedures. Irreversible. General effectiveness around 25–70 per cent in the long term. Ethical considerations. Promising results.

Psychological therapies for OCD

Therapy	Example	Evaluation
Behaviour therapy	Exposure and response prevention (ERP) Cognitive-behavioural	Some success for ERP (Salkovskis and Kirk, 1997) Problems with drop-out Quite fast acting (3–8 weeks) No side effects Both CT (a type of CBT) and ERP are effective at two-year follow-up (Whittal *et al.*, 2008).

Key study

Whittal *et al.* (2008)

Aims: To compare the efficacy of ERP and CT for OCD, using a two-year follow-up of patients treated either individually or in groups.

Sample: 75 individually treated patients and 76 who received treatment in small groups of 6–8. Allocation to CT or ERP was random.

Procedure: Patients were assessed for symptom severity and recovery status. Assessment took place both pre-and post-treatment, and at three-month and two-year follow-up.

Results: No difference in numbers recovered at two-year follow-up.

	CT	ERP
Individual	68 per cent	54 per cent
Group	33 per cent	48 per cent

Conclusions:

■ Most patients do recover with treatment, and gains are maintained over a two-year period.

■ There is no difference between CT and ERP in overall recovery rates.

■ ERP showed more symptom reduction in the group treatment condition.

■ CT had lower drop-out rates.

AQA Examiner's tip

When you are evaluating a therapy you should address its appropriateness and effectiveness.

Think about it

What are the ethical issues that apply to the use of psychosurgery for OCD?

Apply it

Which psychological therapy would you choose for a patient who was going to receive individual treatment? What is the drawback of that choice?

Which would be the best choice if finances were limited?

Make sure that you can justify your answers by using evidence.

Psychopathology

Exam-style questions

You will probably have revised one of the four topics represented in the four examples below.

Example 1

| 0 1 | Outline and evaluate **two or more** therapies used in the treatment of schizophrenia. | *(8 marks + 16 marks)* |

Example 2

| 0 2 | Outline clinical characteristics of depression. | *(4 marks)* |

| 0 3 | Explain issues associated with the classification **and/or** diagnosis of depression. | *(10 marks)* |

| 0 4 | Outline and evaluate **one** biological therapy used in the treatment of depression. | *(4 marks + 6 marks)* |

Example 3

| 0 5 | Outline **two or more** explanations for phobic disorders obsessive compulsive disorder. | *(8 marks)* |

| 0 6 | Evaluate explanations for phobic disorders. | *(16 marks)* |

Example 4

| 0 7 | Outline the clinical characteristics of OCD | *(4 marks)* |

| 0 8 | Outline any **one** psychological therapy for OCD | *(4 marks)* |

| 0 9 | Evaluate the use of psychological therapies for OCD | *(16 marks)* |

Sample answers

Suggested content for the other example questions for this section can be found at
www.nelsonthornes.com/psychology_answers

Example 4

0 7 *The clinical characteristics of obsessive compulsive disorder (OCD) include obsessions, compulsions and anxiety. It occurs in young adulthood and affects both men and women. Obsessions are intrusive thoughts, impulses or images which are disturbing and cause anxiety. For example, someone could have an obsession with locking the door when they go out. Compulsions may be physical or mental behaviours which the person does in order to reduce this anxiety, e.g. checking several times that the doors are locked. Both obsessions and compulsions lead to anxiety, making it the main symptom.*

• Could have mentioned the diagnostic criteria, but just about enough to gain marks in the top band

0 8 *ERP (exposure-response-prevention) is one type of behavioural therapy used for OCD. It is done in two parts, exposure and response formation. OCD sufferers try to avoid the stimulus in order to prevent anxiety, instead of stopping themselves completing the compulsive act. Obsessions and compulsions are reinforced by classical and operant conditioning.*

• Small mistake describing ERP

This is not really about the therapy – it is more focused on
• the explanation.

In ERP, the therapist gradually exposes the sufferer to the stimulus, a bit like systematic desensitisation. The patient is given a list of targets which will prevent them from doing compulsive acts. Sessions last 13–20 weeks and booster sessions may be used to prevent relapse.

• The difference is not made clear.

No mention of response prevention

AQA — Examiner's comments

A lot of this answer to question 8 is not about the therapy, and so as a whole the account is limited. A mark in the basic band would be awarded.

0	9

Psychological therapies are more effective than drugs and have less side effects, so they should be tried first.

One researcher found that ERP reduced OCD without any side effects, — Some repetition.
making it effective. There is no long-term evidence that this is the case though. ERP is also appropriate because the exposure part causes desensitisation and the rest stops compulsive acts from occurring. Some studies have found it isn't effective, but that could be down to lack of — A bit vague here.
motivation in the patient. Individual differences also mean that some people may be better off with drugs.
Freud developed psychoanalysis to treat mental problems, but this therapy — It would be a good idea to explain why it is not suitable.
isn't suitable for OCD sufferers.

Cognitive therapy can also be used to deal with the mental side of OCD. — Unfortunately this is description, not evaluation.
Patients are asked to bring thought records in a diary and bring it to the therapy sessions. The aim is to prove that patients' beliefs are wrong and hopefully they will change their beliefs as a result. For example, they might be told not to worry about doors being unlocked. This will deal with the obsessions. The therapist can then discuss the compulsions and try to prove that they are unnecessary.

Research has found that CT alone has a good effect on reducing OCD — This is better, but lacks detail.
symptoms, but other studies have shown that it is better when combined with drug treatment.

There are also computerised and self-report methods of therapy which — This could be clearer.
have proved just as effective as CT carried out by a therapist.

In conclusion, a combination of ERP, CT and drugs would probably work best for OCD.

AQA   Examiner's comments

There is limited elaboration in this answer to question 9, and ideas are not always clearly expressed. There are several points, so it just manages to get marks in the higher part of the basic band.

Overall, the answers in Example 4 would achieve a mark in the basic band.

10 Media psychology

Media and persuasion

> ### You need to know how to
>
> ✔ describe the Hovland-Yale and the elaboration likelihood models of persuasion
>
> ✔ evaluate both models of persuasion in terms of their strengths and weaknesses
>
> ✔ explain how television advertising uses psychological principles to persuade people.

Attitude change

Every day, many attempts are made to persuade you. Adverts aim to get you to buy things. Music videos persuade you to download tracks. Newspapers and websites try to sway your views about current issues and topics, and politicians try to get you to vote for them. How?

Key model

The Hovland-Yale model of attitude change (1953)

The Hovland-Yale model was the first attempt at explaining the process of attitude change. Developed by Carl Hovland at Yale University, the model suggested that attitude change took place in a sequence of four stages:

- Attention: the first stage was to notice the attempt to persuade you.

- Comprehension: the second stage was to understand what was being said.

- Reactance: the third stage was to believe (accept) or ignore (reject) the message.

- Attitude change: if the message was accepted, attitude change took place.

The Hovland-Yale model also drew attention to the components of attitude change. These were:

- the source (who put the message forward)

- the message (what was said and how)

- the target (who it was aimed at).

Each of these factors (e.g. source, message and target) could influence whether the message was noticed, understood or believed.

Commentary

- The Hovland-Yale model has been supported by many experimental studies and has dominated the topic of persuasion for more than 30 years. It is still used today in marketing and advertising as the basis of most persuasive campaigns.

- The model makes clear predictions and has been easy to test using laboratory experiments. For example, the same message can be presented by two people – an expert and a non-expert – and the number of people persuaded can be compared.

- Experimental studies have explored the different components of persuasion, finding out which factors make sources persuasive (credibility and physical attractiveness) and what kinds of people are more easily persuaded (those with lower self-esteem or intelligence). Messages that inspire fear can be very persuasive (Meyerowitz and Chaiken, 1987).

- It is widely agreed that persuasion takes place in stages, although there is some disagreement about what the stages are.

- The Hovland-Yale model took the view that people are rational, that they think carefully about the information given before being persuaded. More recent approaches to persuasion (e.g. like the elaboration likelihood model) have emphasised that people are 'cognitive misers'. They do not like to think too carefully about most things and prefer to take 'short cuts'. It is only when issues are really important that people think carefully about the arguments presented.

Persuasion

Key model

The elaboration likelihood model (ELM) of persuasion (Petty and Cacioppo, 1986)

Petty and Cacioppo agreed with Hovland's claim that people think carefully about important arguments and attempts to persuade them. However, they argued that much of the time people do not do this on less important matters, but make rapid decisions and jump to conclusions. In the ELM model, there are two 'routes' to persuasion:

- The central processing route is used when the topic is important. People think carefully about the arguments and the evidence for them.

- The peripheral processing route is used when the topic is trivial/ unimportant. People do not pay attention but use shortcuts and jump to conclusions.

The ELM also argues that people vary in a dimension called 'need for cognition' (NC). Those with a high NC tend to think carefully and use the central route, whereas those with low NC generally use peripheral processing.

> **AQA Examiner's tip**
>
> The ELM and Hovland-Yale models are both mentioned on the specification using the word 'including'. This means that questions can be set specifically on them. Make sure you learn these models.

Commentary

- The ELM is supported by the heuristic-systematic processing model (Chaiken), which agrees with the claim that there are two different kinds of processing.

- The ELM model draws on recent developments in the field of cognitive psychology and processing effort. For example, studies on attention have shown how we can process perceptual information consciously or automatically, which uses a similar framework to the idea of central/peripheral processing. The view of people as limited information processors is also drawn from cognitive psychology.

- The ELM model takes into account individual differences between people by proposing the idea of NC. Vidrine, Simmons and Branden (2007) studied more than 200 smokers who were given either a fact-based quitting leaflet or an emotion-based leaflet. Those with a high NC were more easily persuaded by the fact-based leaflet, showing that information and evidence is important to them.

- Other studies have shown how differences such as mood can also affect how easily we are persuaded (Mackie and Worth, 1989).

- The ELM also acknowledges that the topic is important when someone is trying to persuade us. This makes intuitive sense.

> **Think about it**
>
> Identify **two** attempts that have been made to persuade you recently, one about a serious topic and the second a trivial topic. Did you think carefully about the arguments using the central route or did you use the peripheral route suggested by the ELM?

Strategies used by TV advertisers

Television is a powerful medium for persuasion. Political parties invest heavily in election broadcasts to persuade people to vote for them. Advertisers pay heavily for prime-time TV slots, such as intervals in World Cup matches or in episodes of a popular series. This is despite the fact that around eight out of 10 people leave the room during advert breaks and most people are strongly resistant to TV adverts. The aim of advertisers is to manipulate consumers' attitudes and to influence their behaviour. What strategies are used in TV adverts to makes them persuasive?

Attention and comprehension

Because people are resistant to adverts, advertisers have to 'get clever' and capture our attention and make us remember them. Some adverts are very subtle; they do not mention the product they are promoting until the end – if at all.

↓

Favourable associations

Product endorsement

This refers to the use of a celebrity to promote the product. In 1990 about 20% of TV adverts used product endorsement (Fowles 1996). The reasoning is that celebrities are seen as reliable and trustworthy as well as objective sources of information. They become the public 'face' of the product.

Product placement

A simpler strategy is to use product placement. This approach is used in American TV advertising and was finally legalised in the UK in 2011. Product placement involves the overt use of a product (e.g. drinking Coca-Cola) in a TV programme by a character or celebrity.

↓

Repetition

Adverts are repeated regularly. Through repetition, even irritating adverts are remembered making them effective.

Commentary on the effectiveness of television

Each of these strategies builds on the psychology of persuasion. Most people are resistant to the idea of advertising and do not like to think they are being persuaded. Advert breaks are an ideal time to leave the room or do something other than watch. For this reason, advertisers need to catch the viewers attention and often use outrageous ways of doing this:

■ Petty and Cacioppo's ELM pointed to the way in which many people like to be made to think and have a higher need for cognition. Cryptic adverts are often the most popular and create the greatest discussion. Goldman (1992) argues that the extra thought required by cryptic adverts is what makes them memorable.

■ The widespread use of celebrity endorsement implies that it must be an effective method of advertising. However, some studies (Fowles 1996) indicate that viewers often remember the celebrity but forget the product they are promoting.

■ An experiment on product placement showed that it was only effective in reinforcing people's existing attitudes. Smoking and non-smoking participants watched one of two clips of *Die Hard*. Clip 1 showed the actor Bruce Willis smoking and clip 2 showed a scene in which he was not smoking. Smokers liked the character more in clip 1 whereas non-smokers rated him as less attractive in clip 1 (Gibson and Maurer 2000)

■ Zajonc (1968) identified the 'mere exposure effect' which has been demonstrated in many experimental studies. The effect shows that familiarity generally increases liking. By repeating an advert, time and time again, advertisers build up familiarity making us more likely to choose a product when faced with a shelf of alternatives in the supermarket

Apply it

Make a note of adverts which use the tactics described. Try to think an example for grabbing attention, favourable associations and repetition and how this was achieved.

Media influences on social behaviour

You need to know how to

✔ describe at least two explanations of how TV and films influence antisocial and pro-social behaviour

✔ provide relevant evidence to evaluate these explanations

✔ describe research into the possible effects of computer games on behaviour.

Media influences on pro- and antisocial behaviour

The study of media affects has a very long history, starting in the 1950s and continuing today. Many people believe that watching violent films or playing violent computer games, leads to aggressive behaviour especially in children. This belief is fuelled by high-profile coverage of violent incidents, such as the Columbine High School shootings. However, the evidence has been far from consistent in this area – partly due to the difficulties of investigating media effects. Influences on antisocial behaviour have attracted far more research than pro-social behaviour (i.e. behaviour that is constructive). This is because social psychology has traditionally been 'problem driven'. One important difference between pro- and antisocial programmes is the intent of the makers. People who produce pro-social programmes intend them to have an effect whereas makers of violent films intend them to entertain.

Two explanations of media influence are:

- Social learning theory – this claims that people copy aggressive behaviour that they have seen on TV.
- Cognitive priming – this argues that watching aggression leads children to develop beliefs about aggression, known as schemas or scripts, that influence how they interpret the world around them and how they behave.

Key theory

Social learning theory (Bandura, 1963)

Bandura argued that both pro- and antisocial behaviours could be learned through the same mechanism of watching and copying the actions of role models. The focus in this theory is on the link between watching violence and aggressive behaviour:

- Children learn behaviours through the observation of other people, who are called role models.
- If a role model behaves aggressively or helpfully and receives a reward for their actions, the child is likely to copy the behaviour in order to receive a similar reward.
- This is known as learning through vicarious experience.
- If the child repeats the behaviour and receives a reward, this is learning through direct experience or operant conditioning.

The original theory offered little room for children to think and was roundly criticised by many people who pointed out that behaviour is more complex. In later revisions of the theory, Bandura modified this to include cognitive elements.

- In order for a child to imitate a role model, he or she must first of all attend to the behaviour, then store a mental representation of it in memory (remember it) to be able to physically reproduce it, and lastly be motivated to use the behaviour.

Key explanation

Cognitive priming (Berkowitz, 1984; Huesmann, 2003)

Cognitive priming focuses on the idea that watching violence affects our cognitions and beliefs about the world, leading us to interpret situations differently and possibly respond aggressively. This approach suggests that violence does not have direct effects on behaviour for most people (e.g. most people do not watch a violent film and go out and copy it), but it does affect how people process the situations they see around them:

- Berkowitz (1984) argued that unconscious memories of violent scenes from films are stored in our memories. These memories are activated in situations where similar aggressive cues exist.
- Huesmann (1986) developed the idea of priming further, to suggest that watching violence leads people to store schemas and scripts of violent actions.
- Schemas include beliefs, for example that the world is a dangerous and violent place. Scripts are plans of how to behave in a particular situation. These may be retrieved in similar real-life situations and they 'prime' similar behaviour.
- Priming can also occur from media sources such as song lyrics. There is quite a lot of interest in the possible effects of rap lyrics on cognitive priming.

AQA Examiner's tip

Different methods have been used to study imitation/media effects. Each of these has strengths and weaknesses and you should be able to refer to some of these when you are discussing research studies and the conclusion that can be drawn from them. You can view an example of how to do this successfully in the sample essay on page 156.

Research studies of antisocial behaviour

Reference and method	Procedure	Findings
Bandura, Ross and Ross (1963) Laboratory experiment	Bandura studied nursery-school children, divided into three groups. One group observed a film of an adult behaving aggressively to a bobo doll. The second group observed the adult playing peacefully with the doll. The control group were not exposed to a role model.	Children who had been exposed to the violent role model performed significantly more aggressive acts towards the bobo doll than the control group or those who watched the non-aggressive model.
Phillips (1983) Natural experiment	Phillips compared US homicide (murder) figures in the 10 days before and 10 days after major prize fights (boxing matches).	There were significantly more murders after a match. Victims were more likely to be from the same ethnic background as the winner.
Gunter et al. (2002) Natural experiment	Gunter compared the rates of aggressive behaviour in 47 children aged three to four before TV was introduced to the island of St Helena and for a number of years after TV was introduced.	Gunter found no overall increase in aggressive behaviour, but children who watched more cartoons behaved more aggressively. The children who had the highest antisocial behaviour scores before TV was introduced were more likely to watch cartoons.
Huesmann et al. (2003) Correlational study	Huesmann studied more than 550 children from Chicago aged five to eight years old. They measured how much violent TV the children watched. Four hundred were followed up in their early twenties and aggressive behaviour was measured again.	There was a positive correlation between the amount of violent television watched in childhood and how aggressive the participants were as adults. For men, this included both physical and verbal aggression, but for women the correlation was simply for verbal aggression.

Research studies of pro-social behaviour

Reference and method	Procedure	Findings
Baron, Chase and Courtright (1979) Field experiment	Children aged between seven and nine were randomly allocated to watch one of three clips from The Waltons, an American TV series. The first group watched a clip showing cooperative behaviour, the second watched a clip with non-cooperative behaviour and the third watched a neutral clip. Following this, an accomplice of the experimenter walked past the classroom and dropped a pile of books.	Children who had watched the cooperative clip were quicker and more likely to help than those in the neutral group.
Rosenkoetter (1999) Correlational study	Rosenkoetter studied a sample of American children aged between five and nine and measured the amount of time they spent watching sitcoms (e.g. The Cosby Show) and studied reports from their parents about the amount of helpful behaviour they demonstrated.	There was a positive correlation between the two variables. Children who watched more pro-social sitcoms showed high levels of helpful behaviour.

Commentary

There is some evidence from laboratory experiments that young children copy behaviour that they see on television. They act out the behaviour almost immediately afterwards, whether it is pro- or antisocial in nature (e.g. Bandura *et al.*, 1963; Baron *et al.*, 1979). Laboratory experiments produce the largest effect size (Anderson and Bushman, 2002) of all research methods.

- Laboratory experiments look at immediate effects in very young children. It is not clear whether similar imitation would occur in older children or adults who have a more developed moral sense.

Other studies (e.g. Gunter *et al.*, 2002) that have used natural environments and longer follow-up periods suggest that simply watching violence does not have much of an effect on most children. Natural experiments suggest that children who already have an interest in aggression may pay more attention to violence and be more susceptible to it. This points to the importance of factors over and above simple imitation.

Correlational studies (e.g. Huesmann *et al.*, 2003; Phillips, 1983; Rosenkoetter, 1999) identify a correlation between watching TV and both pro- and antisocial behaviours. However, most people who watch boxing matches do not go out and commit murders. This suggests again that the explanation is not based on simple imitation but on cognitive priming in susceptible individuals.

- This is the view taken by the third variable theory (Comstock and Paik, 1991) who argue that the link between watching aggression and acting aggressively is caused by a third variable.
- It is hard to isolate the roles played by imitation and cognitive priming in aggression. Most evidence suggests that the majority of people who watch violence do not imitate what they see, and only a few individuals are more susceptible and may be influenced by media violence.

Social learning theory highlights the importance of nurture (experiences and upbringing) in the development of aggressive behaviours in children. However, it overlooks the role of nature – inbuilt differences in personality or temperament that may make some people more aggressive than others. Bandura's original research showed how children who were viewed by teachers as already more aggressive copied the range of violent adult behaviours. Similarly, Gunter's study of St Helena found that children judged as more aggressive before TV was introduced were more likely to select and watch aggressive programmes.

> **Think about it**
>
> If you are also revising the chapter on aggression, you could present a short summary of biological/ genetic evidence on aggression in order to 'criticise' the over-emphasis on nurture in social learning theory.

The effects of computer games

Playing violent computer games is different from watching violence in films or on television. In games like *Grand Theft Auto IV*, the player takes an active role in deciding what types of aggression will be used, and where, when and how the aggression will be used. Improvements in graphics make today's games increasingly realistic. What do we know about the effects of gaming on aggression?

Key study

Computer gaming (Anderson and Bushman, 2001)

Method: A meta-analysis of over 30 research studies with a combined total of more than 4,000 participants. Each study had examined the effects of playing violent computer games either through experimentation or non-experimental methods. The meta-analysis focused on two questions:

- Does playing violent computer games lead to a significant increase in aggression?

- If so, how does the exposure to gaming lead to increased aggression?

They measured the effects of computer games (the independent variable or IV) on different aspects (the dependent variables or DVs). For each of these, they calculated the effect size.

Here are their results.

Dependent variable	Effect size	Number of participants in the calculation
Aggressive behaviour	0.19	3,033
Aggressive thoughts	0.27	1,495
Aggressive feelings	0.18	1,151
Physiological arousal	0.22	395

Findings: The greatest effect of playing games was on aggressive cognitions, followed closely by physiological arousal.

Anderson and Bushman argue that gaming leads players to develop aggressive ideas about the world. They expect other people to behave aggressively and have stored scripts about how to act when confronted with situations that could potentially involve violence. These ideas have been incorporated into their general aggression model (GAM).

Commentary

- Anderson and Bushman's meta-analysis involved a large number of participants. This increases the reliability of the findings.

- The study was carried out in 2001. Since then, computer graphics have become far more realistic, implying that they may have an even greater effect than that found in 2001.

- Many studies of gaming are carried out in the laboratory where participants are given short exposure to games. In real life, gamers can continue to play for many hours or even days, e.g. when a new game comes out.

- Subsequent studies have begun to indicate how gaming may affect brain regions. Bartholow (2006) compared the brain activity of a group of regular gamers with non-gamers and found that the gamers showed reduced responses in brain activity to images of real-life violence. This indicated that they were desensitised to the violence.

The psychology of celebrity

You need to know how to

✔ describe at least one social psychological explanation why people enjoy 'relationships' with celebrities

✔ describe at least one evolutionary explanation for the attraction of celebrity

✔ explain why some people go on to stalk celebrities or become intense fans

✔ outline and evaluate research evidence relating to the attraction of celebrity and celebrity worship.

Evolutionary explanations of attraction to celebrity

Films and television have the power to make people famous and turn them into celebrities. Many people have a real fascination with celebrities and dream of becoming famous, as shown by the numbers who audition for television talent shows every year. A feature of modern culture is parasocial relationships with celebrity figures who we do not know in real life. These are unlike real relationships as they are entirely one-sided. At a low level, they are generally fairly harmless, but sometimes they can replace real face-to-face relationships and become obsessional and intense. How does psychology explain our cultural fascination with celebrity and its more extreme form of stalking?

Key theory

The evolutionary approach

The evolutionary approach assumes that behaviours exist today because they brought survival advantages to our ancestors in the past. In parasocial (celebrity) relationships, the individual looks up to someone famous and successful, often imitating their behaviour. What kinds of survival advantages could be brought by these behaviours?

■ In the hunter-gatherer environment, paying attention to the most successful members of the group and imitating their behaviour would have been a useful strategy that could have aided survival.

■ The prestige hypothesis (Henrich and Gil-White, 2001) argues that it is often difficult to establish which specific behaviours lead to success in a famous individual. Therefore, it makes sense in evolutionary terms to copy all of the behaviours of a successful individual

■ The desire to become famous (the attraction of celebrity) is explained by the status and power achieved by celebrities. In the past, having high status or resources meant greater opportunities for reproduction with other successful mates. A celebrity lifestyle offers ample opportunities for reproductive success.

Commentary

■ The evolutionary explanation of attraction to celebrity (i.e. the desire to become famous and live a celebrity lifestyle) can be seen as a loosely linked collection of ideas or a 'meta theory' sharing the common underlying assumption of survival advantage. These kinds of explanation are almost impossible to test scientifically, as we cannot go back in time to establish whether our ancestors had relationships of this kind in hunter-gatherer societies.

■ Some behaviours exist today simply because they have not been selected out by natural selection. The assumption that all behaviours once brought survival advantages is disputed by many people.

■ Social psychological explanations focus on the importance of low self-esteem in attraction to celebrity and there is considerable evidence to show that psychological factors play an important role in the development of parasocial relationships.

Social psychological explanations of attraction to celebrity

Key theory

The social psychological approach

The pathological view of celebrity relationships (Maltby, 2001) argues that people attach themselves to celebrities and form para-social relationships with them because of deficits in their own lives and/or relationships. In common with the evolutionary explanation, there are different components to the pathological explanation:

■ Poorer mental health: People seek celebrity relationships when they struggle with real, face-to-face relationships. This is sometimes known as the absorption-addiction model (McCutcheon, 2002). A more recent version of this model suggests that celebrity relationships are most attractive to people with lower self-esteem.

■ Insecure attachment styles: These types are most attracted to parasocial relationships because they make no demands and there is no risk of rejection. Insecurely attached people are also more likely to develop intense celebrity worship and to stalk their idols (McCann, 2001).

> ### Think about it
>
> The evolutionary and the social psychological explanations directly contradict each other. One assumes that attraction to celebrity is instinctive and the other assumes that it arises from upbringing and early childhood attachments. You can use the two explanations to evaluate each other by highlighting that supporting evidence for one explanation contradicts the other explanation. This is one way to develop your critical argument.

Commentary

■ The hypothesis about poorer mental health has received some support. Maltby *et al.* (2001) examined the link using a sample of more than 300 British students who were asked to complete measures of attraction to celebrities and a health questionnaire that measured loneliness and depression. They found that people who were attracted to celebrities often had some degree of social problems and were more likely to experience anxiety and/or depression.

■ There is also some evidence that self-esteem is important, especially in adolescents. Giles and Maltby (2004) measured celebrity attraction in a sample of nearly 200 British teenagers aged 11 to 16. They found that intense interest in celebrities was most common in teenagers who lacked close relationships with their parents. They suggest that celebrities provide adolescents with 'pseudo-friends' when they are making the transition to adulthood. Close attachment to celebrities can indicate difficulties with this transitional stage.

- McCutcheon (2006) has tested the attachment hypothesis (insecure attachment styles) using 300 students. She found no link between insecure attachments and celebrity relationships.

There is quite a lot of support to suggest that psychological factors – particularly low self-esteem – play an important role in the attraction to celebrity. This explanation contradicts the claims of the evolutionary approach.

These theories have very different views on the cause of celebrity relationships. The evolutionary approach sees them as driven by biological factors and programmed in genes, taking the nature side of the nature–nurture debate. In contrast, social psychological explanations view parasocial relationships as 'psychological' in origin, coming from our relationships with other people. This takes the nurture side of the nature–nurture debate.

Obsessive fandom and celebrity stalking

Very few fans stalk celebrities, but cases where they do receive considerable media attention. Stalking can involve different kinds of obsessive behaviour. Some common examples include:

- attempts to establish a close relationship by sending letters and gifts
- non-consensual communication (repeated ringing/emailing)
- malice and making threats.

Stalking typically occurs between people who are known to each other – often stalkers are ex-partners or potential partners. Cases of celebrity stalking make up only about 1 per cent of the total stalking cases, which makes them very rare (Hoffman and Sheridan, 2008).

McCutcheon (2004) has identified three stages or levels of celebrity fandom. The third level is commonly thought of as stalking:

- Entertainment social: attracted to the celebrity because of the fun it brings, which is shared with other people (talking about a celebrity, going to gigs, joining a fan club, reading a fanzine).
- Intense personal: an intense engagement with some obsessive thoughts about the celebrity ('He/she is my soulmate').
- Borderline pathological: obsessional behaviour and pursuit of the celebrity including trying to contact the celebrity ('If he/she is asked me to do something illegal, I would do it').

Causes of intense fandom/stalking

- Keinlen (1998) and McCann (2001) suggest that stalking behaviour is related to insecure attachment patterns. There is some evidence for this: McCutcheon et al. (2006) found that people with insecure attachment styles were more likely to believe that extreme following and stalking of celebrities was acceptable.
- Although articles about celebrity stalking abound in the popular media, academic study is relatively limited. It is difficult to investigate celebrity stalking due to its (thankfully) rare nature. There is a need for more case study research. This involves serious ethical considerations and also prevents generalisations being made.

Exam-style questions

Example 1

Content analysis has shown that many video games have violent themes. Many of these games are aimed at adolescents. There is a growing concern that such games encourage violent behaviour in young people who play them.

0 1 Explain some of the difficulties of conducting research into the effects of violent games. *(4 marks)*

0 2 Discuss what psychological research has told us about some of the effects on young people of playing video games. *(4 marks + 6 marks)*

0 3 Discuss how social psychology explains the attraction of celebrity.
(4 marks + 6 marks)

Example 2

0 4 Outline the elaboration likelihood model of persuasion/attitude change. *(4 marks)*

0 5 Discuss what psychological research has told us about the influence of the media on pro-social behaviour. *(4 marks + 8 marks)*

0 6 Evaluate explanations for the effectiveness of television in persuasion.
(8 marks)

Example 3

In an experiment, 70 teenagers were asked to complete a rating scale to assess their hostility, anger and anxiety. They were then randomly allocated to play a violent or non-violent video game. After the game, they completed the rating scale again. Scores on the scale before and after playing the game were compared.

Both groups had higher ratings on hostility and anger after playing the games, though the effect was more pronounced for the group playing the game with the violent content.

0 7 Discuss the findings of this study in relation to research into media influence on aggression. *(16 marks)*

0 8 'There is an increasing body of psychological research into the phenomena of intense fandom and celebrity worship.' Outline what psychological research has shown about intense fandom and/or celebrity worship. *(8 marks)*

Example 4

0 9 Outline **one** explanation of media influences on pro- and/or antisocial behaviour.
(4 marks)

1 0 The Department of Health wish to plan a television campaign to encourage people to take more exercise with the aim of reducing rates of obesity. Using your knowledge of the Hovland-Yale model, discuss the factors they may take into account when planning the campaign. *(10 marks)*

1 1 Discuss how evolutionary psychology explains the attraction of celebrity **and/or** celebrity worship. *(4 marks + 6 marks)*

Sample answers

A table of suggested content for the other examples is not provided for the Psychology in Action sections because the questions are more open and involved. You will need to interpret the questions and apply your knowledge of the topic and evaluative skills to answer them.

Example 1

0 1 One difficulty of conducting research into violent video games is ethics. It's very hard to carry out studies in this area because it would be unethical to ask people to play games such as Mortal Combat or GTA 4 if there is any chance that they could affect them badly. Another problem is that most studies that are carried out are in unrealistic situations: people are asked to play a game in a lab experiment for about half an hour and are then measured for aggression immediately afterwards. This isn't how people play in real life: many people will play a game for two or three days when it first comes out, so you can't really tell after half an hour. It lacks validity.

Two appropriate points here about ethics and validity, although they could have been expressed in a better way.

0 2 Quite a lot of studies have shown that game playing has effects similar to watching violent films – but maybe even worse. Anderson and Bushman conducted a meta-analysis of more than 30 studies of gaming with thousands of participants. They measured the overall effect of playing on different aspects of behaviour and found that playing had a big effect on aggressive thoughts and on arousal (feeling stressed/increased heart rate, etc.) although there was less of an effect on behaviour. But this comes to back to the answer in 01. People are only followed up in these studies straight after so you aren't going to see long-term effects. Anderson and Bushman's meta-analysis involves a large number of participants which meant that the findings should be quite reliable.

Description of the findings of a relevant study, but there could have been a bit more detail about them.

Remember that the examiner may not have marked any of the student's other answers, so try not to refer them.

Two relevant critical points here.

A different study by Bartholow (2006) has shown using brain scans that people's brains stop reacting to violence when they play games – this is desensitisation and some people argue that it is important in understanding later aggressive behaviour Many of the studies in this area are quite old: this is important because games have got much more realistic lately due to better computer graphics and we don't really know the impact of these better games. Finally, the view that games affect behaviour is on the nurture side of the nature–nurture debate; but it does ignore how aggressive people are in the first place (nature) and it could be that only aggressive people are drawn to play games or affected by them – a gene–environment interaction.

Good critical point.

An ambitious ending here with a link to relevant issues and debates.

03 *Social psychological explanations of celebrity argue that people develop a passion for celebrities because their own lives have problems or they are unbalanced (the pathological view). There are different hypotheses such as low self-esteem or insecure attachments. There is some evidence that celebrity relationships are more common in people with poorer health. Maltby (2001) studied more than 300 British students who were asked to complete measures of attraction to celebrities and a health questionnaire which measured loneliness and depression. She found that people who were attracted to celebrities often had social problems and were likely to experience anxiety and/or depression. Self-esteem is also proved to be important. Giles and Maltby (2004) measured celebrity attraction in a sample of nearly 200 British teenagers. They found that intense interest in celebrities was most common in teenagers who didn't have good relationships with their parents. But there isn't any real evidence that it is all to do with attachments. Poor attachments are used to explain everything in psychology – depression, etc. But people can get earned security so it isn't to do with that.*

• Basic coverage of explanation

• Two good studies, accurate and well used

AQA

Examiner's comments

Answer 01 is sufficient to gain marks in the top band, as is answer 02. For answer 03, the basic coverage and lack of detail in the description is the main flaw. The evaluation is much better and the answer overall would achieve marks just below the top band.

11 The psychology of addictive behaviour

Models of addictive behaviour

You need to know how to

✔ describe and evaluate the biological, learning and cognitive models of addiction

✔ describe and evaluate research evidence relating to these models

✔ describe and evaluate explanations and research relating to smoking and gambling addiction

✔ describe and evaluate explanations of initiation, relapse and maintenance of addiction and their application to smoking and gambling.

Biological model of addiction

Genetics

It is more likely that multiple genes play a role in addictive behaviour rather than a single gene. There may be a link between tobacco smoking and genes involved in dopamine regulation (e.g. Lerman *et al.*, 1999). Family studies of alcohol use disorders show high concordance rates between relatives for alcohol disorder (e.g. Merikangas *et al.*, 1998). Twin studies also show that there is likely to be a genetic component in addiction. For example, Kendler's twin study (1999) estimated the heritability of nicotine dependency to be 60–70 per cent.

Commentary

Although there may be a genetic component in addictive behaviour, it is not clear how this might work. It could be that genes influence the biology of individuals so they react to addictive substances differently, or it could be that genes affect their behavioural response to the addictive response. Also, it is likely that genetics will only cause a predisposition to become dependent on a substance – an environmental trigger is needed to start the addiction off.

Biochemistry

The dopamine reward system may be important in the development of substance addiction, in particular the mesolimbic dopamine system. People who are susceptible to addiction may have a more sensitive mesolimbic dopamine pathway than other individuals. Serotonin may also be involved in the regulation of impulsive behaviour. It has been found that some people with addictive behaviour have low levels of serotonin, possibly suggesting that the serotonin system that helps to limit reinforcing and pleasurable behaviours may be faulty in these individuals.

The endogenous opioid system may also be key. Opioid neurotransmitters in the brain include encephalin and endorphins. These systems are activated by pleasurable states and also by drugs such as alcohol and nicotine. Naltrexone, a drug used in the treatment of alcohol addiction, works by blocking opioid receptors in the brain and so stops alcohol having its rewarding effect.

Think about it

To what extent would you say that this approach to addiction is reductionist? What other factors should be taken into account as well as genetic and biological factors when trying to explain addiction?

Commentary

■ Alcohol and nicotine affect the nervous system by increasing dopamine levels (Altman *et al.* 1996).

■ The fact that Naltrexone works suggests that there may be an effect of the opioid system. Studies have also shown that long-term smoking disrupts the opioid system (e.g. Krishnan-Sarin *et al.* 1999).

■ It is very likely that brain systems are involved in addiction to substances and perhaps in behavioural addictions too. However, much of the data is correlational so it is hard to draw inferences about cause and effect from it.

Learning models of addiction

The learning approach sees addiction as a set of learned behaviours that can therefore be unlearned. Learning may take place in a number of ways. Two of these ways are operant conditioning and social learning theory (SLT).

Operant conditioning

Addictive behaviour is more likely to be repeated if it is reinforced or rewarded, e.g. gaining approval of friends. Some addictive behaviours – such as smoking – may be repeated because of negative reinforcement. This means the removal of unpleasant consequences. In the case of smoking, the negative reinforcement is the removal of unpleasant withdrawal symptoms.

Social learning theory

This approach takes into account cognitive factors as well as the fact that we may learn from our peers, family and friends. Expectancy, attributions and imitation are all included in the theory.

If an alcoholic passes a pub where people are drinking outside, they may experience a physiological response to the smell/sight of alcohol as well as other processes such as memories of drinking and so on. These reactions may be interpreted as a need to drink, hence the addiction.

Also, addicts have expectations when they experience cues for the addictive substances. When people are seen drinking outside a pub, the addict may see how drinking is enjoyable and realise that they would enjoy drinking. This may encourage them to drink again.

Commentary

Operant conditioning can explain many aspects of addictive behaviour but it does not take into account people's cognitive processes. For example, people make decisions about their behaviour based on costs and benefits (see below). In contrast, SLT *does* take these cognitive factors into account. It also emphasises the importance of role models in shaping behaviour and can explain the importance of the media in developing and maintaining addictions. The behavioural approach to addiction can of course be taken in conjunction with the biological approach. For example, it may be that the physiological effects of addictive substances are in themselves reinforcing.

Cognitive models of addiction

The cognitive approach puts an emphasis on learning, memory, problem solving, planning and other cognitive processes in explaining addiction.

AQA Examiner's tip

If you can link research that you talk about in your answers to wider issues in psychology, such as the nature–nurture debate, then this will show the examiner that you have a good awareness of these issues.

Apply it

Try to make brief notes in bullet-point style to list what research evidence shows about the possible genetic and biochemical factors involved in addiction.

AQA Examiner's tip

When you use research to support a point that you make in the exam, try to use other research to substantiate or to critically evaluate the research. This will help you to improve your AO2 and AO3 marks.

- One key process is self-regulation, which is about weighing up the relative importance of social and physical factors as well as the individual's own goals when planning behaviour.
- Some cognitive psychologists suggest that people who engage in potentially self-destructive behaviour may have faulty systems that control their actions. They seem to be unable to control their actions despite wanting to. This may be due to people attaching a higher weight on the present than on the future consequences of an action. This is a preference for immediate gratification rather than future benefits and has been called cognitive myopia by Herrnstein and Prelec (1992).
- The cognitive processing model suggests that addictive behaviours become automatic, and so they are difficult to stop. Facing situations that trigger automatic responses is difficult for addicts and requires a lot of mental effort. This can be particularly true when there are other stresses in an addict's life.

Commentary

Cognitive models can be useful to describe the thought processes involved in addictive behaviour. Some therapies have been developed as a result of this approach, and they have been helpful in working with people with addiction. This approach is also quite effective at explaining why relapse occurs when people are trying to give up addictive behaviours. However, the cognitive approach does not really address the issue of initiation.

Explanations for smoking

Four kinds of factor may contribute to people smoking:

- biological
- social
- cognitive
- individual differences.

Biological

There may be a genetic factor. (Shields' twin study (1962) found high concordance rates for smoking behaviour).

Commentary

- Twin studies never show 100 per cent concordance rates, which means that some other factor or factors must be involved.
- Twin studies do not control for the fact that twins have usually grown up together, so similar behaviours may be due to this as well as genetics.

Social

SLT explains that children imitate the behaviour of role models and this may be why some smoke. Parental smoking increases a child's likelihood to smoke by a factor of 2. If parents are anti-smoking, a child is seven times less likely to smoke.

AQA Examiner's tip

If a question is focused on one of these approaches or models, remember that you may be able to gain AO2/3 marks by comparing or contrasting the model with the other two. For example, the learning theory approach may be used in commentary about the cognitive model.

Apply it

Divide your page into three columns and try to summarise the three approaches to addiction – biological, learning theory and the cognitive approach. Then, using a different colour pen, include some commentary on each of the areas you have included.

Commentary

- A 1996 study by Michell and West showed that adolescents are not as susceptible to peer pressure in relation to smoking as might be thought.
- Peer pressure seems to work in a complex way and is probably a key influence.

Individual differences

Some studies have found evidence for links between smoking and poor school performance, low self-esteem and risk-taking behaviour.

Commentary

Much of this research is correlational and so a causative link cannot be made.

Cognitive

A study investigated reasons for 11- and 12-year-olds starting to smoke and found that children's behavioural intentions were a good predictor of subsequent smoking behaviour. This may be a universal effect as similar results were found in Chinese children.

Commentary

Cognitive factors may be key in planning anti-smoking campaigns and they can direct policymakers and planners to ways of making campaigns effective.

Commentary regarding all of the explanations

It is likely that an interaction of factors is the best explanation for smoking addiction. We know that smoking is strongly influenced by family and peer behaviour, but there may be other personality factors too, and these may well have a biological basis. As smoking is still seen as a social habit by many people, we should expect that social factors and psychosocial factors are key as well as biological ones.

Initiation, maintenance and relapse

The table on page 162 summarises some of the processes that may underlie initiation, maintenance and relapse in smoking behaviour from the perspective of three different models of addiction. Physical addictions such as smoking, where nicotine can lead to physical dependence and withdrawal symptoms, also involve cognitive expectancies about the effects of smoking besides modelling and imitation of parents and peers. The pleasure of smoking is a positive reinforcer for the behaviour, while avoiding withdrawal symptoms acts as a negative reinforcer for continuing smoking. So each model has something to say about initiation, maintenance and relapse in smoking addiction.

AQA Examiner's tip

Remember that if you outline some of the processes in your answers, AO2/3 marks are likely to be given for research supporting their involvement in addiction. Also remember that there is no 'correct' model.

A complete explanation for smoking addiction will involve biological, cognitive and learning models. Relevant commentary on this interaction between the models can gain excellent AO2/3 marks.

Think about it

To what extent do you think that smoking is still seen as a social habit? Is it now seen as more antisocial? If this is the case, do you think that the explanations for people taking up and continuing to smoke need to be rethought?

AQA Examiner's tip

This introductory paragraph about the table contains important information about how to use effectively the information for evaluation. It will be useful to find and use relevant research studies to support the models.

	Biological model	Cognitive model	Learning model
Initiation	Genetic vulnerability Sensitivity of dopamine reward system to nicotine	Expectancies that smoking will have positive effects; stress reduction, weight loss, improve mood, etc Negative effects are minimised by high self-efficacy: 'I can control my smoking'	Modelling and vicarious reinforcement (peers and parents) Positive reinforcement from peers Direct reinforcement from positive effects of smoking – weight loss, reduced stress, etc.
Maintenance	Activation of dopamine reward pathways Avoid withdrawal symptoms caused by physical addiction to nicotine	Belief in positive aspects of smoking Expectancies that abstinence will lead to negative consequences High self-efficacy: 'I can give up any time'	Reinforcement from peers and social group. Also from improved concentration, reduced stress, etc. Negative reinforcement by avoiding withdrawal symptoms and loss of peer group support.
Relapse	Abstinence leads to physical craving and withdrawal symptoms, making relapse likely.	Perceived negative consequences of abstinence – weight gain, increased stress, irritability, etc. High self-efficacy: 'I can give up any time'	Exposure to cues classically conditioned to smoking Negative reinforcement by avoiding withdrawal symptoms Abstinence directly 'punished' by weight gain, increased stress, etc.

Explanations for problem gambling

Three kinds of factor may contribute to problem gambling:

- biological
- sociocultural
- psychological.

Biological

As with smoking, twin studies suggest there may be a genetic vulnerability to problem gambling. It may be that the genes controlling some of the neurotransmitters in the brain are involved. After a win, some of the levels of neurotransmitters in the brain rise, and elevated levels have also been found when the person is getting ready to gamble. Stopping gambling and stopping taking drugs have been found to have similar physiological effects, for example, insomnia, loss of appetite (e.g. Rosenthal and Lesieur, 1992). This suggests that a biological mechanism may be involved. Some studies have found frontal lobe and EEG abnormalities in problem gamblers (e.g. Cavedini *et al.*, 2002).

Commentary

- Twin studies do not ever show 100 per cent concordance rates, which means that some other factor or factors must be involved. Twin studies do not control for the fact that twins have usually grown up together, so any similar behaviours may be due to this shared upbringing.

- Any link between levels of brain chemicals and problem gambling is only an association. It does not necessarily mean that the altered levels of chemicals are the cause of the problem gambling.

Apply it

Interview someone you know who is trying to give up smoking or who has already given up smoking. Talk to them about the addiction and about how they felt – physically, psychologically and socially as they tried to give up. Try to link what they say to what you have learned about the main factors that may be involved in smoking – for example to psychological, biological and sociocultural factors.

Sociocultural

If people have more access to gambling opportunities, they are more likely to become problem gamblers. Alcohol may increase gambling in young people who already gamble.

Commentary

- In Australia, there are different laws in the various states and territories relating to the availability of gambling, but the pattern of gambling is similar nationally. However, there is no clear evidence to prove that availability affects problem gambling. Also, in the UK, the introduction of the National Lottery did not increase problem gambling.

- There is inconsistent evidence relating to alcohol and gambling. For example, regular casino gamblers actually drink less when they are gambling.

Psychological

Impulsivity in childhood is a risk factor for problem gambling. Attention deficit/hyperactivity disorder (ADHD) is characterised by risk-taking. A higher rate of childhood ADHD is reported in problem gamblers than in non-gamblers. Operant conditioning may be key in the maintenance and initiation of problem gambling. Cognitive processes may also be involved in the origin and maintenance of gambling. For example, gamblers may engage in irrational self-talk when gambling, and this irrationality may maintain arousal in gambling episodes (Sharpe *et al.*, 1995).

Commentary

- Again, the link between ADHD, risk-taking and gambling needs to be investigated further. For example, could it be the case that both ADHD and gambling are caused by the same underlying biological mechanism, or are other factors involved?

- Although it seems intuitively that operant conditioning is key, operant conditioning cannot explain why problem gamblers continue to gamble even when they consistently lose money.

- Evidence for a link between faulty cognitions and problem gambling is convincingly strong, e.g. Delfabbro and Winefield, 1999).

Commentary regarding all the explanations

There are a variety of gambling activities such as the lottery, casino gambling and betting on horses. It is unlikely that any explanation is powerful enough to account for problem gambling in all of these. Sharpe (2002) suggests that a biopsychosocial model, incorporating all three sets of factors in interaction, is the most likely to explain the initiation, reinforcement and maintenance of problem gambling.

Blaszczynski and Nower (2002) suggest a different model, and propose that there may be three different routes to problem gambling:

- behaviourally conditioned people who are not pathologically disturbed but who make poor judgement calls

- emotionally vulnerable gamblers who use gambling as a way of achieving emotional stability and

- antisocial impulsive problem gamblers who have a biological dysfunction and may have a range of problems of which gambling may be only one (e.g. criminal activity, substance abuse).

Apply it

Imagine you are a psychologist working with someone with a gambling problem and try to link biological, psychological and sociocultural factors to their gambling behaviour. You might want to draw up two tables to do this (one for smoking and one for problem gambling). Include a commentary for each of the points you make about the person's behaviour.

Initiation, maintenance and relapse

The table below summarises some of the processes that may underlie initiation, maintenance and relapse in gambling behaviour from the perspective of three different models of addiction. Gambling has been shown to activate dopamine reward pathways in the brain while minimising the costs and maximising the chances of winning is an important cognitive bias found in gambling addiction. Partial reinforcement through occasional wins is a powerful means of maintaining gambling behaviour, but relapse can occur if the gambler tries to avoid the pain of not gambling.

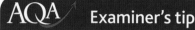 **Examiner's tip**

The introductory paragraph about the table contains important information about how to use effectively the information for evaluation. Researching and finding relevant research support studies for the processes will be useful.

	Biological model	Cognitive model	Learning model
Initiation	Genetic vulnerability Sensitivity to arousing effects of gambling	Expectancies of pleasurable effects of gambling Cognitive biases minimising costs and exaggerating chances of winning High levels of impulsivity	Modelling and vicarious reinforcement Positive reinforcement from peer approval Rewarding effects of arousal and excitement
Maintenance	Activation of dopamine reward system Avoidance of physical withdrawal effects	Perceived positive effects of gambling such as improved mood, winning Need for immediate gratification and loss of inhibition High self-efficacy: 'I can stop at any time'. Cognitive bias exaggerates chances of winning.	Rewarding effects of arousal and excitement Partial reinforcement (occasional wins) powerfully sustains gambling. Direct reinforcement from peers and social support
Relapse	Avoidance of withdrawal effects such as increased anxiety and physiological arousal	Perceived loss of positive aspects of gambling such as improved mood, monetary gains, etc. High self-efficacy: 'I can stop gambling at any time'.	Direct punishment from loss of positive aspects of gambling Widespread exposure to cues classically conditioned to gambling (shops, arcades, etc.) lead to anticipated rewards of relapse.

AQA Examiner's tip

Remember that if you outline some of the processes in your answers, AO2/3 marks are likely to be given for research supporting their involvement in addiction. However, as with smoking addiction, there is no 'correct' answer.

All three models (biological, cognitive and learning) can make significant contributions to explaining gambling addiction, and a complete explanation will involve all of them. Relevant commentary on the need for this interaction in explaining gambling is an effective route to AO2/3 marks.

AQA Examiner's tip

At A2, not many marks are available for AO1 in paper 4 answers (only 8 marks out of 24). So you need to make sure that you practise writing clear succinct descriptions and outlines of research.

Vulnerability to addiction and the role of the media

You need to know how to

✔ describe risk factors in the development of addiction including stress, peers, age and personality

✔ provide informed commentary for these risk factors

✔ describe and evaluate research into the role of the media in addiction.

Risk factors in the development of addiction

Factor	Description	Evaluation
Stress	Addicts who cope badly with stress are more prone to relapse than those who deal with stress effectively. Understanding this link may help to pinpoint factors in the development of addiction (Cleveland & Harris 2010).	The practical application of the research is it suggests that developing ways of coping with stress is a better way of resisting addictive behaviour (e.g. relapse) than trying to avoid stress.
Peers	Peers have an influence on the development of addictions. Associating with others using drugs, for example, may be one of the biggest single risk factors in the development of addiction.	Other evidence suggests that experimenting with drugs while alone is also a key factor in the development of addictions. Recent work has suggested that the influence of peers is often over-emphasised. (Bauman & Ennett 2006)
Age	Teenagers who start using alcohol or other drugs at an early age have a higher risk of developing an addiction later on, in comparison to those who first use drugs when they are older. A similar link exists for smoking.	The effect described, of starting younger being linked to a higher risk of later addiction, could be due to genetic or to learned factors. Further research is currently being undertaken to try to identify the exact mechanism involved.
Personality	Neuroticism is a personality trait that may be linked with addictive behaviours. People with high levels of neuroticism are likely to experience anxiety or depression and may self-medicate with tobacco, alcohol, or drugs as a coping mechanism.	Researchers found that smoking only accounted for up to 40 % of the association between high neuroticism and death rates in neurotic individuals, so other factors must also be considered taken into account. (Mroczek, Spiro & Turiano 2009)
Gender	Gender differences depend on what the addiction is. Currently male smoking rates in the West are remaining stable/declining. Female rates are increasing slightly.	Evidence has shown that smokers weigh less than non-smokers, and smokers who give up do gain weight. Also, smoking may be used by females as a diet strategy (Ogden and Fox, 1994).
Family influence	Parents are influential models for children. If parents use drugs then adolescents are more likely to use drugs sooner and more often. The same applies if parents demonstrate relaxed attitudes to drug use.	There are empirical studies showing a link between parental attitudes and addictive behaviour, e.g. Fisher (1999) in relation to gambling. However, there are children whose parents drink/use drugs but they do not, so other factors must be considered.

AQA Examiner's tip

If you can make informed commentary on studies and research that you talk about in your answers and relate your comments to methods in psychology, this will show the examiner that you have a good awareness of these issues. In this area, for example, you could make the point that there is a lot of correlational research and that correlational research does not allow us to make cause and effect links.

AQA Examiner's tip

Remember to use research to support each of these points in the exam and try to use other research either to support or to critically evaluate the research. This will help you to improve your AO2/3 marks.

The role of the media in addictive behaviour

	Description	Evaluation
Advertising	Advertising is used both to increases sales of things like lottery tickets and alcoholic drinks as well as to increase awareness of government health interventions such as drink-driving campaigns. Advertising may make people more likely to start gambling. TV adverts for the lottery focus on the benefits of winning – they do not mention the non-winners. In young people, advertising of alcohol increases awareness and shapes attitudes. (e.g. young drinkers show a preference for heavily marketed products).	It is very hard to measure the effects of advertising as other factors are involved that can affect people's decisions. The fact that tobacco advertising is now illegal and alcohol advertising is subject to severe restrictions suggests that it is in fact effective.
Models in the media	For many years TV programmes showed people smoking and drinking alcohol. This is now less acceptable. This modelling was both positive and negative. Social learning theory suggests that individuals can learn behaviour though observation and vicarious reinforcement. So positive consequences for TV characters would be more likely to encourage someone to engage in the addictive behaviour.	If models (i.e. behavioural models) are seen being negatively reinforced or punished for their behaviour then it is less likely to be repeated, so TV can have a beneficial effect as well as a negative one. The effects of behavioural models on TV are also hard to measure.

AQA Examiner's tip

Remember: you need to be able to back up each of these points with research evidence from your reading.

Reducing addictive behaviour

You need to know how to

✔ describe the theory of planned behaviour (TPB) in the context of addiction

✔ evaluate TPB in explaining prevention and reduction of addictive behaviour

✔ describe and evaluate psychological, biological and public health interventions and legislation in reducing addictive behaviours.

Theory of planned behaviour (TPB)

This theory attempts to explain how people come to choose their behaviours regarding things like addictive behaviours such as smoking. TPB proposes three factors:

- attitude – personal beliefs about the behaviour
- subjective norms – what they think others think about it
- perceived behavioural control – can they successfully carry out the behaviour

People have different attitudes and norms and ideas about whether or not they think they can actually achieve what is being considered. These factors vary in strength and determine whether or not a behaviour occurs. Decisions will vary depending on the person and the situation.

Perceived behavioural control in an individual can be affected by internal factors such as motivation but also external factors such as practical or financial barriers to be overcome to change behaviour.

Commentary

It can be hard to find out what people's attitudes and intentions are. Not all measures that ask people about these necessarily predict subsequent behaviour. For example, Sheppard et al. (1988) suggest that there are other factors that may have an effect on behaviour that are not always measured, such as the number of choices available to a person in a given situation. Also, it may be that being under the influence of an addictive substance, such as alcohol, changes a person's intentions.

Research has shown that the assumptions of the TPB do predict subsequent behaviour. However, TPB does not take into account factors such as feelings and emotions. Emotions may need to be studied as well in order to get a full picture of how TPB can really explain people's behaviour in relation to changing their addictive habits.

Types of intervention

Four kinds of intervention are on the specification:

- psychological
- biological
- public health interventions
- legislation.

Apply it

Annabel is trying to give up drinking alcohol. The theory of planned behaviour (TPB) could be used to explain how she might try to do this. Make a flow chart that shows how the theory might describe Annabel's attempts to give up alcohol.

Think about it

Do you think that the smoking ban has made any difference to people's smoking behaviour? Do you think that the effect on the smoking behaviour of teenagers (who may not be old enough to go into pubs) is the same as that on adults? What do you think is the most effective way of getting people to stop smoking?

Apply it

You are a therapist working with a team of doctors who are trying to devise an anti-smoking campaign for teenagers in their area. Summarise the main types of intervention that you could put in place and (for each) suggest reasons why the intervention may not work.

Examiner's tip

At A2, many marks are available for AO1 in paper 4 answers (only 8 marks out of 24) so you need to make sure that you practise writing clear and succinct descriptions and outlines of these interventions. Spend some time thinking about intervention strategies too – you might be asked to devise/recommend strategies or give advice about how to prevent addiction.

Interventions and their effectiveness

Intervention	Description	Evaluation
Psychological	Aversion therapy – based on classical conditioning. For example, Antabuse is a drug that, when taken (by alcoholics), makes them vomit when they consume alcohol. The association between vomiting and alcohol is made.	Found to be effective, e.g. Lang and Martlatt (1982). The person has to be motivated to take the drug, although given as an implant solves this issue. Also, it fails to address the reasons for the addiction unless given in conjunction with therapy.
	Self-management techniques, e.g. keeping a diary of addictive behaviours and noting triggers and feelings	Seem only to be useful as part of a broader programme, not on their own. (Hall *et al.*, 1990).
	Cognitive approach. For example, CBT – training in communication and problem-solving skills and strategies for preventing relapse, often involving the addict's family and friends as support	Reasonably effective but more so when used with medication (Feeny *et al.*, 2002).
Biological	NRT (nicotine replacement therapy), e.g. nicotine patches or gum. A low dose of nicotine to help to reduce withdrawal symptoms and are positively reinforcing, e.g. relieve stress. May also desensitise nicotine receptors in the brain, so a cigarette while on patches is less satisfying.	The low nicotine doses are not satisfying and so some people will give up the therapy. Although it removes the effects of tar etc. in cigarettes, nicotine itself may be harmful. Despite this, a cost benefit analysis would suggest that NRT is a better option than smoking cigarettes.
	Bupropion – drug that increases brain levels of dopamine. It also seems to reduce the pleasurable effects of smoking.	Has reasonable success rates (Watts *et al.*, 2002)
	Varenicline also causes dopamine to be released in the brain and blocks the effects of nicotine.	Higher success rates than Bupropion and also reduces relapse rates in the medium term
Public health interventions	Doctors can give out advice and leaflets and are in the ideal position to follow this up.	Parkes *et al.* (2008) study of five GP practices found it was effective, especially when patients were told their true lung age. Doctors are in the ideal front-line position and may be able to give advice at an early stage. These interventions are less effective for dependencies on alcohol or other drugs.
Legislation	From 1989 to 2000, there was a strong correlation between the amount spent on advertising alcoholic products and their consumption by underage drinkers. In November 2000, the European Commission made recommendations regarding advertising to help address this problem. More recently, the rules regarding advertising alcohol in the UK (effective from September 2010) have had a strong emphasis on making sure that advertising does not appeal to under 18s.	Studies seem to suggest that a reduction in advertising does reduce the behaviour (e.g. Pekurinen, 1989). But there are many other factors that it is hard to control for (e.g. tighter restrictions on sales or simultaneous health campaigns).
	In 2003, cigarette advertising in the UK was banned. Since July 2007, in the UK, smoking in public places has been illegal.	Cigarette sales have decreased since 2007 (by 7% in the first month after the ban) and cigarette consumption seems to be falling by 2% annually. Also, the amount of air pollution in pubs and clubs has decreased. These figures suggest that early worries that smokers would continue to smoke but just do it at home are unfounded. Again, many factors are involved so it is hard to assess the effects of the smoking ban on its own.

Exam-style questions

Here are some examples of the kind of exam-style questions that you could encounter for this topic and some sample student responses and associated examiner feedback.

Example 1

A recent large survey on behalf of the Gambling Commission provided a number of interesting findings about gambling behaviour in Great Britain. For example, 57 per cent of the population had gambled on the National Lottery Draw in 2007, although the rate of problem gambling in the adult population was only about 0.6 per cent.

0 1 Explain some of the difficulties of gathering data about problem gambling. *(4 marks)*

0 2 Outline and evaluate **one** explanation of gambling addiction. *(4 marks + 6 marks)*

'The relapse rate for smokers in the first three months after trying to give up is estimated at 70 per cent.'

0 3 Discuss reasons why relapse occurs in people with addictive behaviour. *(4 marks + 6 marks)*

AQA 2010

Example 2

'Children who experiment with smoking can very quickly get hooked on nicotine and it only takes a few cigarettes to turn them into regular smokers, a new study has found. Two other studies published today show that smoking by peers and teachers can also independently influence the take up of smoking by young teenagers.' (Action on Smoking and Health, 2002)

0 4 Explain why policymakers would be more inclined to accept the evidence of these 'published studies' rather than mere opinion. *(4 marks)*

0 5 Outline and evaluate the learning model as an explanation of initiation and maintenance of smoking addiction in young people. *(4 marks + 6 marks)*

0 6 'We are all exposed to models of addictive behaviour, yet not everyone becomes addicted.'

Discuss individual differences in vulnerability to addiction. *(4 marks + 6 marks)*

AQA 2007

Example 3

'Sally is a young woman who puts herself down all the time. She thinks that she is overweight and has started to diet. Like her parents and some of her friends, Sally smokes cigarettes. Her smoking habit has recently become excessive and she has become addicted to nicotine.'

0 7 Using your knowledge of the psychology of addictive behaviour, explain some of the likely reasons why Sally has become addicted to smoking. *(6 marks)*

0 8 Outline the theory of planned behaviour. *(4 marks)*

0 9 Outline **two** examples of public health interventions aimed at reducing addictive behaviour. *(4 marks)*

1 0 Assess the effectiveness of public health interventions **and/or** legislation in reducing addictive behaviour. *(10 marks)*

AQA June 2010

Example 4

The government is very interested in preventing addictive behaviour and has funded a number of interventions that they hope will be effective in helping to prevent people becoming addicts.

1 1 Explain some of the difficulties of measuring the effectiveness of interventions for addictive behaviours. *(4 marks)*

1 2 Outline and evaluate psychological interventions for addictive behaviour. *(4 marks + 6 marks)*

1 3 Discuss how the theory of reasoned action can be used in explaining the prevention and reduction of addictive behaviours. *(4 marks + 6 marks)*

Sample answers

A table of suggested content for the other examples is not provided for the Psychology in Action sections because the questions are more open and involved. You will need to interpret the questions and apply your knowledge of the topic and evaluative skills to answer them.

Example 1

0 1 *When gathering data it can be hard to get people to be in the study as it could be difficult to find people that were long-term gamblers. So it could be hard to get a sample. Also, gambling may be seen as unacceptable behaviour and so people may lie about their behaviours. Alternatively they might not even realise themselves that they had a problem. Issues like this would mean that any data collected would not be very valid – in other words, it would lack external validity and the results would not be able to be generalised from the sample that was studied. Also, if researchers use questionnaire studies and surveys, we already know that people may not return questionnaires, for example.*

This question is assessing AO2/3 skills. The student has identified some issues and also put them into the context of gambling.

0 2 *Learning theory is one explanation of gambling addiction. For example, operant conditioning would look at the reinforcing effects of gambling. For a gambler it may be that winning is reinforcing, not just the money that is won but also the feelings of success when the gambler wins. There might also be negative reinforcement, so gambling might help the gambler to cope with stress or negative emotions and this would be something else that would increase the likelihood of gambling happening again.*

This student could have chosen risk factors, (e.g. personality). Alternatively, a biological predisposition could have been discussed.

Although this may seem like a good explanation it does not explain why gamblers go on gambling even when they do not win. However, the fact that operant conditioning says that variable reinforcement schedules are the most effective does explain why fruit machines are so addictive – in some ways it is better only to win sometimes than to win every time. In fact though gambling can be seen as quite complex and it is probable that no one explanation can provide a full explanation for gambling behaviours it is probably a combination of biological, social and psychological factors. It may be that nature and nurture are both involved. For example, a gambler may have a genetic predisposition to gambling, but then social factors such as having friends who go horse racing etc. may kick the addiction off. Also, gambling is often associated with alcohol and so the availability of alcohol may be a confounding variable that makes it hard. This means that it is hard for policymakers to make a policy or guidelines which would help gamblers as gambling is such a complex issue.

The explanation has to be evaluated. Cite evidence to support assertions. Need to contrast operant conditioning with other explanations to provide effective evaluation. Nature–nurture is mentioned but other issues and debates could have been discussed too, such as free will and determinism.

0 3 *Smokers are usually biologically addicted to nicotine and this makes it very hard to give up. Some evidence suggests that in fact long-term smoking alters the dopamine system in the brain and so even after many months ex-smokers can relapse. The withdrawal effects from nicotine are commonly described as very unpleasant indeed, so this can make relapse more likely.*

However, usually it is thought that the biological effects of nicotine only last for between two and six weeks so after this time relapse may be due to social and psychological factors. For example, social cues. Smokers may find it hard at the end of a meal when they used to have a cigarette, or when they see an ashtray.

Cognitive psychologists would also include self-efficacy in their explanations of relapse. If the person does not think that they can give up then they are very unlikely to be able to do it. Of course it is likely again that more than one of these factors operates at the same time.

So for example, if a person is experiencing the unpleasant effects of nicotine withdrawal and then they have a bad day at work and then on top of that maybe they do not believe that they will be able to give up then it is going to be much more difficult for them.

It is likely that more than one explanation for relapse needs to be considered at a time.

Also, individual differences should be considered. It is probably true that different people react to giving up smoking in different ways and if you were working with someone and trying to prevent relapse you would have to consider this.

At least two explanations should be given, as the question says 'reasons' not 'a reason'. The student has provided this as they have covered biological, cognitive and social explanations.

To evaluate, you could use research studies. This was not done here. Relevant issues and debates could have been referred to such as ethics, or free will and determinism, or nature–nurture. Commentary based on these could have improved the mark gained.

AQA Examiner's comments

This is a reasonably good set of answers overall and would get marks in the basic/reasonable band. The student has tried to answer the questions and to include commentary on the explanations and ideas that they have covered.

The answer to question 03 is good one that would attract high marks both for description (AO1) and evaluation (AO2/3). Although it seems a little muddled, it covers all of the material and is relatively well expressed. It is a bit short, however, and so although a real attempt has been made to include some sustained commentary, a few more sentences would have helped.

12 Anomalistic psychology

The study of anomalous experience

You need to know how to

✔ explain the scientific status of parapsychology and what pseudoscience is

✔ explain the terms extra sensory perception (ESP) and psychokinesis (PK)

✔ describe and evaluate research into PK and ESP (including the Gansfeld technique) and its methodological issues and controversies.

Psychological research into the paranormal is called parapsychology. Pseudoscience is research that seems to be scientific but actually is not. The main differences between science and pseudoscience are to do with methodology and scientific rigour.

Some of the features of a science are:

■ objectivity
■ replicability
■ use of the hypothetico-deductive method.

AQA Examiner's tip

When you answer a question on this topic, if you make it clear that you understand what science is and how it is different from pseudoscience, this will show your breadth of knowledge.

Differences between science and pseudoscience

Science	Pseudoscience
Findings are peer reviewed.	Peer review is less likely. Results are often communicated directly to the public.
Areas of study are dictated by the advancement of human understanding.	Areas of study are likely to be chosen because of their interest to the researcher.
Hypothetico-deductive method is used. A hypothesis is generated, then data is gathered.	Data is often collected first and then explanations are formulated to fit the data that has been collected.
Hypotheses can be tested rigorously and if necessary falsified.	Rigorous testing is less likely to be a feature of the research.

The study of parapsychological phenomena such as ESP (extrasensory perception) and PK (psychokinesis), by their nature, lend themselves to abuse, but scientific fraud also happens in other areas.

Here are some examples of research into ESP. They attempt to assess whether anomalistic experience is a real phenomenon. These examples were later revealed to be fraudulent.

The Soal and Goldney studies (1938–41)

Soal and Goldney studied ESP in a large number of participants on card-guessing tasks. They appeared to find robust scientific evidence that two participants in their studies did have telepathic abilities. However, subsequent re-analysis of the data suggested that it had been altered and faked.

Commentary

- It may have been that the personal pressure to find evidence for ESP was what motivated Soal.
- His behaviour, however, brought the whole area of parapsychology into disrepute.
- He gave the impression of being scientifically rigorous, but in fact there were a number of flaws in his procedures that meant fraud would have been possible.

Levy Jr (1974)

Levy investigated the ability of rats to anticipate events by ESP or to effect physical changes by PK.

He implanted electrodes into the pleasure centres of rats' brains so that he could stimulate them to cause intense pleasure. A computer generator was set up so that the pleasurable stimulation was given randomly, but overall for 50 per cent of the time. Levy Jr wanted to investigate whether the rats could anticipate the computer by using ESP or influence its mechanism using PK. If they could, their pleasure score would be higher than 50 per cent. Levy Jr found a 54 per cent pleasure score and claimed that the rats had some psychic powers.

Commentary

- One of the electrical engineers who worked on the equipment for the experiment caught Levy Jr cheating by pulling the plug out of the computer selectively so it only registered occasions where the rats did appear to influence the shock generator.
- Even if evidence for psychic abilities in rats had been found, it would not necessarily mean that humans share these abilities.
- It is likely the rats experienced pain – an ethical issue.

The scientific status of parapsychology is brought into question by these examples of fraudulent research. To gain credit in the wider scientific community, research needs to follow the scientific principle of objectivity, be reported accurately and be able to be replicated. However, the nature of what is being studied in parapsychological research can make this difficult. So the value of research must be based on scrutinising the methods of the research on a case-by-case basis.

Apply it

Show your understanding by illustrating the concept of scientific fraud in anomalistic psychology using an example from the research you have read. Try to write a short paragraph briefly outlining this example.

Methodological issues in the study of paranormal cognition (ESP) and action (PK)

In typical Ganzfeld studies of ESP, there is a sender who tries to telepathically send information about pictures to the receiver. The receiver wears opaque goggles or has their eyes covered, and white noise is played. This stops them receiving any cues from their visual and auditory fields during the sending period. The receiver then has to choose which of a small set of pictures was 'sent' to them. Later Ganzfeld studies use the autoGanzfeld techniques, where the researcher, sender and receiver are all kept separate from each other, and the selection of material to be sent is done by a computer. These changes mean that the possibility of fraud is reduced.

Key study

Study of ESP by Sargeant *et al.* (1979)

Method: The Ganzfeld technique was used. The sender was in a different room from the receiver. For 30 minutes, the sender concentrated and tried to 'send' a picture to the receiver. At the end of the sending session, the receiver was shown four pictures and had to give a score to each. Higher scores meant that the receiver thought they had been sent this picture.

Finding: As one picture was sent out of a choice of four, a chance hit rate would be 25 per cent. Sargeant conducted 12 sessions and got six direct hits – a 50 per cent hit rate.

Commentary: Blackmore (1987) did an independent review of the methodology and found that there were a number of ways in which cheating could have occurred. For example, an envelope containing pictures disappeared from the office where the testing was taking place.

At the end of one of the Ganzfeld sessions, Sargeant came into the room where the receiver was being tested. Both Blackmore and a student observer felt that Sargeant had tried to push the receiver towards one particular answer (the correct answer).

AQA Examiner's tip

Remember the commentary points on methodological and ethical issues, which will help you to evaluate this particular study.

Controversy and criticisms of the Ganzfeld method of studying ESP

- Sensory leakage could occur, that is, there were other ways in which information may have reached the receiver. The autoGanzfeld automated slide method countered this criticism to some extent.

- Security – as with the Sargeant studies, the pictures were not always kept securely, thus increasing the opportunities for fraud.

- Meta-analyses on ESP studies often show varying results because of the way researchers select studies and calculate the figures.

- Often the studies are not replicable, so they do not satisfy one of the criteria for science (that of reliability).

- Experimenter effect – some studies have suggested that the expectations/attitudes of the experimenters have an effect on the findings of ESP research.

Think about it

Make a list of the issues with the study of the paranormal. Identify the implications of these issues.

Sheep-goat effect – people who believe in ESP typically show a higher-than-average hit rate in ESP experiments and those who do not believe show a lower-than-average hit rate. This effect may need investigating further, but it seems to show that a belief in anomalistic phenomena shapes an individual's experience of them.

Studies of psychokinesis (PK)

Schmidt (1969)

Schmidt devised a machine that would flip coins randomly (a 'heads' light or 'tails' light would come on) based on the random rate of decay of radioactive particles. This makes fraud very difficult. He asked the participants to try to influence this coin flipping. His results showed that there was a significant deviation from chance.

Commentary

It is important to remember that the fact that there is a statistical deviation from chance is not necessarily evidence of PK. Just because the study showed that the coins did not fall heads half the time and tails half the time, this does not necessarily mean that PK was occurring.

Summary of work on ESP, PK and related controversies

- Some studies of ESP and PK seem to show that some people have abilities that are better than chance.
- There are various methodological issues with many of these studies, which cast doubt on the results.
- Even if the methodology is tightly controlled, a significant statistical deviation from chance in performance of these investigations does not necessarily mean that psychic abilities are involved.
- All extraneous variables must be controlled and studies must be replicable before research into ESP and PK will receive scientific credibility.

> **Think about it**
>
> We know that a significant deviation from chance in studies of ESP and PK does not necessarily mean that psychic powers are involved. Why not? What other factors could be considered and may have an effect? The kind of ideas that you come up with could be useful as evaluation (AO2/3).

> **Apply it**
>
> Try to write a couple of paragraphs to answer the following question:
>
> How might the idea of scientific fraud be used to explain the findings of research studies in the areas of ESP and PK?

Explanations for anomalous experience

> **You need to know how to**
>
> ✔ describe and evaluate the role of coincidence and probability judgements in anomalous experience
>
> ✔ evaluate explanations for superstitious behaviour and magical thinking
>
> ✔ evaluate the role of personality factors in anomalous experience.

The misattribution hypothesis

It may be argued that people misattribute the causes of events to supernatural phenomena instead of attributing them to more mundane explanations.

Some factors that may explain misattribution of the causes of events to supernatural phenomena are described below.

> **Think about it**
>
> Do you think it is true that people do sometimes misattribute the causes of events to paranormal events or experiences? Can you think of any examples from your own experience?

Probability misjudgement

Imagine you thought of someone that you had not thought of for a long time, and then you bumped into them on the street. Some people might think this was more than a chance encounter – they might put the meeting down to a psychic phenomenon. In other words, something that is chance might be wrongly attributed to a psychic event or phenomenon.

Commentary

Blackmore and Troscianko (1985) suggested that some people make poor probability judgements and that these are the people who are more likely to attribute their experiences to psychic phenomena. However, this could also be explained by poor cognitive abilities. For example, people are notoriously poor at estimating probabilities. When asked, 'How many individuals have to be at a party for two of them to share the same birthday', few people believe that the answer is as small as 23 (which it is!).

Examples of precognition in dreams (when dreams supposedly predict future events) are easier to understand if you think about the billions of dreams that happen around the world every night. In terms of probability, it would be surprising if some of them did not predict future events, simply on the basis of chance.

Coincidence

Is coincidence the result of some psychic ability or is it just chance? Marks and Kammann (1980) concluded that when two random things happen, we tend to believe that any link between them is meaningful. However, these coincidences are hard to investigate. We know that our memories are not always accurate. We may not recall all of the coincidental events exactly. So if we do not have accurate memories of every coincidence that seems to occur and of everything that happens to us, it is not possible to tell if there is more to coincidence than meets the eye. In summary, it may be that belief in anomalistic behaviour is partly the result of superstition, self-deception and coincidence.

Cognitive abilities

Some psychologists suggest that believers in psychic abilities have biased cognitive abilities (e.g. Gray, 1987). More reliable research has been done on people's performance in logic tests and it has been found that non-believers perform better (Polzella *et al.*, 1975). This suggests that believers in psychic abilities have problems with logical connections between events.

Commentary

There is some disagreement among psychologists about whether the results of much of the research in the area of cognitive abilities and anomalous experiences are reliable or not.

In many of these studies, the sample is an unrepresentative one comprising university students. So the results may not be generalisable to the wider population.

Spontaneous paranormal experiences

Stanford (e.g. 1974) argues that typical collections of spontaneous experiences may misrepresent the operation of psi in naturalistic situations. He suggests that such psychic experiences seem to come in the shape of thoughts, feelings and mental images, albeit perhaps rather unclear ones, that convey some information to the person experiencing it (e.g. that a loved one is in danger). Stanford's Psi Mediated Instrumental Response (PMIR) model is a theory that suggests that such 'lucky coincidences' represent the operation of non-intentional psi that happens to be just what the person experiencing the coincidence needs at that time.

Apply it

Divide your page into two columns. Try to make brief notes in bullet-point style describing how attribution theory and misattribution attempt to explain psi experiences. Then take a different-colour pen and complete the table to show strengths and limitations of the explanations and research evidence that supports your evaluation.

AQA Examiner's tip

Try to focus on the AO2/3 skills as well as AO1 when looking at material in psychology. In the exam, more marks are available for commentary and for evaluating than for description.

Apply it

In a couple of carefully written paragraphs, summarise what psychologists have said about superstition and coincidence. Next, write two or three sentences of commentary on each of these. Then, try to write another paragraph that explains how superstition and coincidence may partially explain a belief in anomalistic phenomena.

AQA Examiner's tip

Remember that you can gain marks for making comments about correlation and causation. When using or evaluating research that shows an association or correlation, you need to make it clear that you understand that an association or correlation between two variables is not the same as a causative link between them.

Commentary

- Some researchers argue that Stanford has ignored another class of spontaneous psi experiences – those that feature odd coincidences (e.g. unexpectedly meeting someone that you needed to meet). The people that this happens to may be temporarily puzzled, but most are likely to shrug off the coincidence as a happy chance.

- Also, the PMIR model has been criticised. There does not seem to be any link between PMIR and luck when it is studied scientifically. As a result of the lack of support, Stanford has changed the model and has suggested that psi abilities could in fact be more to do with character disposition.

Superstitious behaviour and magical thinking

These are two closely related areas. Magical thinking is when we think we are influencing events by our behaviour or thoughts. We think in terms of cause and event, rather than simple coincidence or correlation. Examples might be the belief that you really will do better in an examination if you wear your favourite T-shirt (this can also be called superstition). In some cultures, there are beliefs that elaborate ceremonies are essential if winter is to end and spring begin. In obsessive compulsive disorder, the person believes that their ritual behaviours are necessary to avoid disaster.

Superstition

Behaviourists have attempted to explain superstitious behaviour.

- Skinner found that even pigeons appear to demonstrate superstitious behaviour. They show bizarre patterns of behaviour in the Skinner box, perhaps turning around twice before pecking at the reward disc. His research with pigeons suggested that the reason for superstitions becoming persistent is that the behaviour is not rewarded every time it occurs. Sometimes the behaviour is rewarded and other times it is not. In pigeons this type of unpredictable, variable reinforcement leads to very persistent superstitious behaviour.

- Work on the behavioural approach shows that variable reinforcement schedules (i.e. when reinforcement is not given all the time) are very effective. This is why fruit machines can be so addictive. For example, if someone puts a lucky mascot on their desk before a test, this behaviour may not always be reinforced with good marks in the test. However, good marks in the test will be achieved often enough for the individual to believe that the mascot has helped, and so the superstitious belief continues.

Commentary

Skinner's original work with pigeons was challenged by Staddon and Simmelhag (1971), who suggested that there were reasons for pigeons demonstrating what looked like superstitious behaviour other than the reasons put forward by Skinner.

However, despite this criticism, it seems to be the case that the variable reinforcement effect is found consistently in different cultures.

Magical thinking

Many of us have beliefs in the paranormal. This raises the question about what the main function of such belief might be. Some of the views about the nature of paranormal beliefs are summarised below.

> **Think about it**
>
> Do you think it is likely that personality factors alone can account for anomalous experience? How might personality be related to cognitive aspects such as probability judgements and coincidence?

> **AQA Examiner's tip**
>
> Although they are separate bullet points on the specification, remember that you can use material from any part of the specification to answer questions. For example, the role of coincidence and probability judgements in anomalous experience can be used to expand and evaluate the role of personality factors.

Psychodynamic explanations

Paranormal beliefs such as magical thinking serve central needs. Fantasy proneness and the belief in paranormal experiences may both originate from the need to deal with trauma or abuse in childhood (Irwin, 1990). People may use paranormal beliefs as a means of gaining control over troubled and chaotic home environments (Lawrence *et al.*, 1995).

Social explanations

Children lack the stability that they would have had many years ago. The divorce rate is rising and there is an increasingly high level of job insecurity. Magical thinking may arise from a child's need to control the familial situation by providing structure and familiarity.

Having studied paranormal beliefs and personality, Irwin has suggested that paranormal beliefs may give some people a purpose and strength. Belief in the paranormal may enable unconfident people to become more self-assertive.

Need for explanation

It may be that some people need magical thinking to explain things that cannot easily be explained in other ways. This function, along with socialisation, can be stabilising. Also, as religiosity dwindles, the belief in the paranormal may take its place.

Need for control in stressful times

Keinan has suggested that when people feel they are in uncontrollable situations, belief in the paranormal increases. The paranormal beliefs, such as magical thinking, provide a sense of control and may also provide an explanation for the situation. Blackmore and Troscianko (1985) supported this idea. Believers in paranormal phenomena felt they had more control over a task where they had to try to influence the flip of a coin than non-believers did.

Cultural significance of magical thinking

Blaisdell and Denniston (2002) investigated a large number of world cultures in relation to paranormal beliefs and found that culture and paranormal belief were closely linked. For example, warlike cultures had vengeance themes as a feature of their beliefs in the afterlife, and kinship in the afterlife is central to societies with large populations. Another example of magical thinking is that behaviour in this life will determine your future in the afterlife.

Culture shapes belief in the paranormal, and belief in the paranormal shapes culture. Bailey's work on Hindu funeral rituals showed that the paranormal belief in the afterlife dictates the ritual surrounding death and the funeral. This research shows that paranormal belief and culture are closely linked.

Commentary

When thinking about paranormal phenomena and psychic abilities, there may also be an element of deception, self-deception and superstition involved. We know that belief in the paranormal cannot be explained by normal means, so it may be thought of as an extension of superstition and magical thinking. We know that deception, self-deception and superstition shape human behaviour. So they must be taken into account in addition to other factors including personality and cognitive factors, plus cultural, subcultural and religious influences.

Think about it

In your experience, are people becoming less religious? Is it possible that belief in paranormal phenomena is taking the place of religion? If so, why?

Apply it

Write a paragraph to explain what research has shown about the possible functions of paranormal beliefs.

AQA Examiner's tip

It is a good idea to practise summarising key ideas precisely and succinctly. Not many marks are available for AO1 in essays at A2 (only 8 marks out of 24) so make sure you can write clearly and succinctly. Having explained what the research shows, make sure you can evaluate the research and provide commentary in terms of its methodology and implications.

Personality factors underlying anomalous experience

Honorton *et al.* (1998) used a meta-analytic technique to investigate the finding that ESP may be linked to extroversion. They found that in over three-quarters of the studies that were analysed, extroverts scored higher on ESP tasks than introverts did.

Commentary

- Low mundane realism – the procedure did not reflect what would happen in real life.

- There may be other variables that have an effect too. One is that in more spontaneous ESP tasks, the personality effect disappears. This may suggest that participants who take part in planned lab situations may have a different (possibly more relaxed) approach to social situations than other people, and that there is a link between this kind of approach and psi abilities.

In 1991, a scientific study by Broughton *et al.* looked at ESP abilities in blood relatives (e.g. parent–sibling pairs) and other pairs of close relatives (e.g. spouse–spouse pairs). It was found that high scores on ESP tasks were more likely with parent–child and sibling pairs than spouse–spouse pairs. If there is an ESP link between relatives, is this due to emotional closeness or genetics? This kind of study does not tell us. Unfortunately, this study separates the two possibilities.

Ramkrishna (2001) tested teenage Indian high-school students to investigate a hypothesised correlation between personality and performance on ESP tasks. It was found that people with high ESP scores had different personality traits from those with low scores. For example, people with higher ESP scores were described using adjectives such as 'warm', 'tough' and 'composed', as opposed to those with low scores ('tense', 'demanding' and 'prone to depression'). Similar results were found by Palmer (1978).

Commentary

- Even if studies find associations or correlations, this does not necessarily mean that the link is causative.

- When ESP tests are given to groups of people rather than to individuals on their own, associations with personality traits (such as those found by Palmer) disappear. This may be due to the fact that people behave differently in group situations. For example, neurotic individuals may be less tense as they are deindividuated in groups, and this may affect anxiety levels and ESP performance.

AQA Examiner's tip

When using or evaluating research that shows an association or correlation, you need to make it clear that you understand that an association or correlation between two variables is not the same as a causative link between them. Remember that you can gain marks for making comments about correlation and causation.

Apply it

Write a paragraph to explain why there may be a link between personality factors and anomalistic experiences. Include research studies in support of what you are saying. When you write about the research studies, include some evaluation of the methodology used – think about ethics, the participants and the procedure. Finish the paragraph with some AO2/3 commentary about the reliability and validity of research into personality and psi experiences.

AQA Examiner's tip

In questions about personality factors and anomalous experience, remember that while research evidence is central, there are broader issues to comment on. For example, the role of cognitive aspects such as probability judgements, and possible genetic influences on anomalous belief.

Research into exceptional experience

You need to know how to

✔ describe and evaluate psychological research into psychic healing, near-death experiences (NDEs), out-of-body experiences and psychic mediumship

✔ describe and evaluate for these exceptional experiences.

Research into psychic healing

Krieger (2000) found that haemoglobin levels were elevated in patients who had received psychic healing compared to a control group. The effects were long-lasting. Bener (2000) identified positive effects in 197 studies of psychic healing. Keller and Bzdek (1986) conducted a well-controlled blind study and showed that psychic healing had a significant positive effect on tension headaches. However, despite the rigorous methodology, Keller and Bzdek used a relatively small volunteer sample, and so more research must be done in this area before firm conclusions can be drawn.

Belief in psychic healing seems to be a key component. A key part of many religions is the belief in healing. Both the therapist and the patient believe that the healing will work. Tang (1998) suggests that there are three reasons why belief in the effectiveness of psychic healing may be part of a logical explanation for its effectiveness. A belief in one or all of these three things ensures that the healing experience has potentially positive effects.

1 The presence of the healer itself detracts the patient's attention from any pain, and so increases relaxation.

2 The connection with the healer activates body self-healing through psychological and mental methods.

3 ESP in the form of psychokinesis interacts with the patient's body.

This idea was supported by a comment made by Lyvers *et al.* (2006) after finding in a well-conducted study that a well-known psychic could not heal people by working with their photographs. They suggested that belief in psychic healing is central to its effectiveness, and the belief may work via the individual's own internal pain response system.

Near-death experiences

NDEs are broadly categorised as either 'pleasant' or 'disturbing' and common features include:

- intense emotion
- the person sees their own body from above (an out-of-body experience)
- movement through darkness towards 'light'
- a life review
- an encounter with someone close who is dead
- for some, a decision to return to their body.

Atwater (2007) suggests that the belief of the individual in the events of the NDE is key. The person's beliefs, religion or cultural background may affect how they interpret what they experience, and the interpretation of the NDE may have an effect on their wider spiritual beliefs. However, some research challenges the research into belief in NDEs. Biological and scientific facts may be used to explain NDEs rather than the idea of belief (Blackmore, 1982).

Think about it

Do you know of any other situations where belief in something seems to alter its effectiveness? Find out about the placebo effect. How might you use this idea to evaluate work on psychic healing?

Apply it

Make brief notes in bullet-point style about research evidence that seems to suggest that belief in psychic healing is central to its effectiveness.

AQA Examiner's tip

When you use research to support a point that you make in the exam, try to use other research to substantiate or to critically evaluate the research. This will help to enhance your AO2 and AO3 marks. For example, to support a point you have made you could use another study that obtained similar results.

Apply it

Write two paragraphs about NDEs. In the first, outline some of the scientific explanations for NDEs. In the second, write a critical commentary of the explanations.

Features of NDEs	Alternative explanations
Anoxia or hypercarbia, with associated visual effects, may explain the common 'light at the end of a tunnel' experience.	Some people have NDEs without anoxia/hypercarbia. There is some controversy about this. Some research has found normal blood gas levels in individuals reporting NDEs, although this research is disputed.
It has been suggested that NDEs may be a product of drugs used in operations and in critically ill individuals. Ketamine may be used to create NDEs, for example.	Not all patients with NDEs have had drugs. Some research shows that painkillers may reduce the likelihood of reporting an NDE.
Temporal lobe stimulation – individuals who have their temporal lobe of the brain stimulated will often report memory flashbacks and body distortions. The temporal lobe seems to be key in NDEs. Abnormal activity in this area of the brain could explain NDEs.	There is some evidence for this idea (e.g. Glannon (1987) stimulating specific brain areas), but other researchers have suggested that the unstable temporal lobe activity may be associated with a personality more prone to NDEs.
Expectation – NDEs often happen to those who think they are dying. Cultural expectation may also influence their form (e.g. Christians may report seeing Jesus; Hindus may see Yamaraj, the lord of death).	NDEs tend to be similar across religions. The differences in religious belief do not account for this. Also, people who have attempted suicide do report NDEs and they are not always disturbing experiences.

Out-of-body experiences (OBEs)

OBEs are often associated with dreams and daydreams. However, scientific explanations for OBEs have also been put forward. For example, OBEs may be induced by anaesthesia or stimulation of the temporal lobe of the brain (e.g. Blanke 2004 produced OBEs by stimulating the angular gyrus, a part of the parietal lobe close to the temporal lobe).

Ehrsson's research study into OBEs shows that the disruption of visual self-perception may explain the feelings reported by those who experience OBEs. However, the study used a small volunteer sample, limiting its generalisability. In addition, it would seem that the nature of the study meant that fully informed consent was not obtained. Despite this, it is positive that there is now a scientific way of studying OBEs.

Some research has investigated belief into OBEs. Gow *et al.* (2004) found that individuals who had experienced OBEs were more likely to have personality features such as fantasy proneness, greater belief in the paranormal and somatoform dissociation (a lessening in sensory integration). Of course, we cannot make assumptions as to causes and effects – does personality shape belief or vice versa?

AQA Examiner's tip

When discussing NDEs and OBEs in essays, you should be aware of issues regarding the nature of a science. If you can make comments about the reliability or robustness of the evidence and research that is done in these areas, your work is more likely to attract marks for commentary (AO2/3).

Apply it

In bullet-point form, summarise the differences between NDEs and OBEs.

Psychic mediumship

There is little research in this area because it is so difficult to do and also because the idea of mediumship does not really fit into accepted ways of thinking about science. However, there has been a long-standing effort to conduct studies scientifically since early research in the 1850s.

Studies of mediumship – description and commentary

Beischel and Schwartz (2007) used a rigorously controlled study, which showed that mediums could give accurate information about dead people when they knew nothing about the sitters who had experienced the death of a parent or peer. Russek and Schwartz (2001) found similar results.

However, despite the tight controls in these studies, it is possible that paranormal phenomena other than mediumship – such as super psi (very strong ESP) – may explain the results.

AQA Examiner's tip

It is a good idea to practise summarising key ideas precisely and succinctly. Not many marks are available for AO1 in essays at A2 (only 8 marks out of 24) so you need to make sure that you can write clearly and succinctly. However, it is just as important to remember that the other 16 marks are for AO2/3, for commentary, evaluation and application.

Cold reading may also explain the apparent ability of some people to provide information that seems as if it could only have come from mediumship skill. Cold reading is a technique of using likely guesses and then focusing on any positive responses in order to give the impression of having information about something.

It may also be that suggestibility has an effect on mediumship. Some mediums have been criticised for targeting bereaved people when they are vulnerable and when they may be more suggestible than usual.

It seems to be the case that belief in mediumship abilities is a key factor to understanding apparent mediumship. The problem that this causes is that 'belief' is a very difficult term to operationalise and to study scientifically.

Exam-style questions

Example 1

A researcher wanted to test the ability of a known 'psychic healer'. Ten volunteers suffering from chronic back pain were selected through newspaper adverts. The volunteers were all given a questionnaire, which rated their belief in psychic healing and another questionnaire, which rated their levels of pain. They were then randomly assigned to either a treatment group or a control group.

Afterwards, all the volunteers filled in the pain questionnaire again. The researcher found that there was no significant effect on pain relief as a result of psychic healing.

Answer the following questions, using your knowledge about research into psychic healing.

0 1 Outline **one** ethical issue in this study and suggest how the researcher could have dealt with it. *(4 marks)*

0 2 The researcher wanted to know whether there was a correlation between belief in psychic healing and improvement in pain ratings. What statistical test could the researcher use? Justify your answer. *(2 marks)*

'It is interesting why, even today in the modern age of science and technology, some people still believe in psychic healing.'

0 3 Discuss research into psychic healing. *(4 marks + 5 marks)*

0 4 Outline and evaluate psychological research into out-of-body experiences **and/or** near-death experiences. *(4 marks + 5 marks)*

Example 2

The 'Ganzfeld' is a technique used to investigate extra-sensory perception (ESP).

0 5 Outline and critically evaluate findings from Ganzfeld studies. *(4 marks + 10 marks)*

'Even if paranormal phenomena do not exist, paranormal experiences do, as surveys have shown that a considerable number of people report experiences which they interpret as paranormal.' (Watt, 2001)

0 6 Discuss personality factors underlying anomalous experience. *(4 marks + 6 marks)*

AQA 2007

Example 3

0 7 Explain what is meant by 'pseudoscience'. *(4 marks)*

During a public demonstration of 'psychic powers', a psychologist witnessed what appeared to be the ability of one person to read the thoughts of another.

0 8 Explain how the psychologist could use the Ganzfeld procedure to investigate this apparent ability. *(6 marks)*

At the same event, the psychologist observed that many audience members appeared impressed by, and expressed a belief in, the abilities of a psychic medium.

0 9 Outline **two or more** factors underlying belief in anomalous experience. *(4 marks)*

1 0 Consider how such factors can be used to explain belief in psychic mediumship. *(10 marks)*

Example 4

A recent study of ESP has found that many people in Great Britain believe in psychic abilities. For example, only 23 per cent of people do not believe in any form of psychic ability.

1 1 Explain some of the difficulties of gathering data about belief in psychic abilities. *(4 marks)*

Out-of-body experiences (OBEs) are not uncommon.

1 2 Discuss research into near-death **and/or** out-of-body experiences. *(8 marks +12 marks)*

Sample answers

A table of suggested content for the other examples is not provided for the Psychology in Action sections because the questions are more open and involved. You will need to interpret the questions and apply your knowledge of the topic and evaluative skills to answer them.

Example 1

Successfully identifies an issue and how to deal with it. More detail needed for top marks. (Deception – if they were not told which group they were in – and informed consent could also have been used.)

0 1 *Confidentiality would be an issue in this study. The researcher would have to say that they would keep all the participants' data safe and confidential and that no one could be identified as an individual from the write-up of the study.*

0 2 *Spearman's rho. This is because the researcher did a questionnaire study.*

This answer would achieve one mark. Spearman's rho is correct, but the justification is not right. To get the second mark, the student should have written that the test is appropriate because the data are ordinal and the researcher was looking for an association between two variables.

0 3 *Psychic healing is a very old form of treatment that seems to work; empirical evidence has shown this (e.g. Krieger, 2000). However, the research seems to show that what is key is belief in the effectiveness of psychic healing. Targ (1998) suggested that there were three possible ways that this might work – firstly, the very presence of the healer might distract the patient from their pain and cause them to feel more relaxed. Secondly, the connection between the patient and the healer might activate the body's self-healing system. Finally, it might be that the healer uses psychokinesis which might help the patient to get better.*

In this paragraph the student has outlined possible explanations that might underlie belief in psychic healing and this material would earn AO1 marks. The outlines are accurate and coherent and would get a mark in the top band.

There is evidence for this idea, as some studies have shown that belief in the power of psychic healing is critical. However, some psychic healers say that it works without the patient believing in it – and there has not been much research into this. One of the problems with research in this area is that is tends not to be scientific – for example, it may not be objective or reliable – both of these are key to a science. For example, belief is very difficult to define and it is also hard to measure. It is hard to create research studies where the results are measurable and where the studies are reliable and also valid. Many studies in this area are based on anecdotal reports or studies where self-report is key and this may mean that their reliability is flawed.

The candidate has neatly divided their answer into a paragraph of AO1 material and this paragraph of AO2/3 evaluation and commentary. The scientific method is discussed effectively and reference has been made to contradictory research evidence. The general comments are sound, but the references to contradictory research are rather vague. However, it is well organised and several relevant points are made. Bearing in mind the marks available, AO2/3 marks would just be in the top band.

0 4   *Belief in near-death experiences has been studied by researchers who have found that common features of NDEs are intense emotion or feeling that you are out outside your own body and looking down on it. On the whole these experiences are described as either pleasant or distressing (Blackmore). It seems as if a person's culture or religion affects the experience that is and NDE. For example Christians often see a figure that is described as Jesus and Hindus report seeing the god of death. However, NDEs are actually experienced in similar ways by people of all religions and this similarity is not explained by these religious differences.*

OBEs are different again although many people have an OBE as part of a near-death experience. Ehrsson (2007) found that he could induce OBEs using a virtual reality technique. Blanke found that stimulating the angular gyrus in female participants could also create an OBE.

Ehrsson's study was well controlled and scientific although it was only a small volunteer sample. He has been one of the first researchers to try to study these things scientifically.

Many people report OBEs or NDEs and it is difficult to assess them as the reports are anecdotal and no controls were in place when the experience happened. Also, maybe trying to understand OBEs and NDEs is taking a reductionist point of view by trying to understand a complex phenomenon in terms of individual components, maybe this is not possible to do with such a subjective and personal area.

For this question, you could talk about OBEs or NDEs or both. Covering both provides more access to AO1 and AO2/3 marks. In this first paragraph, the student has described NDEs and has also brought in cultural issues. The general description of research into cultural aspects would gain AO1 credit, while the closing sentence, although brief, is an effective AO2/3 point.

This paragraph provides some evaluation of methods, together with a link to the nature of science, and it would earn AO2/3 credit. Again it lacks detail, e.g.: Why is it scientific? What is the problem with small samples?

This paragraph outlines studies into OBEs, and gets AO1 credit.

In this paragraph, there is some relevant AO2/3 commentary about anecdotes as well as reference to a wider debate, that of reductionism. It would earn more credit if one or two points were elaborated. For instance, what are the 'components' referred to in relation to reductionism?

AQA   Examiner's comments

The answer to question 04 is slightly imbalanced. AO1 material covers a range of research and refers to several studies. Given the mark allocation, AO1 would just be in the top band. AO2/3 is less effective, with relevant points made but often without sufficient detail to access the top band. AO2/3 is not fully effective and would make the top of 'reasonable'.

13 Psychological research and scientific method

The application of scientific method in psychology

> **You need to know how to**
>
> ✔ discuss the major features of science including replicability, objectivity, the scientific method (hypothetico deductive method) and theory construction
>
> ✔ describe how new scientific knowledge is validated and explain the role of peer review
>
> ✔ discuss some of the problems validating new knowledge.

The features of science

Science is both an approach to studying the world and a system for obtaining knowledge. There are a number of features of the scientific approach:

- Objectivity: Objective knowledge should be free of opinion or bias and based purely on empirical evidence that can be seen by others.
- Replicability: The ability to check and verify this information by repeating a similar study.
- Falsifiability: The ability to demonstrate that a theory is wrong.

One of the other key features of science is the way in which information is gathered. Over time, scientists have developed a number of principles that guide the way they collect data and the way science progresses.

> **Think about it**
>
> Use the key features of science to compare psychology with a non-science subject such as English. Do the key features apply to most of the psychology you have studied? Do the key features apply to English?

The scientific method

The hypothetico-deductive method (sometimes called the scientific method) involves a number of stages:

1 Identify a problem: Through observations, previous research in the area or even a desire to question common-sense assumptions.

2 Develop a hypothesis: This should be predictive and testable.

3 Devise a study to test the hypothesis.

4 Analyse and evaluate the results to determine whether they support the hypothesis or not.

5 Modify and repeat the process in light of stage 4.

6 Develop a theory.

This is a cyclical process that leads to the gradual progress of science that rejects some theories and tests new ones. A crucial element in the progress of science is the falsifiability of theories and development of new theories.

Alternatives to the scientific approach in psychology

Some researchers question the use of the traditional scientific approach in psychology. They argue that it is inappropriate because:

- Psychologists deal with people and therefore interact with their subject matter.
- Past experiences, beliefs and ideas make it impossible to be truly objective about the data from a study.
- Participants cannot behave naturally in traditional psychological research and therefore the studies are of people in psychological studies, not of normal human behaviour .
- The recording of one aspect of behaviour in studies ignores the subjective experience of participants.

An alternative approach has emerged, which has been called 'new paradigm research'. This type of research tries to understand the subjective world of the participant and studies more complex data that cannot be reduced to numbers easily. It focuses on the underlying meaning, values and emotion of the information. New paradigm research regards participants as active collaborators rather than passive participants obeying instructions.

Validating new knowledge

New scientific knowledge is disseminated in scientific journals. These are periodic scientific publications that act as a permanent record of research. In psychology, there are many different journals that are concerned with different topic areas and approaches. When a psychologist has conducted a study and written a report, it is sent to one of these journals. The work is not automatically published. The quality control is the peer review system. Peer reviewers are experts in their field who assess the quality of the work. Only good work is subsequently published and validated.

Evaluation of peer review validation

The system of peer review is seen as the best method of validating new knowledge and is highly regarded in science. However, there are some problems with the system:

- In a very small number of cases, it does not detect fabrication or manipulation of evidence.
- Research that does not 'fit' with previous work is often seen as suspect and can be rejected.
- Peer review is subject to bias by the reviewer. There is some evidence of institution bias (favouring prestigious universities) and gender bias (favouring male researchers).
- The file drawer phenomenon suggests that peer review tends to favour 'positive reports', where the results support the hypothesis, than 'negative reports'. As a result, most negative reports end up in a file drawer.

Designing psychological investigations

You need to know how to

✔ describe different research methods and apply them to psychological investigation

✔ discuss the implications of sampling strategies

✔ describe the different types of validity and how to improve and assess it

✔ describe the different types of reliability and how to improve and assess it

✔ summarise the BPS ethical guidelines and apply them in the design and conduct of research.

Selection and application of research methods

There are many ways of investigating human behaviour and experience. The first stage in designing any psychological investigation is to consider what exactly you want to find and what data is needed, and then choose the appropriate method to find it.

Borden and Abbott (2008) suggest that scientific studies tend to concentrate on one of two approaches:

■ Exploratory data collection: with the collection of descriptive data.

■ Hypothesis testing: identifying links between variables. These links could be causal (in experiments) or relational (in correlations).

Apply it

Use the material you have from your Psychology AS studies to revise the different methods. Remember that you will need to know about different types of experiments and the advantages and disadvantages of different experimental designs.

Decision chart for choosing a research method

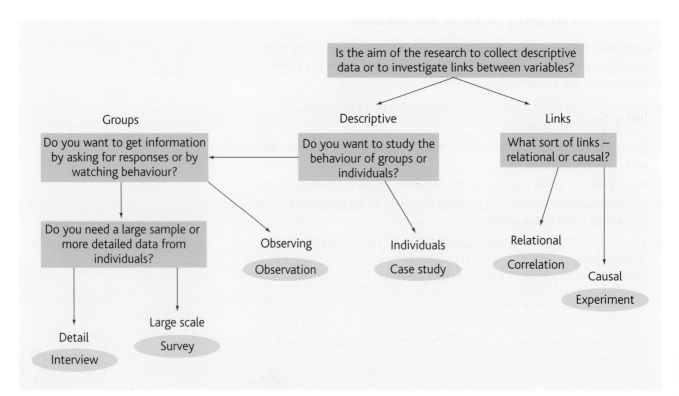

The choice of method is just the first stage in designing the research. The important part is the detail.

For experiments, the first decision is which type of experiment to choose and the experimental design. The next stage is to decide how to manipulate the IV and crucially how to measure the dependent variable (DV) (i.e. how the DV is operationalised or given an operational definition).

There are also a number of issues to be considered if observations are used. The first is whether to use naturalistic or controlled observation. This hinges on whether high levels of ecological validity (naturalistic) or control over confounding variables (controlled) is more important. The second is whether to use participant or non-participant observation. Here the choice is whether ecological validity is more important than reliability of the data.

The major choice when using surveys or interviews is which type of question is most useful. Closed questions provide data that can be quantified and analysed statistically. They are best for quantitative research. However, if the researcher is more interested in qualitative data or detailed information from the interviewee, then open questions are more appropriate.

The choices about what to study in a case history depend on the nature of the case and the reason the case study is being done. For example, a case study of a person with prosopagnosia would tend to focus on what the person could and could not see. The details of the person's childhood experiences, relationships with others and so on. would not be relevant to the case. However, in a case study of someone who self-harms, these types of details would be important. Their perceptual abilities would not be important.

Issues of reliability

Reliability is about the consistency of measurements. A measure is reliable if it gives the same value time after time when assessing a particular variable. There are two types of reliability – external reliability and internal reliability.

- External reliability is the ability to produce the same results every time the test is carried out. It is typically assessed using the test-retest method where the test is used several times with the same or similar groups of participants. When the two sets of scores are correlated, a high correlation value indicates that the test is reliable.

- Internal reliability is concerned with the consistency within tests such as intelligence tests. Individuals should not score above average in one half of the test and below average in the other. It is typically assessed using the split-half method where the scores from each half of the test are compared.

Improving reliability

Reliability depends on the accuracy of measurement. Accuracy of measurement can be improved in the following ways:

- By taking more than one measurement from each participant and then recording the average score.

- Pilot studies can be used to check that the proposed method of measurement works properly.

- When more than one investigator is used in a study, the way that they collect and record data should be standardised to improve inter-rater reliability.

Issues of validity

Validity is concerned with the truthfulness of the measure. A valid measure is one that measures what it claims to measure. It is crucial to consider two types when designing a study: internal validity and external validity.

Internal validity

Internal validity is the ability of the study to test the hypothesis that it was designed to test. Essentially, does the DV measure what it was intended to measure? There are a number of potential threats to internal validity. There is a different way to improve each of them.

Potential problem for internal validity	Improvement of internal validity
Poor operationalisation of the variables – many psychological variables are abstract and it is possible to choose an inappropriate method of measuring them.	One way of avoiding this problem is to use measures or scales that have been validated in previous studies.
Confounding variables – these are variables that vary along with the IV. If there are confounding variables, it is impossible to know whether the IV or confounding variable caused changes in the DV.	Studies need to carefully controlled. All variables except the IV should be kept constant (or controlled).
Demand characteristics – these are cues that lead to the tendency for participants to behave in the way they think is required of them.	The single-blind technique could be used, in which participants do not know what group or condition they are in. Therefore, participants cannot change their responses to suit or foil the researcher.
Experimenter bias – this is the tendency of experimenters to find what they expect or want to show.	The double-blind technique removes both demand characteristics and experimenter bias. In this case, neither the participants nor the experimenter know what each condition or group represents.

> **AQA Examiner's tip**
>
> There can be confusion between confounding variables and extraneous variables. Extraneous variables are variables that might affect the performance of individual participants. They can be situational (lighting, time of day, etc.) or related to the participant (age, mood, etc.). Confounding variables are variables that are accidentally manipulated along with an IV and have unintended effects on the DV for groups or conditions.

Key study

Rosenthal and Fode (1963)

Rosenthal and Fode (1963) asked students to study 'dull' and 'bright' rats. The study involved finding out how quickly the rats learned to run a maze, and the students acted as experimenters. They found that the bright rats learned faster than the dull rats. However, there were no bright or dull rats. They were all from one group that had been randomly assigned.

Rosenthal and Fode found no evidence of any deliberate attempt by the students to distort the results and suggested it happened because of the students' expectations. The students had shown experimenter bias.

> **AQA Examiner's tip**
>
> There is a tendency to confuse ecological validity with mundane realism. However, the mimicking of real-life situations with mundane realism does not necessarily improve ecological validity. Sometimes mundane realism decreases validity because it increases factors such as demand characteristics.

External validity

External validity is concerned with how well the results of a study can be generalised beyond the study itself. A study has external validity if the results can be generalised beyond the limited sample of participants and the setting of the study. If the study can be generalised to other people, then it shows population validity. This can be improved by using representative samples (see 'Implications of sampling strategies' below). If a study can be generalised to other settings, then it shows ecological validity. Improving ecological validity does not necessarily involve doing studies in everyday settings (these are field studies) or trying to copy real life in the laboratory (this is often an example of mundane realism).

Think about it

There can be conflict between the various factors affecting validity. For example, the use of stringent control to remove confounding variables may increase demand characteristics or decrease ecological validity. Often, psychologists have to make a decision about which is most important for their study.

Would you concentrate on internal or external validity in the following studies:

- a study of the duration of the phonological loop in WM
- a study of the effect of anxiety on eyewitness testimony.

Implications of sampling strategies

Type of sampling	Definition	Method	Population validity
Random	A sample in which every member of the target population has an equal chance of being selected	Every member of the target population is identified and a random sampling technique is employed to select the sample.	This is a representative sample and has high population validity.
Opportunity	A sample that consists of those people available to the researcher	The researcher approaches people and ask them to take part in the research. Basically whoever is available and willing.	There is a high chance that the sample will be biased, leading to low population validity.
Volunteer	A sample where the participants self-select, that is, they volunteer to take part in the research	The researcher would advertise their research and the people who respond would be the sample.	A particular type of person is likely to volunteer for research. This has a high chance of bias so we cannot generalise to the target population, leading to low popularity validity.

The main implication when choosing a sample is the effect it has on population validity. Most research uses opportunity or volunteer samples. Ethical guidelines stop psychologists from forcing anyone to take part in studies so there is inevitably some element of volunteer sampling. Both opportunity and volunteer samples can introduce bias as neither type of sample is representative.

Think about it

A random sample would imply that everyone in the target population has an equal chance of taking part in the study. Can samples of participants ever be truly random in psychology?

Ethical considerations of psychological research

BPS guidelines for research with human participants

The British Psychological Society code of ethics, *Ethical Principles for Conducting Research with Human Participants*, covers nine different aspects of ethics that relate to research with human participants:

- **Consent**: participants should give informed consent.
- **Deception**: participants should not be misled.
- **Debriefing**: following the investigation the study should be discussed with participants.
- **Withdrawal from investigation**: participants should feel free to leave the investigation at any time.
- **Confidentiality**: participants have the right to confidentiality.
- **Protection of participants**: this includes both physical and psychological harm.
- **Observational research**: the privacy of participants needs to be respected.
- **Giving advice**: psychologists should only give advice for which they are qualified.
- **Colleagues**: psychologists have a duty to make sure that all research is ethical, and this includes research using colleagues.

Application of BPS ethical principles

The application of the BPS ethical principles is concerned with the potential steps that psychologists can take when designing their studies to ensure that the guidelines are followed. The key for doing so is to always bear in mind the *essential principle* behind the BPS guidelines, which is that 'the investigation should be considered from the standpoint of all participants; foreseeable threats to their psychological well-being, health, values or dignity should be eliminated'.

Many of the ethical issues in psychology can be avoided by gaining informed consent. Researchers can get informed consent by using an information sheet and a consent form. The information sheet should explain the objectives and the procedure and stress to the participants that they can withdraw at any time.

Psychologists want to give full information about a study, but they do not want to cause demand characteristics. Often, full disclosure would reduce internal validity. The BPS recognises that it may be impossible to study some psychological phenomena without withholding some information or misleading participants. If researchers believe this is the case for their study, they should first look for alternatives. When there is no alternative, they have a duty to inform participants about the true nature of the study at the earliest stage.

Debriefing serves three functions:

- To complete the participants' understanding of the study.
- To monitor any unforeseen negative effects of the study.
- To find out whether anything has upset or disturbed the participant.

The participant should leave in the same state as they entered. So if, for example, the study raised the anxiety levels of the participant, then the debriefing should be used to lower their anxiety.

Data analysis and reporting on investigations

You need to know how to

✔ describe the concepts of probability, significance and significance levels, and Type 1 and Type 2 errors

✔ select appropriate graphs and statistical tests and factors affecting choices such as levels of measurement

✔ use inferential analysis and analyse and interpret qualitative data

✔ report psychological investigations according to conventions.

Probability, significance and errors

Very little in life, and in science, is ever certain. Science deals with probabilities and makes judgements about what probability to accept or reject as significant. Psychologists are interested in how likely it was that their results were due to chance.

Probability

Probability, or p, is the likelihood of something happening. It is expressed as a number between 0 and 1, where 0 means an event definitely will not happen and 1 means an event definitely will happen. To calculate the probability that a particular outcome will occur, it has to be divided by the number of possible outcomes.

$$p = \frac{\text{Number of particular outcomes}}{\text{Number of possible outcomes}}$$

The probability of getting a head (one particular outcome) when you toss a coin is 0.5 because that one outcome has to be divided by the two possible outcomes. Probability can be expressed as a decimal or a percentage. 0.5 is 50 per cent and 0.05 is 5 per cent (multiply by 100).

Statistical significance

The role of statistical tests is to find out how probable it is that what we have found in our sample accurately reflects what happens in the population. Hypothesis testing can be viewed as a competition between two hypotheses. These are the alternate (also called the research or experimental) hypothesis (H_1) and the null hypothesis (H_0). Alternate hypotheses state that there will be a relationship between variables (in correlations) or a difference between groups or conditions (in experiments). Null hypotheses state that there will be no such relationship or difference in the *population*. Statistical tests are used to calculate the probability of getting a pattern of results *if* they did not exist in the population. If this probability is small enough, it suggests that the pattern of findings in the sample is unlikely to be due to chance. We can infer that they are likely to reflect the pattern in the population and we can reject the null hypothesis.

This raises the question of what is a small enough probability. The level at which this is set is known as the level of significance. In psychology, the generally accepted level is 0.05 or 5 per cent. This is expressed as $p = 0.05$. Anything less than 0.05 is described as significant. It is unlikely that the null hypothesis is true. Anything above 0.05 is not significant as we cannot reject the null hypothesis.

Sometimes a higher level of significance, such as the 0.01 level, is used in psychological research. This is used when it is important to be certain that the results are not due to chance in, for example, medical or socially sensitive research.

Type 1 and Type 2 errors

The choice of 0.05 as the normal level of significance (i.e. the level at which the null hypothesis is accepted or rejected) in psychology is not arbitrary. It is designed to balance the risk of Type 1 and Type 2 errors. When we do a test and find a p value that is less than our level of significance, we reject the null hypothesis. We accept the alternate hypothesis that a variable had an effect on another or that there was a relationship. However, if there is actually no such effect or relationship, we have made a Type 1 error. At the 0.05 or 5 per cent level, there is a 1 in 20 chance of making a Type 1 error. Sometimes errors are made in the other direction. When we do a test and find a p value that is greater than our level of significance, we accept the null hypothesis. We reject our alternate hypothesis and suggest that there is no effect of a variable or relationship between variables. However, if there is actually an effect or relationship, we have made a Type 2 error.

Dealing with quantitative data

There are typically two stages of dealing with quantitative data:

- Summarising the data. The data needs to be summarised using measures of central tendency and measures of dispersion. Differences or relationships are often best illustrated when data is displayed graphically. The summary data that is produced is called descriptive statistics.

- Analysing the data. With quantitative data, this second stage requires the use of a statistical test. The analysis of data using tests is called inferential statistics.

Descriptive statistics

Graphs allow psychologists to see patterns in the data. Different types of graph are used for different types of data. The three that are most useful are:

- A histogram shows the distribution of a whole set of data. The bars on a histogram are all joined because they represent a continuous scale. The width of the bars are usually equal. The column area represents the frequency of the score.

- Bar charts are a useful way of showing summary statistics. This could be the means or medians of groups but could also be percentages or ratios. As the scale is not continuous, the bars are separated.

- Scattergrams show the relationship between two variables. The two variables are marked on the two axes and then each case is marked on the graph. They show the strength and direction of correlations.

Choosing a statistical test

There are four tests on the AQA A specification: Spearman's rho, Mann–Whitney, Wilcoxon and Chi-squared. The choice of which to use is based on the answers to three questions.

Think about it

Imagine that you had done some socially sensitive research on gender differences and decided to use the 0.01 level of significance.

Compared to using the 0.05 level, are you more likely to make a Type 1 error or a Type 2 error using the 0.01 level?

AQA Examiner's tip

It can be helpful to think of a Type 1 error as the *optimistic* error – we accept the experimental hypothesis when the results were due to chance. On the other hand, Type 2 errors are *pessimistic errors* – we reject the experimental hypothesis when the results did show a difference or correlation.

Apply it

In your Psychology AS course, you studied measures of central tendency and measures of dispersion. You should review these before going on to the next section.

- Revise measures of central tendency including mode, median and mean.

- Revise measures of dispersion including ranges and standard deviation.

What sort of data do I have?

Not all quantitative data are the same and research can generate different types of data. These different types of data represent different levels of measurement. Four levels of measurement are recognised:

- **Nominal data**. Information is put into categories or just named.
- **Ordinal data**. Information or scores are put in order (first, second, third, etc.). Whenever data are ranked, they are ordinal.
- **Interval data**. This is obtained when there are equal intervals on a measurement scale. Using the interval level of measurement we can give scores rather than putting information in order.

> **AQA Examiner's tip**
>
> The two key levels of measurement to understand at A2 are *nominal* and *ordinal*. Chi-squared is used for nominal data. All the other tests require *at least* ordinal data. This means that they can be used for ordinal and interval data.

Do I want to investigate differences or relationships?

If your study is an experiment, you will be investigating differences between two sets of scores. If your study is a correlation, you will be investigating relationships.

What type of design did I use?

Was the experiment a repeated measure or independent groups design?

Decision chart for choosing a statistical test

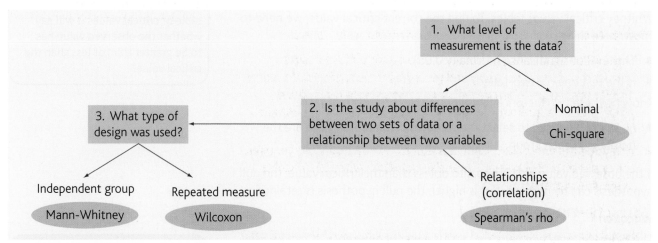

Applying and interpreting statistical tests

Why each test is used and how to interpret the test result for each test.

Ranking

All of the tests here, except chi-squared, require data to be ranked. This involves giving a number to each score in ascending order, so the lowest score is given rank 1, the next rank 2, and so on. If two scores are the same then they share two ranks and are given the average rank. Similarly, if there are three identical scores, they are given the average of the three ranks they occupy.

One- or two-tailed

The results of each of the tests are compared to critical values from the appropriate statistical table. These give different values depending on whether the test is a one-tailed or a two-tailed test. This depends on whether the hypothesis is directional or not. Directional hypotheses lead to one-tailed tests (the direction of difference or correlation is stated). Non-directional hypotheses lead to two-tailed tests (there will be a difference or correlation but the direction is not stated).

> **AQA Examiner's tip**
>
> It is very easy to misinterpret the results of a test because of confusion over whether it is one-tailed or two-tailed. The key to understanding this is to look at whether the hypothesis is predicting *a* difference or correlation (two-tailed) or *the* difference or correlation (one-tailed).

Spearman's rho

Spearman's rho (or Spearman's rank order correlation coefficient) is used to correlate pairs of scores that are at least an ordinal level of measurement (so can be interval). It is based on comparing the ranks of pairs of scores. If these ranks are very similar, it indicates a positive correlation. If they are opposites, it indicates a negative correlation.

When you consult the table, there are three things that you need to know:

■ Whether you look at the figures for a one- or two-tailed test.
■ The level of significance. In most cases, $p = 0.05$
■ The number of pairs of scores (N).

If the observed value is equal to or more than the critical value, the null hypothesis can be rejected. If it is higher, the null hypothesis is retained.

Mann–Whitney

The Mann–Whitney U test is a test of difference. It can be used when the data is at least ordinal and an independent groups design has been used. It works by ranking all the scores together and then comparing the ranks for each group.

The calculated value of U has to be compared to a value from the Mann–Whitney critical values tables. To find the correct critical value, we need to know three things:

■ The level of significance (normally 0.05).
■ Is the test one- or two-tailed?

Knowing these two factors allows you to select the correct table.

■ N_1 and N_2 are used to select the value from the table. These are the numbers in each group.

If the observed value of U is equal to or less than the critical value, the null hypothesis can be rejected. If it is higher, the null hypothesis is retained.

Wilcoxon

The Wilcoxon matched pairs sign test is a test of difference. It can be used when the data is at least ordinal (which means it can be ordinal, interval or ratio) and a repeated measure design has been used.

The value of T has to be compared to a value from the Wilcoxon critical values tables. In order to find the critical value, we need to know:

■ The level of significance.
■ Is the test one- or two-tailed?
■ The number of pairs of scores that have been ranked (N). This may not be all of the pairs in the sample as pairs that have a zero difference are not ranked.

If the observed value of T is equal to or less than the critical value, the null hypothesis can be rejected. If it is higher, the null hypothesis is retained.

AQA Examiner's tip

Remember that Spearman's rho is used when:
- testing for a correlation
- the data is at least ordinal (i.e. it is ordinal, interval or ratio).

AQA Examiner's tip

In an exam, if you are asked to decide whether the observed value is significant, at the bottom of the table of critical values it will say whether the observed value has to be greater than or less than the critical value.

AQA Examiner's tip

Remember that Wilcoxon is used when:
- testing for a difference
- there is a repeated measure design
- the data is at least ordinal (i.e. it is ordinal, interval or ratio).

Chi-squared

The chi-squared (χ^2) test is a test of association that is used when the data are nominal and expressed as frequencies (i.e. numbers in each category). It cannot be used with percentages or averages. The frequency data must be independent so that something recorded in one category cannot appear in another. It compares the observed frequencies in the study with the expected frequencies that would be found if there was no association.

The calculated value of χ^2 has to be compared with the value in the critical values table. To find the critical value, we need to know three things:

■ Is the test one- or two-tailed? A one-tailed test can only be used for a 2 × 1 table with a directional hypothesis. *All* others are two-tailed.

■ Degrees of freedom (df) = (number of rows − 1) (number of columns − 1)

■ The level of significance.

If the observed value is equal to or greater than the critical value, we can reject the null hypothesis.

> **AQA Examiner's tip**
>
> Remember that chi-squared is used when:
> - the data are nominal
> - data in each frequency are independent.
>
> The degree of freedom is determined by the number of boxes with data in them.
>
> Nearly all chi-squared tests are two-tailed tests.

Dealing with qualitative data

Qualitative research involves an in-depth analysis of people's experiences, beliefs, attitudes and involves interpretation and thematic analysis of verbal material. It requires 'rich' data (data that are rich in language that expresses what people feel and believe).

Gathering data

Qualitative data are best collected by semi-structured interviews using open-ended questions, participant observation, focus group discussion or by asking for participants' diaries or notes. The type of method used to get the data is linked to the type of analysis and the purpose of the study. The sampling for qualitative research is very different to that for quantitative research. Qualitative samples tend to be a small, clearly defined group.

Analysing and interpreting data

■ Organising the data. For any method that involves recording speech, this means preparing a transcript.

■ Getting to know the data thoroughly. This typically requires reading the transcripts a number of times before there is any attempt at analysis.

■ Coding the data. The reason for and the emphasis of the coding depends upon the type of analysis.

■ Reflexivity. This is when the researcher reflects on how the research activity and the researcher shape the outcome.

Robson (2002) suggests that the concept of trustworthiness is a good way of assessing qualitative data. One way of establishing trustworthiness is to use an external audit (Smith, 2003). This involves a check of the documentation, from transcript to final analysis, by an external party.

Reporting psychological investigations

The purpose of psychological research is to share findings with others. The reporting of findings is governed by conventions to enable information to be presented clearly and efficiently. One of the conventions is that reports should be in discrete sections, each with their own function.

Report sections

Section	Function
Title	To tell the reader what the report is about
Abstract	To provide the reader with a brief summary of the whole study
Introduction	To introduce the background and rationale of the study, which should lead to the aim and, if appropriate, hypothesis of the study
Method	To describe how the study was done. This should include information about the design, apparatus and procedure.
Results	To summarise the findings. This should include both tables and graphs showing descriptive statistics and, if appropriate, inferential statistical test results.
Discussion	To discuss the findings and their implications such as whether the hypothesis should be accepted. It should also discuss alternative explanations and any methodological problems of the study.
References	To inform the reader about the sources of information
Appendices	These can be used for detailed information not in the report.

Exam-style questions

A psychologist was interested in looking at the best way for students to revise for tests and examinations. Some students believed they did better on tests by cramming all their revision into one intense session the day before the test. Others claimed that repeated, shorter revision sessions over several days was the best way to learn material for the test. The psychologist decided to investigate which of the two methods worked best. An advertisement was placed on a school noticeboard asking students to contact the psychologist if they were interested in taking part. Twenty students agreed to take part in the study and they were put into either the 'cramming' group or the 'repetitive study' group. Both groups were given the same unfamiliar material to learn for a test five days later. The cramming group were asked to learn the material for two hours one day before the test. The repetitive study group were asked to learn the material for 0.5 hours each day on the four days before the test. The psychologist's hypothesis was that participants' scores in the cramming condition would be different to the repetitive study condition.

0 1 Identify the type of experimental design the psychologists used and outline one reason for using this design. *(3 marks)*

0 2 Explain why the students were asked to learn unfamiliar material. *(2 marks)*

0 3 State whether the hypothesis for this study is directional or non-directional. Explain why the psychologist phrased it in this way.

(3 marks)

0 4 Identify an appropriate statistical test to test for a difference between the two conditions. Explain why this is the appropriate test. *(4 marks)*

The psychologists needed to be sure that the participants understood the nature of the study so that they were able to give informed consent.

0 5 Write a consent form that would be suitable for this study. Make sure that there is sufficient information about the study for the participants to make an informed decision. *(5 marks)*

0 6 One important feature of an experiment is control. Briefly describe two factors that might affect the validity of the study and explain how they could be controlled.

(4 marks)

0 7 What is meant by the term 'reliability'? *(1 mark)*

The psychologist found that there was a significant difference between the test results for the two conditions at the $p = 0.05$ level of significance.

0 8 Explain whether a Type 1 or Type 2 error would be more likely if the psychologist had decided to use a 1 per cent significance level.

(2 marks)

The psychologist decided to do a follow-up study to investigate whether the length of revision time was related to the test scores. A second group of 14 participants were given a lesson on some unfamiliar material and then asked to revise the information during the week before a test. Some were asked to revise for 15 minutes, others 20, 25, 30 and so on to 80 minutes. The psychologist's hypothesis was that there is a positive correlation between revision time and test score. She used the Spearman's rho test to analyse the correlation between the two variables. She set the significance level at 5 per cent.

Her calculated value of rho was $r_s = 0.525$.

Extract from table of critical values from the Spearman's rho test

N (number of participants)	Level of significance for a one-tailed test	
	0.05	0.025
	Level of significance for a two-tailed test	
	0.10	0.05
8	0.643	0.738
9	0.600	0.683
10	0.564	0.648
12	0.506	0.591
14	0.456	0.544
16	0.425	0.506
18	0.399	0.475
20	0.377	0.450

For any N, the observed value of r_s is significant at a given level of significance if it is equal to or larger than the critical value.

0 9 Using the table above, state whether the result was significant. Explain your answer. *(4 marks)*

The psychologist later found very similar results with a larger sample and decided to send a report of her study to a peer-reviewed journal that specialises in work on learning.

1 0 Outline what is meant by the term 'peer review' in psychological research. *(2 marks)*

1 1 Explain why peer review is important in psychological research. *(5 marks)*

Sample answers

0 1 *They used an independent group design to avoid practice effects.*

The candidate needs a little more detail about 'practice effects' here. If a repeated measure design had been used, the participants would have learned the information twice.

0 2 *They were asked to learn unfamiliar material to make the test fair.*

The candidate shows some idea of control but should be more precise. The use of unfamiliar material ensures that no one has a better test score because of prior knowledge.

0 3 *The hypothesis is non-directional because the psychologist wanted to look for a difference.*

The hypothesis is non-directional but the reason given is wrong. A non-directional test was used because some students claimed cramming was better and others that repetitive study revision was better (i.e. there was no consistent past evidence of the direction of difference).

0 4 *The Mann–Whitney test because it is a test of difference for independent group design studies.*

The candidate has not included the level of measurement. Mann–Whitney is used when data is at least ordinal.

0 5 *This is a study of the effect of revision technique on test scores. You will be asked to revise some information for two hours before taking a test on it in five days time. Some participants will be asked to do the revision in one 2-hour session and others to revise for half an hour a day for the next four days. The test will last for 15 minutes. The scores from the test are only going to be used to compare the revision method and will be kept strictly confidential. I have read and understood the information and agree to take part in the study.*

The candidate has included information about the amount of time the test may take even though this was not included in the question stem. They have added this to indicate the type of information that should be on the consent form.

The answer would achieve a reasonable mark. Although most of the main information is here, there is one crucial omission: the participant has not been told of their right to withdraw from the study.

The candidate has identified two factors but has only explained how the second could be controlled. In the rush to get information down, they probably thought they had explained how to control the first. This illustrates a basic rule in exams – always reread answers to check them.

0 6 *One factor that might affect the validity of the scores is the material that the students have to revise. Another factor is the test and both groups should have exactly the same test.*

0 7 *Reliability is about the consistency of results.*

0 8 *A Type 2 error is more likely because the psychologist is more likely to reject the hypothesis when they should not at this level than the p = 0.05 level.*

• Top band answer

0 9 *The result is significant. This is because the observed value of rho was greater than the critical value of 0.456 (found when N = 14 at the p = 0.05 level for a one-tailed test).*

The candidate has included all the information needed for full marks here including the three factors needed to obtain the correct critical value.

1 0 *It is when other psychologists look at the report before it is published.*

This is a brief outline that does not elaborate enough for full marks. It lacks a description of the purpose of the peer review process, i.e. to consider the report in terms of its validity and significance. Other ways of elaborating the answer would be to point out that the 'other psychologists' are independent experts working in a similar field.

1 1 *Peer review is very important because it is a way of validating new knowledge. The report is studied by other experts who judge whether the way the study was done was good or not. They also judge how important the work is and whether it adds to overall knowledge. The peers say whether the report should be published or not so that we know that work in journals is good.*

This is not expressed well – this is a scientific method section and it would have been better to refer to the design and procedure.

This is not quite true. Peers recommend whether reports should be published, revised or rejected. The final decision is that of the editor.

The answer shows reasonable understanding and analysis.

AQA Examiner's comments

There are some good points in the answers, although many more marks could have been picked up throughout if more accurate details were included. Overall this answer would achieve marks in the basic/reasonable band.

Glossary

2D:4DR: the ratio between the lengths of the second (index) and fourth (ring) finger.

47 XYY karyotype: the unusual arrangement of the sex chromosomes in which some men carry an extra Y. Most people have only 46 chromosomes. The sex chromosomes are XX for women, XY for men.

A

Accommodation: modifying or changing an existing schema to deal with a new object or situation.

Acculturation: internalising the views of another culture.

Alpha bias: theories that assume real differences between males and females. Sometimes they exaggerate differences that do not in fact exist.

Amygdala: part of the limbic system that recognises emotions like suffering in others.

Androcentric: a theory of female behaviour based only on an investigation of male behaviour.

Androgens: the male hormones produced by the testes. The most important one, testosterone, is thought to cause aggressive behaviour.

Angular gyrus: a location in the brain that is at the junction between the temporal and parietal lobes.

Animism: the belief that everything is alive and has feelings, even inanimate objects.

Anorexia nervosa (AN): an eating disorder characterised by extreme body dissatisfaction and dieting, weight below 85 per cent of normal for age, and loss of three consecutive menstrual cycles.

Anticipated consequences: before we imitate the behaviour we have witnessed, we consider whether there will be positive or negative consequences for us. This will determine whether we repeat what we have observed.

Antisocial behaviour: behaviour that is designed to hurt or cause harm to someone.

Aphagia: failure to eat when hungry. Can be caused by damage to the lateral hypothalamus.

Apnoea: frequent episodes during sleep when breathing stops for a few seconds. This leads to daytime sleepiness and causes insomnia.

Artificialism: the belief that everything is caused by someone, even natural phenomena.

Assimilation: a new object or concept is incorporated into an existing schema without that schema changing.

Attachment: an emotional tie between two people shown in their behaviours.

Attitude: a predisposition to respond in a certain way towards an object, person or situation that involves feeling, thinking and knowing.

Attraction to celebrity: the desire to become famous and live a celebrity lifestyle.

B

Basal metabolic rate (BMR): all cells of the body are continually active and consuming energy, even when the body is at rest. The rate at which this occurs is the BMR.

Bipedal: walking mainly on two legs rather than four.

Body clocks: otherwise known as endogenous pacemakers, they regulate biological rhythms.

Bulimia nervosa (BN): eating disorder characterised by body dissatisfaction, obsession with food, and repeated cycles of bingeing and purging.

C

Carpentered environment: a place where rooms and buildings have geometric shapes. This is a place full of straight lines and angles that do not appear in the natural world.

Cataplexy: sudden loss of muscle tone during waking, leading to collapse. This is a key symptom of narcolepsy.

Central sleep apnoea (CSA): apnoea caused by problems in the brain's control of breathing and respiration.

Cholecystokinin (CCK): a hormone released from the duodenum in response to the presence of food. It acts as a satiety signal to the hypothalamus to stop feeding behaviour.

Chronotype: a personality type defined by when in the circadian rhythm of sleep and waking you are most alert.

Cognition: the term used to describe a range of mental activities associated with thinking. Common cognitive processes include reasoning, problem-solving, paying attention and remembering.

Cognitive consistency: occurs when two related attitudes fit together and agree with each other.

Cognitive development: the development of thinking skills such as reasoning and problem solving.

Cognitive dissonance: occurs when we hold conflicting attitudes that contradict each other.

Cognitive myopia: a short-sightedness in dealing with risk and assessing the consequences of our actions.

Coincidence: a striking occurrence of two events at the same time, apparently by chance. For example, as you are thinking about an old friend, they phone you unexpectedly.

Conditioned response (CR): the response to the conditioned stimulus alone.

Conditioned stimulus (CS): a stimulus that triggers the same response as the unconditioned stimulus after being paired with it.

Conserve: know that quantity remains the same despite changes in appearance.

Constructivist: someone who believes we construct our understanding of what we see by using knowledge beyond that presented in an image.

Continuity hypothesis: the claim that early relationship experiences continue in later adult relationships.

Culture: the behaviours and beliefs of social groups that make them different to each other.

D

Deception: the misrepresentation of information. For example, with deception, someone might be convinced that some information is true when in fact it is not.

Disequilibrium: the state of not understanding how to apply a schema.

Dizygotic (DZ) twins: twins who develop from two separate fertilised eggs and have no more in common genetically than any other siblings. Also known as fraternal twins.

Double-blind study: a method in which neither the researcher involved in the conducting of the experiment nor the participant knows what issue is being examined or what the expected outcome is.

E

Ecological validity: the degree to which the findings of a study can be generalised to other situations, places and conditions (e.g. the findings in one laboratory are the same as in other laboratories).

EEG: a diagnostic test of brainwave activity.

Effect size: a measurement of how much effect the independent variable has on the dependent variable on a scale of 0 (no effect) to 1.0.

Egocentric: not being able to think of your environment from another person's point of view.

Endocrine system: the system of glands in the body that secrete hormones directly into the circulatory system.

Environment of evolutionary adaptation (EEA): many examples of modern human behaviour are thought to have originally evolved many thousands of years ago, when the environment was very different. Behaviours that were able to adjust or adapt then may not be adaptive in today's environment. To understand them now, we have to consider their origins in that EEA.

Equity: the idea that both partners should get out roughly what they put into a relationship.

Ethnocentric: conclusions drawn about a culture without actually testing it; just using research based on another culture.

Ethologist: someone who studies animals' natural behaviour in their own environment rather than in a laboratory.

Exceptional experience: a term that includes experiences that are often thought of as being psychic, such as death-related experiences as well as more normal things like creative inspiration.

External reliability: the ability to obtain the same measurement on repeated occasions.

Extinction: the gradual decline and disappearance of the CR to the CS when it is no longer paired with the UCS.

Extrasensory perception (ESP): the showing of knowledge of an event without being told about the event or experiencing it. ESP could be seen to include telepathy.

F

Falsifiability: the property of being able to be tested to show that a theory is not true.

Fusiform gyrus: part of the temporal lobe that is activated during face recognition tasks (especially in the right hemisphere).

G

Ganzfeld: a German word meaning 'total field', and the name of the method used by anomalistic psychologists to examine ESP.

Gender: a judgement about behaviour, specifically being masculine or feminine.

Gender dysphoria: the belief that you are trapped in the wrong body and should be a member of the other sex. In everyday language, we call this 'transsexuality'.

Gender identity: the classification that the child/adult gives themselves as male or female. In most cases, the child is either male and feels like a boy, or female and feels like a girl.

Genome lag: behaviour changes at a much quicker rate than genes, so there might remain an instinct for a behaviour long after we stop displaying it.

H

High-risk study: the prevalence of schizophrenia in the general population is 1 per cent, which means that an impractically large group of children would have to be studied to find some who go on to develop schizophrenia. Instead, participants are chosen from 'high-risk' populations, i.e. children who have a parent with schizophrenia, and these are studied alongside a control group.

Holistic: taking into consideration the overall image, rather than only individual parts of it.

Hypnagogic hallucinations: REM dreams occurring during the switch from sleeping to waking.

Hypothalamus: part of the limbic system that activates behaviours like fighting, eating and sex.

Hypothetico-deductive method: the basic rule in science that you first generate a hypothesis, then create an investigation to test it and, finally, having tested your hypothesis, you revisit your hypothesis to see whether your original proposal was correct.

I

Idiopathic insomnia: lifelong serious insomnia beginning in childhood with no obvious cause.

Imposed etic: when a researcher imposes their idea and assumes that their view is appropriate irrespective of cultural differences.

Insomnia: a condition where people have difficulty sleeping. This can involve the quality or length of sleep.

Intellectual speech: this is used by older children and adults to think and solve problems.

Internal reliability: consistency of measurement within a test.

Inter-rater reliability: the degree of agreement between different observers.

Interspecific: an act directed towards a member of a different species.

L

Level of significance: the level at which the null hypothesis is accepted or rejected.

Lynch mob: a group of people operating outside the law, who execute someone without a fair trial (sometimes because they suspect them of committing a crime).

M

Macro PK: Psychokinesis (PK) that has clearly observable effects, for example bending keys or stopping watches.

Maintenance of relationships: the processes involved in keeping relationships going smoothly, ensuring that they are rewarding for both partners and repairing them when they go wrong.

MAOA: monoamine oxidase A, an enzyme that causes the breakdown of neurochemicals such as noradrenaline. If this is faulty, there will be higher-than-normal levels in the brain.

Misattribution: when someone makes a wrong assumption about the cause of an event, an assumption about the cause of that event is incorrectly made.

Monozygotic (MZ) twins: twins born from the same fertilised egg. Also known as identical twins, they have exactly the same genetic make-up.

N

Narcolepsy: a genetic condition with symptoms of sleep paralysis, cataplexy, hypnagogic hallucinations and daytime sleepiness.

Natural selection: the selection of behaviours or bodily features that allow an animal to compete successfully for food and shelter and to survive.

Near-death experience: a subjective experience that is reported by people who clinically die, or come close to actual death and are revived.

Need for cognition: the view that some people have a stronger need to know than others and like to get to grips with arguments.

Neologisms: literally 'new words'. Refers to spoken nonsense words that can be the result of brain damage or other conditions.

Neonate: a newborn baby, no more than a few days old.

Neurotransmitters: chemicals in the brain that are important in transmitting information across the synapse. Therefore, they are vital to the brain's normal functioning.

Nominal data: this is obtained when information is put into categories or just named.

NREM: one of the two distinctive types of sleep found in mammals.

O

Ob mice: genetically obese mice.

Objectivity: being based on observable phenomena and not on personal opinion, prejudices or emotion.

Obstructive sleep apnoea (OSA): apnoea caused by obstruction of the upper airways, preventing efficient passage of air to the lungs.

One-tailed test: used with directional hypotheses that state what the direction of difference or correlation will be.

Operant conditioning: this refers to Skinner's idea that the likelihood of any behaviour being repeated depends on its consequences.

Operationalised: a variable is given an operational definition (i.e. it is operationalised) when the researcher defines exactly how a concept is to be measured. For example, aggression is a concept that could be measured by the number of times a child hits other children.

Opioid systems: neurotransmitter pathways in the brain using opioid (or opiate) neurotransmitters such as endorphin and enkephalin.

Ordinal data: this is obtained when information or scores are put in order (first, second, third, etc.). Whenever data is ranked, it is ordinal.

Orexin: a brain chemical (neurotransmitter). Loss of orexin function is associated with narcolepsy.

Out-of-body experience: the feeling of being able to view yourself and the world from outside your own body.

P

Paranormal: phenomena that cannot be explained using conventional scientific theories, although aspects of scientific thought may be relevant to provide a basis for explanation.

Parasocial relationship: a one-sided relationship with a celebrity/media figure.

Parasomnias: these are events occurring during sleep, such as sleepwalking and nightmares, that do not lead to daytime sleepiness.

Parental investment: investment by the parent that increases the offspring's chance of survival at the cost of the parent's ability to invest in other offspring.

Peer review: the scrutiny of research by independent experts.

Perceptual constancies: the perception that objects stay the same even though their appearance (size, shape, colour, etc.) may change.

Perceptual set: being prepared to interpret an ambiguous image in a particular way because of factors like context, expectations and motivation, etc.

Persuasion: a deliberate attempt to change someone's attitude and behaviour.

Phase advance: when we fly from west to east, time differences mean that local time at our destination is later than that indicated by our body clock. This means that our biological rhythms have to advance to catch up with local time.

Phase delay: this particularly applies to air travel and jet lag. If we fly west from London to New York and arrive at, say, 5pm local time, our body clock tells us that it is 10pm (London time). To adjust to local time, we need to delay our sleep time. This is known as phase delay.

Population validity: the degree to which the results can be generalised from the sample to other populations.

Positive reinforcement: this occurs when a behaviour is followed by something pleasant (which increases the likelihood that the behaviour will be repeated).

Prefrontal cortex: this part of the brain is involved in learning, and controls the instinctive impulses caused by the limbic system.

Primary insomnia: insomnia with no obvious external cause.

Pro-social behaviour: behaviour that is constructive, including helping (altruism) and sharing, cooperation and empathy with others.

Prosopagnosia: a condition in which sufferers cannot recognise familiar faces, even those of people they know very well.

Pseudoscience: a set of ideas based on ideas or research that seem to be scientific but, in fact, are not.

Psychic healing: a form of treatment, also sometimes called psychic, faith, paranormal or mental healing. It is usually done by laying on of hands or from a distance. Reiki is an example.

Psychic mediumship: a practice where an individual – the medium – acts as a facilitator for communication between the spirit world and the physical world.

Psychokinesis (PK): an ability to control objects with one's mind, e.g. moving a vase using the power of thought alone.

R

Rapid eye movement (REM) sleep: one of the two distinctive types of sleep seen in mammals. It is characterised by a desynchronised EEG pattern, rapid eye movements and a paralysis of the skeletal muscles.

Reductionism: the term given to explanations of human behaviours at a low level of analysis.

Reinforcement: this occurs when something that follows a behaviour makes the behaviour more likely to be repeated.

Replicability: procedures and/or findings that are able to be reproduced or repeated.

S

Satiety centre: a centre in the brain that inhibits feeding in response to signals from the body. The ventromedial hypothalamus is a key satiety centre.

Scaffolding: the help or support given to a child, which can be varied or withdrawn as the child develops.

Schema: a set of ideas about something. For example, the schema of 'girl' could include ideas about what girls wear, what toys they play with and what games they play.

Secondary insomnia: insomnia secondary to a pre-existing psychological or medical condition.

Self-deception: the process where we mislead ourselves to accept as true or correct something that is untrue.

Sense of self: the knowledge that you are distinct from other people and have unique thoughts, feelings and experiences.

Serotonin: a neurotransmitter that carries messages around the brain. It is also known as 5-hydroxytryptamine.

Sex: refers to the biological classification of being male or female based on bodily features.

Sexual selection: the selection of behaviours that allow an animal to compete successfully for mates and to reproduce.

Sheep-goat effect: the suggestion that the attitude of the participant (whether they believe in ESP or not) can affect ESP scores.

Sleepwalking: parasomnia that occurs during the lighter stages of NREM. It is most common in children.

Social exchange theory: an economic theory of maintenance and breakdown which argues that people aim to maximise rewards and minimise costs involved in a relationship.

Social learning theory: the idea that behaviours are learned through observation of role models and imitation of their actions.

Social speech: this is used to communicate with others.

Somatoform dissociation: a lessening in sensory integration, causing things like loss of motor control or changes in perception.

Stalking: pattern of obsessive behaviour often involving following or making contact, which produces fear or distress in the victim.

Stimulus discrimination: the process of eliciting the CR to a narrower range of stimuli.

Stimulus generalisation: the tendency of the CR to be produced by stimuli that are similar to the CS.

Superstition: the irrational belief that an object, action or circumstance not logically related to a course of events influences its outcome, e.g. putting new shoes on the table will bring bad luck.

Suprachiasmatic nucleus (SCN): a group of neurones in the hypothalamus of the brain. The SCN is our most important endogenous pacemaker and in turn controls the pineal gland and the release of melatonin.

T

Theory of mind: understanding that others have different thoughts and emotions from you, and being to make allowances for that.

Two-tailed test: used with non-directional hypotheses that state that there will be a difference or correlation but not the direction.

Type 1 error: the error that occurs when the null hypothesis is rejected but it should have been retained.

Type 2 error: the error that occurs when the null hypothesis is retained but it is false.

U

Unconditioned response (UCR): a response to a stimulus that is automatic and involuntary (reflex).

Unconditioned stimulus (UCS): a stimulus that triggers an automatic (unconditioned) response.

V

Vicarious learning: learning by observing how others behave.

Vicarious reinforcement: witnessing another person showing a behaviour and being rewarded for it.

Z

Zone of proximal development: the gap between what a child can do currently and what it has the potential to do, initially with help, but ultimately on its own.

Index

2D:4DR 78
47 XYY karotype 49

A

absorption-addiction model 153
accommodation 107
acculturation 39
acetylcholine 8
addictive behaviour 50, 158–68
    media influence in 166
    reducing 166–8
    vulnerability to 165
adoption studies 101, 126
adrenaline 48
advertising 144, 146–7, 166
    resistance to 146–7
afterlife, belief in 179
aggression 43–4, 76
    biological explanations 46–9
    and evolution 50–3
    group displays 50–1, 52–3
    institutional 45, 46
    inter/intra-specific 50
aggressive role models 44
agnosias 23–5
agoraphobia 134
alcohol use 158, 159
alpha bias 113, 118, 189
amygdala 46, 47, 117, 136
anal personality 138
androcentric 113, 118
androgens 47, 48, 79
androgyny 75, 90
angular gyrus 182
animal experiments 25, 57–8, 95–6,
    103, 174, 178
animal learning 94–8
anomalous psychology 173–83
    explanations for 176–80
    personality factors 180
anorexia nervosa (AN) 64–7
antisocial behaviour studies 149
aphagia 57
apnoea 8
appeasement 50
arranged marriages 30, 37–9
assimilation 107
attachment theory 36–7
attention deficit/hyperactivity
    disorder (ADHD) 47, 163
attitude change 144–5
attraction to celebrity 152–4
autism 114, 115, 118
autonomy 65
aversion therapy 168
avoidant personality disorder 134

B

BaMbuti tribe 19
basal metabolic rate (BMR) 70, 71
bias 113, 118, 129, 189, 192, 193
biological rhythms 1–9
    disruption to 3–4
blood glucose levels 58
bobo doll 43, 149
body clock 1–2, 3, 8
body dissatisfaction 65, 67
body mass index (BMI) 69
body temperature cycle 2
Bowlby, John 36
BPS guidelines for research 193–4
brain damage 24, 117
brain size 99
bulimia nervosa (BN) 67–9

C

carnivores 6
carpentered environment 17, 21
cataplexy 9
catatonia 127
celebrity endorsement 147
celebrity, psychology of 152–4
celebrity worship 153
chi-squared test 197, 199
cholecystokinin (CCK) 58
chromosomal abnormalities 77
chromosomes 9, 49, 77
chronotype 9
circadian rhythms 1, 2
classical conditioning 94–5, 97
cognitive development theories
    107–11
cognitive myopia 160
cognitive priming 148, 150
coincidence 177, 178
computer gaming 150–1
congenital adrenal hyperplasia
    (CAH) 78, 79
conservation tasks 107, 108
cortisol 130
crowd behaviour 44
culture and relationships 37–9
culture and socialisation 83

D

data analysis 194–9
dehumanisation 45, 46
deindividuation 44–5
delta waves 5
demand characteristics 121, 192
depression 8, 123, 129–33
    therapies for 132–3

deprivation model 45, 46
depth perception 16–17, 18, 19, 20, 21
determinism 53
diathesis–stress model 10, 13, 127, 131
dieting 62–4, 73, 74
discovery learning 107, 110
dopamine 126, 158, 159, 162,
    164, 168
double-blind technique 192
dreams 5, 9

E

eating behaviour 57–71
eating disorders 64–71
ECT (electroconvulsive therapy) 132
egocentric 116, 118
electroencephalogram (EEG) 4, 5, 24
empathy and lack of 116, 117, 118
encephalin 158
encephalisation quotient (EQ) 99
endogenous pacemakers 1–2, 3, 8
endorphins 61, 158
environment of evolutionary
    adaptation (EEA) 50, 51, 59–60,
    66, 70
equity theory 32–3
ethical principles 193–4
ethnocentric 19, 20
etic, imposed 20
evolutionary stable strategy
    (ESS) 52
experimenter bias 192
expression, facial 22, 23, 117
external reliability 193
extra sensory perception (ESP)
    174, 175–6, 180, 181

F

face recognition 21–2, 113
facial expression 22, 23, 117
false belief task 114–15
family dynamics 65, 68
famine hypothesis 66
fandom 154
fast foods 69
feminine 76
filter theory 29–30
finger length 78
fMRI scans 24
food and culture 61–2
food neophobia 60
food preferences 59–62
    in children 60–1
fraudulent research 174, 175
frustration–aggression theory 45
fusiform gyrus 24–5

G

'g' 91, 92
gambling 162–4
Ganzfeld technique 175
Gardner's theory 92–3
gender 75–87
    behavioural approach 81
    bias 113, 118, 129, 189
    development 79–80, 82–3, 84–5
    differences 76
    dysphoria 78, 80
    identity disorder (GID) 80
    psychological explanations 84–7
    role reinforcement 81
    and sex hormones 78–9
    schema theory 85–6
    traits 76
genome lag 50, 75
ghrelin 58
guided learning 109, 110

H

hallucinations 9
hand–eye coordination 16
hebephrenia 127
herbivores 6
hibernation 1, 6
hippocampal abnormality 126
homeostasis 73
hormones 70
    eating 58, 59
    sex 77, 78–9
        testosterone 47, 48, 76, 77, 79
    stress 8, 48, 49, 130, 132
Hovland-Yale model 144–5
hypnagogic hallucinations 9
hypocretin 12
hypothalamus 2, 8, 46, 47, 57–9,
        70, 77
hypothesis, misattribution 176–8
hypothesis testing 195–6

I

illusions 15, 16, 17, 20
immune system 3
imposed etic 20
infidelity 51
infradian rhythms 1
injunction words vi
insomnia 7–8
institutional aggression 45, 46
intelligence
    animal 97–8
    human, evolution of 98, 99–100
    Machiavellian 98
    psychometric theories 91–2
    tests 91, 92, 101
        and environmental factors 102
    triarchic theory 92
    types of 92

intelligences, multiple 92–3
inter/intra-specific aggression 50
internal reliability 192
'inter-sex' 78
IQ (Intelligence quotient) tests
        91, 92, 101
    factor analysis 91, 92
ironic processes 64

J

jealousy 51, 52
jet lag 3, 4

K

kibbutzim 123
Klinefelter's syndrome 77
Kohlberg's theory 111-13, 120
Koko 97

L

labelling people 124, 125
language 100, 109
learned helplessness 132
learning, discovery 107, 110
learning, vicarious 148
leptin 59, 70, 71
light–dark cycle 2
limbic system 46, 47, 117
Lucifer effect 45

M

magical thinking 178–9
Mann–Whitney U test 198
masculine 76
media influence
    in addictive behaviour 166
    on social behaviour 147–50
    in eating disorders 65, 67, 68
mediumship 182–3
melatonin 2–3, 4, 8
menstruation 1, 48, 65
metabolic rate 6, 64, 69, 70, 71, 74
minimax principle 31
mirror neurons 117–18
misattribution hypothesis 176–8
modelling 135
moral development 111–13, 115–16
moral dilemmas 111, 112, 113, 115,
        121
moral understanding 111–13
mundane realism 192
murderers' brain scans 47

N

narcolepsy 9, 10, 12, 13
natural selection 75
nausea 60
near-death experiences 181–2
needs 29

neuroticism 165
neurotransmitters 8, 61, 158, 162
    serotonin 8, 47, 48–9, 66, 68,
        138, 158
new paradigm research 189
nicotine 158, 159, 160–2
noradrenaline 8, 48, 49, 132
NREM sleep 4–5, 7
NRT (nicotine replacement
        therapy) 168

O

obesity 69–71
object permanence 113
obsessive–compulsive disorder
        (OCD) 137–40, 178
    therapies for 139–40
omnivores 59
one-tailed test 197
operant conditioning 95–6, 97, 105,
        148, 159, 163
opioid system 158, 159
optic flow 14, 15
optical illusions 15, 16, 17, 20
orbital frontal cortex (OFC) 138
orders, disobeying 45
orexin (hypocretin) 9
out-of-body experiences (OBE)
        181, 182

P

paranoia 127
paranormal beliefs, explanations 179
parapsychology 173–83
parasocial relationships 152–4
parasomnias 8–10
parental investment 35, 76
Pavlov 94
peer pressure 161, 165
peer review validation 189
perception theories 14–16
perceptual abilities of babies 21
perceptual constancies 17–18
perceptual development 17
perspective theory 115–16
persuasion 144–7
    elaboration likelihood model
        (ELM) 145–6, 147
phase advance and delay 3–4
phobias 60, 134–7
    therapies for 136–7
Piaget's theory 107–8, 110
pineal gland 2, 3, 8
poisons 59
positron emission tomography (PET)
        scans 47
prefrontal cortex 47
prisoners' experience 45, 46
probability 195–9
product endorsement 146
product placement 146, 147

promiscuity   34, 35, 51, 76, 77
   choosiness   76, 77
prosopagnosia   23–5
pseudopatients   124
pseudoscience   173, 174
psychic healing   181
psychic mediumship   182–3
psychodynamic behaviour   122
psychokinesis (PK)   174, 176, 181
psychological research   188–200
   ethical considerations   193–4
psychopaths   117
punishment   96

Q

qualitative data   199
quantitative data   196–7

R

rape   39, 77
rapid eye movement (REM) sleep
   4, 5, 6, 7
reductionism   53
reinforcement   96, 97, 178
relationships   29–39
   and culture   37–9
   parasocial   152–4
reports, writing   200
reproductive behaviours   33–4
reproductive success   76, 77
research   188–200
   ethical considerations   193–4
   fraudulent   174, 175
   methods   190–1
   new paradigm   189
   validity   192–3
reward/need satisfaction theory
   29–30
ritualised displays   50, 52, 53
role models   44, 148, 149, 159

S

sampling strategies   193
scaffolding   109, 110
schemas   85–6, 107, 148
schizophrenia   8, 123, 125–8
   explanations for   126
   therapies for   127–8

seasonal affective disorder (SAD)
   129, 132
self-efficacy   68
self-esteem, low   63, 65, 67, 153,
   154, 161
self-recognition   97–8, 114
sense of self   113–14
serotonin   8, 47, 48–9, 66, 68,
   138, 158
sex   75
sex chromosomes   49
sex hormones   47, 48, 76, 77, 78–9
sexual reproduction   33–4
sexual selection   33–4, 75
sexual strategies   34, 35
sheep-goat effect   176
shift work   3
Siffre, Michel   2
single-blind technique   192
size constancy   19
Skinner box   95–6, 103, 178
sleep   4–10
   apnoea   8
   changes over life   5, 6
   deprivation   7
   disorders   7–10
   explanations   6–7
   across species   6
sleep–waking cycle   1, 2
sleepwalking   10
smoking   158, 159, 160–2
social behaviour, media
   influence   147–50
social cognition   113–17
social exchange theory   30–2
social learning theory (SLT)   43–4,
   81, 97, 148, 159, 160
socialisation study   83
Spearman's rho   198
split personality   125
stalking   153, 154
statistical tests   196–9
stigmatisation   125
stress   165
stress hormones   8, 48, 49, 130, 132
'super males'   77
superstition   178
suprachiasmatic nucleus (SCN)
   2, 3, 8

T

taste   59
taste aversion learning   60
teasing   81, 82, 89
television influence   146–7, 149, 150
   see also media influence
temporal lobe stimulation   182
territory   50
testicle size   76
testosterone   47, 48, 76, 77, 79
theory of mind   114–15
theory of planned behaviour
   (TPB)   167
theta waves   5
thought-action fusion   139
treatment aetiology fallacy   127, 138
twin studies   9, 10, 66, 67, 68, 70, 101
two-tailed test   197

U

ultradian rhythms   1, 5

V

vengeance   179
ventromedial nucleus   57, 59
vicarious learning   148
violence, desensitisation to   151
violence in the media   149, 150–1
visual cliff   18
Vygotsky's theory   108–10

W

weight control   59
'what the hell' effect   63
Wilcoxon test   198

X

xenophobia   51

Z

zeitgebers   2, 3
zone of proximal development
   (ZPD)   109, 110